Reviving the Social Compact

Explorations in Contemporary Social-Political Philosophy (ECSPP)

**Series Editors: Naomi Zack (University of Oregon) and
Laurie Shrage (Florida International University)**

As our world continues to be buffeted by extreme changes in society and politics, philosophers can help navigate these disruptions. Rowman & Littlefield's ECSPP series books are intended for supplementary classroom use in intermediate to advanced college-level courses to introduce philosophy students and scholars in related fields to the latest research in social-political philosophy. This philosophical series has multidisciplinary applications and the potential to reach a broad audience of students, scholars, and general readers.

1. *Beyond Blood Oil: Philosophy, Policy, and the Future*, by Leif Wenar, Anna Stilz, Michael Blake, Christopher Kutz, Aaron James, and Nazrin Mehdiyeva, 2018
2. *Reviving the Social Compact: Inclusive Citizenship in an Age of Extreme Politics*, by Naomi Zack, 2018

Reviving the Social Compact

Inclusive Citizenship in an Age of Extreme Politics

Naomi Zack

Foreword by Ruth Sample

ROWMAN & LITTLEFIELD
Lanham • Boulder • New York • London

Published by Rowman & Littlefield
A wholly owned subsidiary of The Rowman & Littlefield Publishing Group, Inc.
4501 Forbes Boulevard, Suite 200, Lanham, Maryland 20706
www.rowman.com

6 Tinworth Street, London SE11 5AL, United Kingdom

British Library Cataloguing in Publication Information Available

Library of Congress Cataloging-in-Publication Data

Names: Zack, Naomi, 1944– author.
Title: Reviving the social compact : inclusive citizenship in an age of extreme politics /
    Naomi Zack.
Description: Lanham : Rowman & Littlefield, 2018. | Series: Explorations in contempo-
    rary social-political philosophy ; 2 | Includes bibliographical references and index.
Identifiers: LCCN 2018035964 (print) | LCCN 2018038837 (ebook) | ISBN
    9781538120132 (electronic) | ISBN 9781538120118 (cloth : alk. paper) | ISBN
    9781538120125 (pbk. : alk. paper)
Subjects: LCSH: Social contract. | Citizenship. | Belonging (Social psychology) | Right
    and left (Political science) | Group identity.
Classification: LCC JC336 (ebook) | LCC JC336 .Z33 2018 (print) | DDC 320.1/1—dc23
LC record available at https://lccn.loc.gov/2018035964

♾ ™ The paper used in this publication meets the minimum requirements of American
National Standard for Information Sciences Permanence of Paper for Printed Library
Materials, ANSI/NISO Z39.48-1992.

Printed in the United States of America

To Alex, Bradford, Jessica, Coco, and Winnie

If a long series of abuses, lies, and tricks, all tending the same way, make the design visible to the people so that they can't help feeling what they are oppressed by and seeing where they are going, it's not surprising that they should then rouse themselves and try to put the ruling power into hands that will achieve for them the purposes for which government was at first established.

—John Locke, *Second Treatise of Government*, 1689, Chap 19, S 225

The Revolution was effected before the war commenced. The Revolution was in the minds and hearts of the people.

—John Adams, to Hezekiah Niles, 13 February 1818

Sometimes when you win, you really lose, and sometimes when you lose, you really win, and sometimes when you win or lose, you actually tie, and sometimes when you tie, you actually win or lose. Winning or losing is all one organic mechanism, from which one extracts what one needs.

—Gloria Clemente: Rosie Perez, "White Men Can't Jump" (1992) IBDb, https://www.imdb.com/title/tt0105812/characters/nm0001609

I fell asleep and had a dream that a king was liquidated by a group of kind faces.

—Maquita Donyel Irvin, #Black Lives Matter https://www.goodreads.com/quotes/tag/black-lives-matter?page=2

Contents

Foreword

Ruth Sample

Can citizenship in the era of Trump be saved? If our government has broken the social contract and no longer serves the interests of the people, can citizens have faith that they are better off with government than without it? What happens when our government promises fair and equal treatment, but it has become obvious (and sometimes visible through camera-phone video) that people of color, immigrants, women, and poor people are not truly equal citizens? Is it time to shift our focus from the idea of a social contract— between the government and citizens—to the idea of a social *compact*— direct interaction and agreement among citizens and social institutions for the common good?

Naomi Zack answers that, yes, we must recommit to the fundamental duty of citizenship, going beyond just political participation and voting. Good citizenship will require that we create institutions, structures, and practices that advance the common good even when our government and political system will not or cannot. It also requires that we push for a humane culture that is truly inclusive and treats all with true equal concern and respect—not simply in the formal legal sense but in actual practice. If the government cannot or will not undermine racism and gender discrimination, we must do it ourselves. If the government cannot wipe out poverty and homelessness, we must move our engagement to the local level and do it ourselves. The social contract may be broken, but the social compact is still here, pushed underground, waiting to be revitalized.

This is a timely and surprisingly optimistic manifesto by a philosopher ideally situated to write one. Professor Naomi Zack has been a leading synthesizer of philosophical questions regarding race, class, gender, and more recently ethics for disaster and political philosophy. Now we find ourselves in a series of disasters—political, environmental, social—with no clear solution forthcoming from our government. Our new, intensified politics is driven by a series of malignant forces, some external to politics, some internal to it. These forces "turbocharge" or "supercharge" our political system, robbing it of its ability to effectively respond to the needs of the people. The result to date has been oppositional, irrational, and unpredictable outcomes for voters and citizens. We go from President Obama to President Trump. Elections may be regime changes, but we cannot rely on any change from politics to last; it will soon be supplanted by a swing in the other direction. The solution, Zack argues, is direct, local action on the part of citizens. We must protect ourselves from the vicissitudes of our new overheated politics by designing projects and life-plans that are to some degree insulated from those politics, while at the same time promoting a more inclusive citizenship that transcends traditional notions of who belongs. We can and must, she argues, "reach a consensus about democratic values in the realm of the social compact." This means a humane culture of inclusion, a welcoming attitude toward immigrants, and a guaranteed housing income. The social compact requires us to respond to social and environmental disasters—and help to forestall them—when there is no longer a reliable governmental response in the offing. While our politics may follow a cycle of constant upending, swinging from extreme to extreme, citizens can create a (nonviolent) revolution from below the buffers us and continues to move us forward.

This is not a book of political philosophy in the conventional sense. The era of Trump has created a feeling that we are living through an emergency, and this emergency requires theorizing about race, class, and gender in real time. Zack's recent work in the philosophy of disaster and applicative justice has prepared her for just this moment. The depth and breadth of Zack's unique perspective are on display here, marshaling a wide range of philosophical perspectives as well as historical, scientific, and legal knowledge on the issue of citizenship. This engaging book will captivate philosophers, historians, and social scientists, as well as critically minded citizens and, of course, students. This is philosophy we can use, here and now, for the times we live in.

Ruth Sample
Department of Philosophy
University of New Hampshire

Preface and Acknowledgments

My political memory goes back to the Eisenhower–Stevenson election campaign, when I was in middle school (or junior high school, as it was called then). I was a freshman in college when JFK was assassinated. I was in a park in Chicago (Grant Park, I think) when a cheer went up at the news that Nixon had resigned. I was not shocked by the Clinton–Lewinsky affair. On 9/11, I had moved to Oregon from New York earlier that summer and could not believe the headline on my computer, "ATTACK ON AMERICA." I did not know if the attack was ongoing or over, after hits to the World Trade Center in New York City, the plane crash in Pennsylvania, and the fire at the Pentagon. I noticed that branches of the U.S. military were ceremonially represented, as well as the religions of Christianity, Judaism, and Islam, during Bush's memorial service for the victims of 9/11 at the National Cathedral on September 14, 2001.

In 2016, I thought Trump would win because there was a strange vitality to his campaign. When he won, the immediate reaction from Democrats and progressive intellectuals was as though dictatorship and fascism were upon us. Then progressives and the liberal establishment began to fight back. Since November 8, 2016, I have learned a little about Americans I don't usually interact with, who continue in their loyalty to Trump. I have been heartened by the media and intellectual opposition since he's been in office. But I have been struggling to create an interpretation or a worldview of what is happening. Some of my theories have been crazy, such as that Trump and Bannon were deliberately operating as agents provocateurs to bring about a massive left-wing revolution—although history may still make it look that way.

I have been thinking about and attending to politics as never before in my life, and it may be obsessive, as well as compulsive. I started organizing the subject matter for this book at the beginning of 2017 and settled down to writing at the beginning of 2018. The subject of current politics more broadly includes culture, because politics is part of culture. This means that one has to know a certain amount of history in order to understand current politics. There is no real separation of skills between the more restrained academic work I do and my ongoing project of cultural criticism. The only difference is in the subject matter, what I call here "philosophizing the unphilosophical." I try to follow world news, but my understanding of the United States is better developed because I have lived here for almost three-quarters of a century. This book is my present interpretation of the time we are living through. I have had good support in crafting the manuscript, and many have helped without realizing it. Here I will thank just a very few people who have been directly involved in this project, mention recent audiences who have heard different versions of some of the main themes, and then document the small parts of the book that are versions of small parts of earlier publications and unpublished talks.

The penultimate manuscript benefited a great deal from Simon Rackham's copyedits and from external review commissioned by the press. I am very grateful to Laurie Shrage, my coeditor of the series in which this book appears, who spurred me on to more clarity in chapter 5 and provided many detailed edits throughout the penultimate manuscript. The book appears in our joint series and we have been colleagues for decades, but I believe that she submitted it to her most rigorous criticism, from which this final version has benefited. Natalie Mandziuk, acquisitions editor for philosophy at Rowman & Littlefield, is a firecracker—she makes things happen right away, and we are lucky to work with her. We are also lucky to work with Michael Tan, editorial assistant, who has so ably and expertly implemented preproduction mechanics and details. I am very grateful to Jehanne Schweitzer, senior production editor at Rowman & Littlefield. Thanks to Rebecca Saxon in the University of Oregon Philosophy Department Administration for help with the index.

I am grateful to the Philosophy Department audiences at Kent State University, Seattle University, and the University of Oregon graduate students at the What Is Community? conference, for which I read papers based on chapters 1, 2, and 3 in February and May 2018. Some of the discussion comments have led to last-minute additions and qualifications in the manuscript.

Parts of chapter 3 rely on my discussion of the White Mass Recently Politicized (WMRP) in "Contemporary Claims of Political Injustice: History and the Race to the Bottom," *Res Philosophica* (Online First: October 18, 2017, https://doi.org/10.11612/resphil.1613). In chapter 5, the section on Locke's meaning of property and interpretations is a development of the section "Propriety" in chapter 6, "Propriety and Civic Identity," from my *Bachelors of Science: Seventeenth Century Identity, Then and Now* (1996, pp. 86–93.) The case studies of natural disasters in New Orleans, Haiti, and Chile presented in chapter 6 were first described by me in the 2009 paperback edition of *Ethics for Disaster*. For chapter 8, I am grateful to the graduate students and faculty audience of the Philosophy Department at the University of Oregon for discussion when I gave an early version of some of the ideas at the What Is Materialism? conference at UO in May 2014. Since then, I have benefited from audience and panelist feedback when presenting "How the Homeless Are Us and Why We Can't Stand Them," Public Library, Brooklyn, New York, January 2016; "Philosophical and Activist Aspects of Homelessness," colloquium paper, Department of Philosophy panel presentation, Georgia State University, Atlanta, March 2015; and "Homelessness: An Urgent, Growing Problem That Cannot Be Solved But Must Be Addressed," American Philosophical Association Central Division Meeting, March 2016. Thanks especially to John Abbarno for encouraging my work on homelessness and his plan to include chapter 8 in the forthcoming second edition of his edited volume *Ethics of Homelessness*. In chapter 9, the section "The Harsh History of U.S. Immigration" draws on accounts and sources from the section "Ethnicity and US Immigration" in chapter 5 of *Philosophy of Race: An Introduction* (2018).

Of course, I am completely responsible for errors, stylistic awkwardness, missteps in arguments and conclusions, and the transgressions against academic philosophy that go along with writing so much about contemporary events.

Naomi Zack
Eugene, Oregon

Introduction

This book is only superficially about the United States in the early years of Donald J. Trump's presidency. This particular time and place has served as a node for broad changes in reality that have been a long time in process but seem to have popped out instantaneously and simultaneously: The tempo of events is faster. Politics is expanding. Public discourse is harsher. Oppression is more arbitrary and disruptive. Unarmed civilians are killed by terrorists everywhere and (in the United States) by police officers. There are egregious human rights abuses in Syria, Myanmar, North Korea, and other countries. Safety nets are shrinking in the United States. Women are asserting themselves as never before. Natural disasters strain government response. The natural environment faces new human-made and political threats. Homelessness is increasing. Immigrants and refugees are increasingly subject to deportation. However, more people are willing to take to the streets to express resistance. The citizenry appears to be divided as never before, about racial justice, gender, culture, climate change, immigration, and myriad other extant and forthcoming issues, including gun control (in the United States). But the citizenry is also newly regenerated, in criticism and activism. Democracies throughout the world are undergoing parallel changes, but direct comparisons with the United States are complicated by parliamentary systems of government.

There is great division and opposition in the United States two-party political system. What it all comes down to is that government is breaking the social contract, by not benefiting the people and by not functioning as expected. This is not a matter of theory but of the fundamental structure of organized society under representative democratic government. The idea of the social contract has a long tradition in political philosophy, but its intellectual history is only broadly at stake here. Specifically at stake is the basic premise that people implicitly consent to a unified government that has a monopoly on legitimate force, because they are better off with it than without it. Government is set up by those governed for their own benefit. Exactly how government functions and the nature of its benefits depend on historical circumstances and the will of the people. In democracies with elected representative government, the functioning of government and its benefits are constantly subject to debate, political debate. But what is not up for grabs is that government must function and that its functioning must benefit the people. This basic social contract structure is rule governed, based on founding documents that are constantly being reinterpreted. For instance: Who are the people? Do they include nonwhites, women, and immigrants? What is the job of elected government officials? What is the line between politicking and governing?

Progressive political groups in democratic societies, such as abolitionists, suffragists, civil rights advocates, and environmental advocates, have largely assumed that a broad social contract of functional government for the people exists in the background and that their missions have been to *perfect* the social contract by making it more just and more inclusive, in specific ways, for specific communities and constituencies. U.S. examples include the right to vote for women and the right not to be obstructed in voting for African Americans. Many progressives have thought it possible to further their causes by invoking principles based on humanitarian and egalitarian moral laws that are more basic than any politics of the moment. And they have also assumed the continuing existence of a functional government of laws that will carry out such principles after they have prevailed in their causes. This is the project of *applicative justice*, applying the rules for justice already in effect for some, to others for whom they have not been applied.

In progressive academic scholarship, theorists have worked within liberatory categories that advocate for members of specific groups: race (African Americans and people of color, generally), gender (nonmen), humanitarianism (refugees, poor people, and homeless people), disaster (survivors and vulnerable populations), environmentalism (the natural environment and nonhuman life), and immigration (resident immigrants and applicants). As categories, such taxonomy is for progressive scholars and intellectuals to think with. We use the liberatory categories with the goal of improving life for humans and natural beings toward greater freedom and flourishing, and without losing the freedom and flourishing that have already been gained. But it is more important that these categories, as tools of thought for progressives, are for the good of those who populate them. We cannot know if or how or when the work of theorists with these categories will change the world; the categories are not blueprints for reality, and even definitive, normative explication does not automatically lead to plans for immediate action with the wherewithal for change to be put into effect. But even when it is impractical or incomplete, our work is part of the fabric of higher education and the ongoing archive of collective knowledge.

However, we should constantly check the relevance of our work within these liberatory categories to the history of our time. If the basic social contract, as it is popularly understood, is breaking, this should have implications for scholarly liberatory works. The history of our time has resulted in the need for a shift within these categories, from perfecting the social contract now in place as a background posit, to reviving and reinterpreting and developing the social *compact* instead. This is a shift from projects in applicative justice, with appeals to functioning government, to a public and private civic realm that is outside of government. In the realm of the social compact, dysfunctional government is bypassed because citizens, residents, organizations, and institutions interact directly with each other, for the good of the whole.

As a work of philosophy or theory, this book is unusual in being about contemporary political events, many of which occurred in the process of writing. The reader will have lived through the same events, and I hope that she/he/they will philosophize or theorize along with me and provide new criticism, analysis, and perspectives, through consideration of what I offer. Many contemporary subjects and controversial issues have been omitted, for reasons of time and space, as well as expertise and relevance. Here is a synopsis of the book:

> *Reviving the Social Compact* offers new concepts for understanding and acting through political and social upheaval and distress post-2016. Politics as contest has become *turbocharged*—it is boosted by its own exhaust in an expanding, closed system. In a very agonistic two-party system, candidates and then elected officials and the public become more focused on winning than governing and holding government accountable for the benefit of the people, as the *social contract* requires. Race has now exceeded intersection—it is a wild track after a *junction*; the junction results from the contradiction between formal rights and ongoing racism. Class is no longer based on real-life interests but has been manufactured for political contest and manipulated through social media. For politics, race, and class, organic preexisting organizations of citizens and residents willing and able to speak out and demonstrate provide powerful resistance, as spectacle and aspiration. It is the job of progressive scholars to provide theorics for what transpires in those arenas. Women, through feminism, have been amazingly successful so far, most lately in #Me-Too. But in terms of transgender people, sex workers, and nonwhite and poor women, even progressive women's movements remain *top-rest*, because low-status and obscure members are left out. This motivates revitalizing the *social compact* for society outside of government, which also retains the right of revolution. But we are not talking about violence or force here. In our time of extreme politics, getting the other party in office is in itself a regime change tantamount to revolution. The vitality of those in the realm of the social compact is evident in disaster resilience when people are on their own in natural

disasters in society and work to save the environment from disasters in nature. Homelessness is a static condition of disaster that unlike immediate disasters in society and nature could be effectively counteracted with broad profit incentives, in the usual capitalistic way. The catch is that a universal guaranteed housing income would be required. Much of the foregoing comes to a point in immigration. U.S. history shows many reversals in immigration policy, but never has expulsion been such a cruel tool and never has *good citizenship* so strongly required *hospitality*. Good citizenship, from within the domains of both the social contract and the social compact, will be the abiding response and solution to current political abuses, insults, and afflictions. There are many scripts for good citizens at this time, and they not only remain to be written but will be invented as existential responses.

I wrote this synopsis after I finished writing all of the chapters. The chapters take up the themes mentioned in the synopsis with the use of concrete examples "plucked from the headlines." Here is a more systematic account of chapter contents and themes.

Part I, "Politics, Race, Class, and Feminism," takes up the classic liberatory categories in terms of the breakdown of the social contract and contemporary resistance against that. Our customary assumptions about these categories require revision at this time. Chapter 1, "Turbocharged Politics," begins with an engine metaphor for present politics. Politics is not government or rule, but contests that lead to that. At present, politics has expanded into governing and ordinary life. In a two-party system, this creates dramatic divisions, but the losing side is still able to resist and express its aspirations in the realm of the *social compact*. This losing side now has revived momentum in organically organized resistance such as MoveOn.org and discourse from observers and theorists, which together may neutralize the apparent threats to democratic norms and structures.

Chapter 2, "The Junction of Race," shows how race, especially pertaining to African Americans, is more of a wild track after a junction than a subject that can be understood through *intersectionality*. The contradiction of formal equality and ongoing prejudice and discrimination entails that anything can and does happen with the introduction of race into encounters with law enforcement, criminal justice, social life, and within institutions. The resulting and ongoing life spoilage has resulted in new debate about whether racism is a fundamental social and psychic ill or the result of economic and status interests. Grassroots movements such as Black Lives Matter serve to drive progress and keep public attention focused on injustice. Chapter 3, "The Political Creation of Class," examines how social class identities are no longer based on interests but subject to almost instantaneous creation by turbocharged politics drawing on fake news and new forms of white supremacy. However, here the resistance is already structured, to be organized through official political action seeking to further the real class interests of those who need better health care and educational opportunities, as well as social justice, and there have also been nascent popular interest-based initiatives, such as Occupy Wall Street.

Chapter 4, "The Amazing Success of Feminism," shows how the core mission of feminism has been realized in educational and employment opportunities for women, as well as in LGBTQ and transgender rights. Unlike racial liberation theories, feminism has not relied on essentialist identities—one does not have to be a woman in the traditional sense in order to identify as a woman or with women, in the feminist sense. It is not even necessary that everyone who is a feminist in practice identify as a feminist, for instance among the participants of #MeToo. But feminist success is often a *top-rest* phenomenon, leaving out poor white women and women of color, as well as transgender people and sex workers who are not famous or already middle class. The numerical size of this "rest" within a progressive movement is part of the motivation for thorough examination of the difference between the social contract and the social compact, which comes in chapter 5.

Part II, "The Need for the Social Compact," shifts from the received liberatory categories to a social compact posit or lens for viewing political history, natural disasters and environmental destruction, homelessness, and immigration. Chapter 5, "The Social Contract and the Social Compact," re-examines John Locke's influence on the U.S. founding documents through his notion of the social contract. That those governed consent to government because it will benefit them is the core idea of the social contract. However, Locke, unlike his heirs, did not think that the social contract was an agreement between citizens and government. Instead, it was an agreement among citizens that they would set up a government, reserving the right to revolution (an interpretation shared by Thomas Jefferson). The citizens before, during, after, and altogether apart from government have a social compact among themselves. The social compact is an imagined agreement between each individual and the whole collective for the benefit of all. It is through this social compact domain that progressive movements, as well as society more broadly, could become more egalitarian.

Chapters 6 and 7 are a pair: natural disasters in society and disasters within nature likely have the same human-made causes. Natural disasters such as Hurricanes Katrina, Sandy, Harvey, and Maria have received variably effective government response, depending on preexisting infrastructure. The difference in recovery between earthquakes in Haiti and Chile were also the results of differences in prior infrastructure and government practices. But infrastructure is not the full story, insofar as weather disasters are likely to become more intense as climate change progresses and government response capabilities may be stressed beyond effectiveness. At this time, the natural disasters in society with the best apparent recovery are those providing profit incentives for reconstruction. Disasters within nature or environmental pollution and degradation are more obviously human made than natural disasters in society, sometimes directly, as with the BP oil spill, and sometimes indirectly, insofar as CO_2 fossil-fuel emissions will likely result in further climate change that in turn causes more extreme local weather events. This problem is global, but the U.S. government has not yet responsibly addressed it. Fossil-fuel industry ties with the current EPA head do not help. The idea that God gave the earth and all its fruits to mankind to use without restriction was first stated by Locke in *The Second Treatise*, but it now lives on long after 1689 in federal policies supported by conservative Christians, based on the Protestant religious premise that it is neither necessary nor desirable to protect or preserve the natural environment. For natural disasters in society and unnatural disasters in nature, both first response and new negotiations with industry do, and will, continue to occur in the social compact realm. This is not to say that the social contract, as expectations from government, should not continue to be invoked, but that its time may just run out as both kinds of disasters get worse and government is unable to fulfill its obligations.

Chapter 8, "Homelessness and Monetization," shows how homelessness functions as a slow disaster for increasing numbers of Americans. Every problem and pathology associated with those unhoused occurs among the housed. Unhoused people are perceived as repellant because they are forced to satisfy biological needs, especially sleeping, in public view. However, housing resources that provide basic shelter remain unavailable for everyone in a culture where the symbolic value of material things has become more important than their functionality. Solving the problems of the homeless might thereby increase the numbers of the unhoused because there would be help in sight if those barely hanging on let go. In an era of tightening social safety nets, a universal guaranteed housing income would provide stable profit incentives in a capitalistic society. Those willing and able to earn more would be free to do so, and those subsisting on those funds could be required to spend a certain percentage on housing, which would provide a stable market for a new segment of the housing and real estate industries.

Chapter 9, "Immigration and Expulsion," recounts the history of assimilation of non-Anglo European immigration in Anglo-dominant U.S. society. Although all of these groups became recognized as racially white, discrimination against Italians and anti-Semitism persisted longer. Acceptance of nonwhite racial and non-European ethnic immigrants has been more grudging, at present very discriminatory against MENA (Middle Eastern and North African) and Hispanic/Latino immigrants. Mexico has provided the most immigrants to the United States, which is not surprising because large parts of the West and Southwest were part of Mexico before the Mexican-American War. Undocumented immigrants, as well as DACAs (Deferred Action for Childhood Arrivals), bring moral problems underlying legal immigration policies to light. Without advocacy of open borders, it is possible to support hospitality toward both documented and undocumented immigrants and develop that virtue as a corrective to policies and practices that arbitrarily violate due process when immigration becomes eclipsed by expulsion.

The conclusion is of course inconclusive, because in attending to current events we cannot know what will happen. There are ironies in mismatches between the intentions and consequences of political action and transmogrifications of past political villains into nostalgic teddy bears. However, certain structures are evident. First, since the 2016 presidential campaign, there has been a Super Jumbo News Story that encroaches on all aspects of U.S. life. Second, the balkanizing of news through social media has enabled distorted solitary interpretations of what is going on. Third, it is important that adult residents recognize the *duty* of good citizenship. The good citizen goes beyond fulfillment of the necessary requirement of voting to engage in thought, conversation, and active participation in civic life. The good citizen brings moral values to political life and expects that government practices will reflect moral values.

Part I

Politics, Race, Class, and Feminism

Chapter One

Turbocharged Politics

Winning isn't everything; it's the only thing. (UCLA Bruins football coach Henry Russell; see Wikipedia 2018c)

THE ENGINE METAPHOR

For a useful metaphor, please consider the following:

A main difference between the turbocharger and the supercharger lies in the power supply. A turbocharger uses the exhaust stream for its energy. The exhaust will run through a turbine that will itself spin the compressor. . . . The source of the power for the supercharger is in a belt connected directly to the engine. A supercharger will compress air of the atmospheric pressure, and create the boost by forcing air into the engine. (ProCar Mechanics 2018)

Politics is the activity of political contest, who gets elected, their rule, and resistance to that. The political is the entire sphere of activity that includes government and discourse about government. As the engine metaphor suggests, supercharged politics is an intensification of politics with input external to politics. Turbocharged politics is revved up by its own by-products. When politics is turbocharged, the political system is more enclosed than when it is supercharged. But that does not prevent politics from expanding over other areas of life and preempting other claims for attention (just as a turbocharged engine may burn more fuel and create a louder exhaust). There is, of course, a third option, returning to the engine metaphor:

Naturally aspirated engines draw air into the engine through an air intake, which depends on creating a vacuum to feed air into the engine's intake manifold as needed. . . . The benefit of a naturally aspirated engine is that they are in general more reliable than forced induction engines, or engines that rely on a turbo or supercharger. The big drawback is that to have a high-output naturally aspirated car usually means having a large, heavy and gas guzzling engine. (Oneshift 2018)

When politics is naturally aspirated, it is more integrally connected to the rest of society than if it is super- or turbocharged. Naturally aspirated politics is motivated by political concerns and aspects of government that are shared and widely understood before political contests begin, and it is brought into political contests to structure both the content (what is said, about what) and the form of discourse (how it is said). It is less likely that issues will be invented in naturally aspirated than super- or turbocharged politics. There is also a shared loyalty and conformity to basic political principles, such as the limitations and structure of government, as set forth in founding documents (the U.S. Constitution) and their interpretation (judicial rulings). There is an expectation that elected officials will carry out their duties of governing, according to certain norms and in democratic societies, an expectation that those governing will be fair to those who constitute opposing political interests. For example, U.S. presidents are supposed to be presidents of those who did not vote for them, as well as of those who did and those who did not vote at all. Overall, there is a continuity in government, as well as predictability. Indeed, naturally aspirated politics is usually boring to the majority of the population because it lacks dramatic events, scandals, or high-wattage personalities. Conversations about politics are neither intense nor urgent under such normal conditions. Politicians may use high-flown inspirational language and even invoke existing, traditional, widespread ideals and values, such as love of country, the importance of family, or blessings from God. But most of the body politic tunes out such rhetoric and does not consider it directly relevant to their actual lives.

THE FUNDING OF SUPER- AND TURBOCHARGED POLITICS

Supercharged politics usually derives its impetus from other, natural (i.e., nonpolitical) aspects of society, especially when there are social problems or needs that it is believed government should address. Compared to turbocharged politics, the result might be a slower and more ponderous political engine, but it doesn't boost itself in a self-enclosed sphere. Opposition and criticism remain a normal part of the political process. Examples include Roosevelt's New Deal, Johnson's War on Poverty, attempts to institute national health care under the Clinton administration and the Affordable Care Act under the Obama administration, and attempts to institute gun control in the wake of school shootings. The supercharge in these cases has come from intense interest and concern about problems and interests that are not in themselves political, although they can quickly become politicized at a time when politics has expanded. The result of that politicization may be governmental dysfunction if it is the obligation of government to address such issues and a thoroughly politicized dominant political party either pushes through or blocks legislative or executive action on such issues. (The 2017 tax cut is an example of the former, the Republican blockage of President Obama's nominee to the Supreme Court is an example of the latter.)

However, supercharged politics can also be more limited to the sphere of political contest and the supercharge can be instantly enabled by judicial decisions. The last occurred in two recent U.S. Supreme Court decisions: *Citizens United v. FEC* (Federal Election Commission) (2010) and *McCutcheon v. FEC* (2014). In *Citizens United*, the court reversed the Bipartisan Campaign Reform Act (BCRA) of 2002 (U.S. Congress 2002), which had limited independent campaign spending and political messages and media broadcasting by unions, corporations, and nonprofit and profitable organizations to within sixty days of general elections and thirty days of primary elections. The court held in a 5–4 decision that the BCRA violated the First Amendment. At issue was whether *Citizens United*, a conservative political organization, could advertise and broadcast a partisan film, *Hillary: The Movie*, within sixty days before the 2008 Democratic primary election, in which Hillary Clinton was running for president.

More than this, in *Citizens United*, the court held that unlimited amounts of money could be spent on political activities if it was done independently of a political party or a specific candidate. The result of that decision was that unlimited amounts of money could be spent by PACs (political action committees) and super PACs, often with only nominal independence from candidates and parties. In the case of corporations, such contributions need not be made public—because corporations have a legal status as "persons," with the privacy rights of individual human persons (Levy 2015). By 2015, such spending was estimated to have doubled, reaching billions in contributions (Childress 2015). (Disclosure of campaign contributions from foreign entities can still be required on state levels, given relevant legislation [Weintrab 2016].)

The *Citizens United* ruling paved the way for the First Amendment–based 5–4 ruling in *McCutcheon v. FEC* four years later. *McCutcheon* struck down limits on campaign donations for federal elections. The plaintiff was Shaun McCutcheon, an Alabama businessman who during the 2011–2012 period had donated $33,088 to sixteen federal candidates and more than $25,000 in noncandidate contributions. The Federal Election Campaign Act of 1971 (U.S. Congress 1972) had capped the amount of political contributions that individuals and associations could make within a two-year period. The court ruled that there could be no limits on total contributions to federal campaigns. Chief Justice John Roberts wrote, "The government may no more restrict how many candidates or causes a donor may support than it may tell a newspaper how many candidates it may endorse" (*McCutcheon v. FEC* 2014). The court left the individual limit on how much individuals could contribute at $2,700 per candidate (Gold 2014), although later in 2014 Congress increased the amount of individual contributions tenfold (Childress 2015).

At this time (several years before and after the 2016 U.S. presidential election), politics seems to have become the overriding media preoccupation and mechanism of power in society. And politics is both supercharged and turbocharged. Economic interests are funneled into political victories, which is the supercharge; then lobbyists influence the rule of elected officials, who are capable of rapidly changing course or staying the course; in changing or staying the course, elected officials constantly reenergize their missions, as politicians rather than as legislators or executives who discharge their duties as such. It is also at least arguable that decisions made by members of high courts are politicized. In addition, officials are no sooner elected than they begin the politics of their reelection. For example, Donald Trump began his reelection campaign in November 2016, right after he was first elected (Wikipedia 2018a). And it has long been widely known, earlier than Trump's election, that members of Congress begin fundraising for their next elections as soon as they take office (Lewis and Arkedis 2014). Altogether, what happens in politics changes what follows in politics, very quickly, and that is the turbocharge.

The culture provides the raw material and inspiration for the ideological and rhetorical vote-getting aspect of politics, but what politicians say to get votes may bear little relation to what they do in office. Politics now has a life of its own, given its super- and turbocharged nature. Politics is the activity attending who gets elected, their rule, and resistance to that rule. Politics is a zero-sum activity. At the end of any given episode, one side wins and the other side loses. However, *political activity*, more broadly, is not a zero-sum game, because it allows for collaboration and compromise among opposing factions. In the United States, only a Democrat or a Republican can win an election, and that is part of the nature of politics. But political activity after elections can involve both parties working together; certainly this has occurred in the past. But when the political activity of postelection governing itself becomes politicized, politics has expanded into the political sphere, or normal political activity has become politicized.

THE DANGER OF POLITICS

The danger of politics to rational, progressive, as well as just peacefully traditional democratic life lies in its nature as constant contest. Each side has winning as its primary goal, in contrast to holding goals that are of benefit to society or even to its own political party. When an organization, institution, society, or even small groups become politicized, common goals go out the window in favor of winning a contest. All human activity and interaction involves some form of power, but the power in politics is often no more than gaining and holding a winning position. For example, in January 2018, the Pennsylvania State Supreme Court struck down the congressional map of eighteen districts because it "clearly, plainly and palpably" violated the state constitution in order to favor Republicans (Weigel 2018). In February, the U.S. Supreme Court refused to hear the Republican-dominated state's appeal. When Democratic Governor Tom Wolf vetoed a new map drawn by the Republican majority legislature, lower-level federal courts let stand a map drawn by the state court that would improve the chances of Democrats in the next congressional election (Liptak 2018). Twelve Republican lawmakers then moved to impeach the original state court justices, who were Democrats (Crook 2018).

The Pennsylvania dispute reveals the hypercompetitive nature of politics after the 2016 election. The fairness of government rules are not considered in the light of party politics, and neither do partisans accept a general obligation to their national or state constitution. A change of this nature changes the quality of political life. The right turbocharged vehicle may leave its supercharged and naturally aspirated competitors in the dust. All future vehicles in this kind of race may become turbocharged in order to keep up. For any given race, there is only one winner, and drivers are willing to take both calculated and impulsive risks to get there. The attention given to the race and resources committed to it may expand into other areas of life. Politics now dominates the U.S. media and has expanded into culture, as well as government and erstwhile political discourse. Let's now examine a sample of the effects of this encroachment of politics and several areas in which political life has changed: debate and ignorance, politics and community, and the threat to democracy.

CONTEMPORARY POLITICAL DEBATE AND IGNORANCE

Political debate is the intellectual and rhetorical exchange by candidates of contesting perspectives, intentions, plans, and worldviews. Political debate has changed: candidates freely slander their opponents; populists and neo–white supremacists dismiss and insult progressives and progressives respond by censoring them; emotional responses have supplanted cognitive discourse; chanted slogans no longer sum up political messages but may be the whole of such messages. Part of this change is the result of media that deliver sound, visual images and effects, and entertainment as a substantial part of political messages. That elected officials and their opponents use Twitter instead of interviews and press conferences to communicate directly with the public injects spontaneity and instantaneity. Blogs and news feeds constantly enliven the spectacle, and the circus unfolds 24/7, even in the absence of real political events. This circus is present to everyone, at any time, at no direct cost of admission (people pay for their devices, cable services, and data used, independently). Everyone can be both alone and in public at the same time, at any time, which has caused drastic revisions in the nature of political communities—as we will soon see. These electronic innovations have radically changed the medium for the transmission of politics and rendered erstwhile ideals of debate quaint, boring to most people, and generally irrelevant.

Phenomenologically, the experience of politics is now a lot richer than passive audiences quietly listening to talking heads with robotic arm gestures or reading what has been said and recapping and discussing it, logically, with decorum. Politics has always had a certain amount of hoopla for prospective voters, but its circus aspects have not before been this omnipresent or loud enough to drown out older methods of discourse and resources for them. Two of those resources have been history and science, specifically, but now specialized knowledge in general is no longer a vital component of political debate. Progressives in the academy have struggled in recent years to understand the inadvertent and willed ignorance of those who have newly taken up oppressive doctrines of nativism and white ethnic nationalism, with reliance on nineteenth-century racist racial science that has been discredited since the 1930s. However, much of the theoretical work in epistemic ignorance that was relevant in 2008 is not useful for understanding what is happening in 2018.

In their edited volume *Race and Epistemologies of Ignorance*, Shannon Sullivan and Nancy Tuana present philosophical analyses of ignorance of racial difference and racism, and cultural examinations of how it serves the interests of white supremacy and privilege to ignore certain kinds of knowledge (Sullivan and Tuana 2007). All of this work remains relevant as examinations of how knowledge selection by white people leaves out the kind of information that would need to be shared by people of all races in an egalitarian society. The white racial identities of white people (Alcoff 2007), their interests in maintaining white racial dominance based on false ideas of their superiority (Mills 2007), and their willingness and ability to select what counts as knowledge and history, in ways that deliberately or inadvertently favor them (Outlaw 2007), all result in official knowledge that falsifies the experience of nonwhites or ignores it outright. Such falsification and omission would be politically important if politics were still based on knowledge. Insofar as politics is based on spectacle and circus, knowledge is no longer relevant to much of current political debate. Still, knowledge originally left out can come back and demand attention through expressive and demonstrative ways, including entertainment, art, and comedy.

Can we describe debate-as-political-circus in terms of epistemic ignorance? The idea of ignorance suggests a lack or absence of truth or knowledge, analogous to the idea of evil as a privation of good. Insofar as the political circus does not even purport to rest on knowledge, it is a plenum, with nothing and no one receptive to knowledge, as such. No one performing in such a circus or organizing it has concerns that go beyond funding and the number of spectators and their "likes" at any given time. Furthermore, as we shall see in chapter 3, the culture wars in terms of social class have also produced the situation of an epistemic plenum for individuals who might otherwise be accurately called ignorant. Here, in considering the realm of turbocharged politics, which feeds on itself after elections, we can see that only a competing circus has the power to intervene with the performances in a dominant circus.

For example, President Trump's legal spokesperson shocked members of his own party with announcements, backed up by the president's own Twitter feed, that the Mueller investigation into connections between Trump's presidential campaign and Russian interference in the 2016 election, together with possible obstructions of justice by members of the administration, was bogus and should be curtailed. Democrats and other progressives immediately became apprehensive that Trump would soon fire Special Counsel Robert Mueller, who had been appointed by his own attorney general's office to independently investigate these matters. The response included the usual countercharges and insistence on what had been documented by Republicans as well as Democrats concerning Trump's obstruction of justice, which were normal knowledge claims in response to epistemic ignorance or falsification. But more noteworthy was MoveOn.org's immediate preemptive organizing efforts, which, on their website, promised an oppositional circus should Mueller be fired. Their text is worth quoting in full to convey its practical urgency:

Nobody Is above the Law—Mueller Firing Rapid Response

Donald Trump is publicly considering firing Special Counsel Robert Mueller, the person leading the Department of Justice investigation of possible criminal actions by Donald Trump and members of his presidential campaign, as well as the efforts to conceal those activities.

It's also possible that, rather than firing Mueller, Trump will obstruct Mueller's investigation by **issuing blanket pardons** of key figures being investigated, **firing Deputy Attorney General Rod Rosenstein** (the person overseeing Mueller), or taking other actions to prevent the investigation from being conducted freely.

Any one of these actions would create a constitutional crisis for our country. It would demand an immediate and unequivocal response to show that we will not tolerate abuse of power from Donald Trump.

Our response in the hours following a power grab will dictate what happens next and whether Congress—the only body with the constitutional power and obligation to rein Trump in from his rampage—will do anything to stand up to him.

That's why we're preparing to hold **emergency "Nobody is Above the Law" rallies** around the country, in the event they are needed.

Use the map or search below by ZIP code to find an event near you, or create one if none exists.

Rallies will begin just hours after national events are triggered:

- If actions are triggered **BEFORE 2 p.m.** local time —> events will **begin @ 5 p.m.** local time.
- If actions are triggered **AFTER 2 p.m.** local time —> events will **begin @ noon** local time the following day.
- This is the general plan—**please confirm details on your event page**, as individual hosts may tailor their events to their local plan.

This is our moment to stand up to protect our democracy. Let's mobilize to show that we won't let Donald Trump become the authoritarian that he aspires to be. The law applies to all of us, and it's essential that it also applies to the most powerful people in our country.

Use the search tool to find an event near you, or create one if none exists.

If you choose to attend an event, you agree to engage in nonviolent, peaceful action, to act lawfully, and to strive to de-escalate any potential confrontations with those who may disagree with our values.

[insert zip code] Search

Create an event in your area! (MoveOn.org 2018)

MoveOn.org's response was rapid, but as a type of response it had precedence in earlier reactions to the 2016 election: The hugely symbolic Women's March on Washington following the 2017 inauguration, in which participants wore pink "pussycat" hats in defiance of the campaign revelation that Trump had bragged about grabbing women by their genitalia, was likely the largest protest in U.S. history (Chenoweth and Pressman 2017; Przybyla and Schouten 2017). New York City airports were immediately brought to a standstill by demonstrators and lawyers to assist detainees after President Trump's first ban on immigration from a list of specific Middle Eastern and North African countries (Gambino et al. 2017). The ensuing court battles over Trump's revised bans remain inconclusive over a year later, although the U.S. Supreme Court has not shown eagerness to support decisions by lower courts on the unconstitutionality of Trump's bans (Gerstein 2017a, 2017b).

Mass demonstrations may delineate specific goals that can lead to political change, but their expressive nature is an important component of democratic life—the people thereby make themselves seen and heard. The Women's March was at the time criticized for an absence of clearly stated goals, but #MeToo erupted in the same year (Lapowsky 2017; also see chapter 4). In addition, the 2017 Women's March in Washington was an international event, anticipated as such and carried out by 2.6 million people worldwide (Schmidt and Almukhtar 2017; Chenoweth and Pressman 2017; Przybyla and Schouten 2017).

Because mass expressions of resistance and calls for change receive wide media attention, politicians eager to become candidates cannot help but take notice and voters may become somewhat activated. In anticipation of the 2018 midterm congressional elections, a number of Democratic victories have occurred in Republican strongholds throughout the United States. While it is difficult to draw direct connections between mass demonstrations and how people vote, it is also difficult to dismiss the influence of mass demonstrations, especially for those who were previously undecided or politically passive. More to the point, such public expressions have resulted in evident tampering down of oppressive or undemocratic positions expressed by the Trump administration at different times. For example, although the Republican party's reaction to Trump's float of firing Mueller was mixed, after several days the idea was "walked back" when the White House issued a statement that the administration intended not to intervene in the completion of the investigation (Day, Tucker, and Lemire 2018).

To track such political details and use them to draw broad conclusions is a dicey business, tedious and exhausting for academic theorists who are at their best in developing perspectives that will hold over many, rather than just a few, "news cycles." But nonetheless, it becomes necessary to pay attention when politics-as-contest overrides normal political life. Parallel to the hegemony of politics has been the hegemony of instant digital communication, which facilitates the spontaneity and instantaneity of turbocharged politics, as noted. This means that erstwhile political theorists need to stoop to the immediate, in order to be apprised of current events at times when current events are the most important events.

POLITICS AND COMMUNITY

Many at this time use the word *community* very loosely. To call a group a community or to append the idea of community to a favored cause or a social identity adds substance to the group, cause, and identity for rhetorical purposes. Thus, the word may be applied to members of groups who do not know one another or do not realize that they have interests in common.

Often, a community is an imagined entity, and even though many may bond over imaging the same community, imaginary entities do not have the same material force as real entities—apart from what people do in their name. Philosophers have emphasized in recent decades the importance of communities as anchors and sources of cherished values, if not values in themselves. Communities thus emphasized contain individual identities that are advocated for and supported, such as LGBTQ communities, Latinx communities, African American communities, academic communities, deaf communities, and for more traditional epistemological purposes, knowledge communities. And this is all fine on the level of discourse, because it signals that a writer or speaker is aware of social issues and has a sense of social responsibility shared by others. But if we are talking about historical events or who supports a given side or cause in politics, it might be helpful to think about what is required for the reality of a community. If we had an idea of what constitutes a real community, it might be possible to predict the outcome of certain political contests, in terms of their influence outside of turbocharged politics.

It would be archaic to restrict the reference of *community* to actual geographical neighborhoods, but it would be too futuristic to call any group participating in an immediate internet craze a community. There should be some material and epistemic cohesion, as well as a geographical foundation of some kind, for a group to constitute a real political community. For example, Kenneth Burke noted very early on during World War II that Hitler understood the importance of centering the Third Reich in Munich as a Nazi mecca (Burke 1939). And in the early twenty-first century, no new community is likely to be viable without a website and a physical office somewhere. A real community should also have a commonality already shared by constituents. Besides such general requirements, one would expect any real community to have the resilience to endure over time, with continuity in its history and resilience in its reaction to external threats and attacks.

As of this writing, just before spring 2018, while Steve Bannon, exiled from the White House and defunded by the powerful Mercers, attempts to peddle nationalist populism in Europe, there is robust protest and police presence at his orations (Farrell 2018). Bannon is trying to build a community or a coalition of communities. But the resistance he meets in Europe, like the current resistance to alt-right speakers on U.S. college campuses, likely issues from already existing communities, of students, teachers, progressives, and others who have supported liberatory causes, as part of their work and aspirations, for some time. The alt-right does not at present have an army, and its prospects for gathering military force seem dim. No matter how many guns individuals in the United States may have, they are not organized for systematic assault against existing police and military. Of course, one doesn't want to give such people ideas and the situation could change, as it did leading up to World War II. We may be one Great Recession or Depression away from alt-right populism finding fertile soil for organized violence. There are plenty of threats to individual freedom and rights violations under the rule of vanilla Republicans, not to mention individual life tragedies for victims of hate crimes and deported immigrants. But, on the ground of community, the establishment or center does hold, and as Nietzsche might have said, so far tragedy is merely repeating itself as farce.

The immediate question is whether the contemporary alt-right constitutes a community for political purposes that go beyond the politics of any given moment, namely the recent political past. Observers concur that this contemporary right-wing element in U.S. politics became visible due to its internet presence after 9/11. More theoretically, there is little doubt that this amalgamation of neo-Nazis, nativists, white supremacists, ethnic nationalists, and so forth received a boost in mainstream media coverage after the 2016 election. And there is no question about the rise in hate crimes during the age of Trump (BBC News 2017; Beirich and Buchanan 2018). Indeed, David Neiwert begins his book *Alt America: The Rise of the Radical Right in the Age of Trump* with the observation that Dylann Roof killed nine African Americans in a church in Charleston, South Carolina, the day after Trump announced his presidency (2007, 1). However, despite widespread internet presence preceding Trump's election, by December 2017 many alt-right websites had been banned from mainstream servers and many of those that had been reconstituted on alternative serves had been abandoned by members and users (Roose 2017).

We should also ask whether the alt-right is a political community in any sustainable material sense. At this time, apart from still random terrorist acts and hate crimes, the alt-right has been a creature of the internet. MoveOn.org, by comparison, is capable of using the internet to organize for public expression by its geographical, ideological, identity, and knowledge-based communities, which there is every reason to credit as real. If this seems speculative about the membership of MoveOn.org, we should note that beyond its effectiveness, its organizational nature defies categorization. Andrew Chadwick described MoveOn.org's internet-based hybridity as borrowing from the nature of interest groups, political parties, and political movements (Chadwick 2005). So the real contrast is that the alt-right remains on the level of politics as contest, whereas MoveOn.org has spilled out of politics into political life. Moreover, MoveOn.org has millions of members, and the membership of the alt-right has been estimated at fifty thousand according to Stephen Pinker, or about 0.02 percent of the U.S. population (Wikipedia 2018b; Pinker 2018, 341).

THE THREAT TO DEMOCRACY

Intellectuals and progressives have a tendency to respond to the content of ideas without regard for the number of people who hold them or their causal efficacy. Thus, the threat of the alt-right is interpreted from the menace of its ideas rather than its practical force. Similarly, politics itself may be interpreted as a threat to democracy that goes beyond self-contained rhetoric, in those cases when it is only that.

Democracy is a political system. Politics is made up of contests. Turbocharged politics can only threaten democracy if it results in a political system that is not democratic. But turbocharged politics is its own self-contained system of expression, contest, resistance, and new context. It may supplant normal political life, but it is not clear that it can change a political system. For that to happen, as it has in the past, the winning side needs material backup, usually the military, and the wherewithal to put campaign promises into reality. Executive directives have to be able to withstand challenges in the courts, and the legislature must be willing and able to pass new laws that can be administratively implemented and enforced. The political *atmosphere* may change in an era of turbocharged politics, but a change in atmosphere is not a change in the fundamental structure of government, especially if the party in power loses participation in the legislature through elections that remain more or less democratic.

The expansion of politics-as-contest and the hegemony of politics over political life described in this chapter may be temporary. The people may rise up and insist on a return to naturally aspirated or even just supercharged politics, but it is important to note that they will have to do that as part of politics, opposing circus with circus or fighting fire with fire. Or these changes may be followed by the kind of dictatorship and totalitarianism that many now fear. In either case, or something in between, the new phenomena are important to recognize if not fully understand. The importance of these phenomena rests on distinguishing politics from what is political. To interpret events, gestures, and rhetoric on the level of politics, as deep political changes and existential threats to democracy, may be precipitous. In *How Democracies Die*, Stephen Levitsky and Daniel Ziblatt analyze transitions from democracy to authoritarian rule in Venezuela, Turkey, and Hungary and draw cautionary parallels with recent changes in the United States. Democratic regimes have been tested by demagogues gaining mainstream political acceptance, subversion of democratic institutions, and transgression of unspoken norms of toleration and restraint in partisan politics. This transgression leads to extreme polarization, the deathblow to democracy (Levitsky and Ziblatt 2018, 1–9). They write, "Many Americans are justifiably frightened by what is happening to our country. But protecting our democracy requires more than just fright or outrage. We must be humble *and* bold. . . .

And we must see how citizens have risen to meet the great democratic crises of the past, overcoming their own deep-seated divisions to avert breakdown" (2018, 10).

The threat to democracy remains a threat that has so far mostly been confined to the sphere of politics, which has taken all of the oxygen out of public attention and not met strong or effective resistance from governing powers. How could it be stopped, given current First Amendment protection? There have been incursions into political life itself, but so far no irrevocable damage has been done that cannot be corrected if partisan politics flips toward Democrats—which is not to minimize the inevitable perils of the other side taking over in the same way. Livitsky and Ziblatt caution that intolerance increases divisions, which can kill democracy. But what if most of this combat is on the level of politics and the vast majority of Americans already know that?

It is true that the Republican-dominated U.S. legislature has taken what it wants according to party goals from Trumpian politics, such as the 2017 tax cut (Kaplan and Rappeport 2017). But it has also perforce compromised somewhat with Democrats on social issues in the March 2018 federal budget (Kaplan 2018). At the same time, the U.S. Supreme Court has been conservative along Republican lines, but that was expected long before politics loomed so large. We should not minimize the massive disruption to public attention and normally aspirated political activities caused by super- and turbocharged politics, but democracy yet lives, although sometimes this is evident only agonistically, in pushback.

Until recently, turbocharged politics has been a tool of the Republican Party. But this could change if Democrats learn how to deploy similar tools for framing issues. In April 2018, a new organization called Navigator published its first report of online findings regarding degrees of concern among Republicans, Democrats, and independent registered voters about controversial contemporary issues, including the long-term future of the economy, corruption in Congress, the motivation for passing the 2018 tax plan, President Trump's norm breaking, and the influence of the NRA. The purpose of Navigator is to provide progressives with information about what the American electorate already cares about so that they can better communicate with and influence members of that electorate through relevant framing or "messaging." On some questions, respondents with very negative opinions of Trump were left out of the surveys, and quotations from respondents were limited to those who were not extremely partisan (Hohmann 2018; Navigator Research 2018). Navigator will either prove to be a tool of turbocharged politics for Democrats or a project for leaders in the Democratic Party and other progressives to become accurately informed about what their constituents think. Insofar as Navigator's mission is explicitly Democratic, it risks the former. But if Navigator manages to avoid becoming overpoliticized or manipulative, it could represent what we will see in chapter 5 is a commonwealth enterprise, originating in the realm of the *social compact*, so as to change the government side of the social contract. Also, as will be addressed in forthcoming chapters, how those both inside and outside of the academy think about recent changes and resistance to them may play some part in eventual real-life outcomes.

REFERENCES

Alcoff, Linda. 2007. "Epistemologies of Ignorance: Three Types." In *Race and Epistemologies of Ignorance*, ed. Shannon Sullivan and Nancy Tuana, 39–58. Albany: State University of New York Press.

BBC News. 2017. "FBI: US Hate Crimes Rise for Second Straight Year." November 13. http://www.bbc.com/news/world-us-canada-41975573.

Beirich, Heidi, and Susy Buchanan. 2018. "2017: The Year in Hate and Extremism." Southern Poverty Law Center, February 11. https://www.splcenter.org/issues/hate-and-extremism.

Burke, Kenneth. 1939. "The Rhetoric of Hitler's Battle." *Southern Review* 5:1–21.

Chadwick, Andrew. 2005. "The Internet, Political Mobilization and Organizational Hybridity: 'Deanspace', MoveOn.org and the 2004 US Presidential Campaign." Paper presented at the 55th Annual Conference of the Political Studies Association of the United Kingdom, University of Leeds, April 4–7.

Chenoweth, Erica, and Jeremy Pressman. 2017. "This Is What We Learned by Counting the Women's Marches." *Washington Post*, February 7. https://www.washingtonpost.com/news/monkey-cage/wp/2017/02/07/this-is-what-we-learned-by-counting-the-womens-marches/?utm_term=.b5c8d292b968.

Childress, Sarah. 2015. "Report: After Citizens United, Outside Spending Doubles." *Frontline*, January 14.

Citizens United v. Federal Election Commission. 2010. 558 U.S. 310.

Crook, Oliver. 2018. "Pennsylvania GOP Moves to Impeach Democratic Supreme Court Justices." *WhoWhatWhy*, March 23. https://whowhatwhy.org/2018/03/23/pennsylvania-gop-moves-to-impeach-democratic-supreme-court-justices/.

Day, Chad, Eric Tucker, and Jonathan Lemire. 2018. "Some in GOP Alarmed as Trump Tweets against Robert Mueller." Associated Press, March 19.

Farrell, Nicholas. 2018. "I'm Fascinated by Mussolini: Steve Bannon on Fascism, Populism and Everything in Between." *Spectator/USA*, March 12. https://usa.spectator.co.uk/2018/03/im-fascinated-by-mussolini-steve-bannon-on-fascism-populism-and-everything-in-between/.

Gambino, Lauren, Sabrina Siddiqui, Paul Owen, and Edward Helmore. 2017. "Thousands Protest against Trump Travel Ban in Cities and Airports Nationwide." *Guardian*, January 29. https://www.theguardian.com/us-news/2017/jan/29/protest-trump-travel-ban-muslims-airports.

Gerstein, Josh. 2017a. "Supreme Court Drops One Trump Travel Ban Case." *Politico*, October 10. https://www.politico.com/story/2017/10/10/trump-travel-ban-supreme-court-243657.

———. 2017b. "Appeals Court Rules against Trump Travel Ban 3.0." *Politico*, December 22. https://www.politico.com/story/2017/12/22/trump-travel-ban-appeal-block-317892.

Gold, Matea. 2014. "Fundraising Expansion Slipped into Spending Deal Could Power Financial Bonanza for Parties." *Washington Post*, December 10. https://www.washingtonpost.com/news/post-politics/wp/2014/12/10/fundraising-expansion-slipped-into-spending-deal-could-power-financial-bonanza-for-parties/?utm_term=.8e4f0ea3f8d7.

Hohmann, James. 2018. "New Coalition Aims to Improve Democratic Messaging against Trump." *Washington Post*, April 18. https://www.washingtonpost.com/news/powerpost/paloma/daily-202/2018/04/18/daily-202-new-coalition-aims-to-improve-democratic-

messaging-against-trump/5ad6951530fb046acf7bccee/?utm_term=.6d45b6465ffe&wpisrc=
nl_daily202&wpmm=1.

Kaplan, Thomas. 2018. "Congressional Leaders Agree on $1.3 Trillion Spending Bill as Deadline Looms." *New York Times*, March 21. https://www.nytimes.com/2018/03/21/us/politics/congress-spending-deal-government-shutdown.html.

Kaplan, Thomas, and Alan Rappeport. 2017. "Republican Tax Bill Passes Senate in 51–48 Vote." *New York Times*, December 19. https://www.nytimes.com/2017/12/19/us/politics/tax-bill-vote-congress.html.

Lapowsky, Issie. 2017. "The Year Women Reclaimed the Web." *Wired*, December 26. https://www.wired.com/story/year-women-reclaimed-the-web/.

Levitsky, Stephen, and Daniel Ziblatt. 2018. *How Democracies Die*. New York: Crown.

Levy, Gabrielle. 2015. "How *Citizens United* Has Changed Politics in 5 Years: The Controversial Supreme Court Ruling Has Remade How Campaigns Are Run in the U.S." *US News*, January 21. https://www.usnews.com/news/articles/2015/01/21/5-years-later-citizens-united-has-remade-us-politics.

Lewis, Lindsay Mark, and Jim Arkedis. 2014. "So You've Won a Seat in Congress—Now What?" *Atlantic*, November 6. https://www.theatlantic.com/politics/archive/2014/11/so-youve-won-election-to-congressnow-what/382421/.

Liptak, Adam. 2018. "Supreme Court Won't Block New Pennsylvania Voting Maps." *New York Times*, March 19. https://www.nytimes.com/2018/03/19/us/politics/supreme-court-pennsylvania-voting-maps.html.

McCutcheon v. Federal Election Commission. 2014. 572 U.S.

Mills, Charles W. 2007. "White Ignorance." In *Race and Epistemologies of Ignorance*, ed. Shannon Sullivan and Nancy Tuana, 11–38. Albany: State University of New York Press.

MoveOn.org. 2018. "No One Is above the Law—Mueller Firing Rapid Response." March 17. https://act.moveon.org/event/mueller-firing-rapid-response-events/search/.

Navigator Research. 2018. "A Guide for Advocates: What Americans Think and How to Talk to Them About It." https://navigatorresearch.org/wp-content/uploads/2018/04/04_2018_Navigator_Final.pdf.

Neiwert, David. 2017. *Alt America: The Rise of the Radical Right in the Age of Trump*. New York: Verso.

Oneshift. 2018. "Turbochargers." March. http://www.oneshift.com/features/8284/naturally-aspirated-vs-turbocharged-vs-supercharged-vs-twincharged-engines/2.

Outlaw, Lucius T., Jr. 2007. "Social Ordering and the Systematic Production of Ignorance." In *Race and Epistemologies of Ignorance*, ed. Shannon Sullivan and Nancy Tuana, 197–212. Albany: State University of New York Press.

Pinker, Stephen. 2018. *Enlightenment Now: The Case for Reason, Science, Humanism, and Progress*. New York: Viking.

ProCar Mechanics. 2018. "Differences between Superchargers and Turbochargers." March. http://procarmechanics.com/differences-between-superchargers-and-turbochargers/.

Przybyla, Heidi M., and Fredreka Schouten. 2017. "At 2.6 Million Strong, Women's Marches Crush Expectations." *USA Today*, January 22. https://www.usatoday.com/story/news/politics/2017/01/21/womens-march-aims-start-movement-trump-inauguration/96864158/.

Roose, Kevin. 2017. "The Alt-Right Created a Parallel Internet. It's an Unholy Mess." *New York Times*, December 11. https://www.nytimes.com/2017/12/11/technology/alt-right-internet.html.

Schmidt, Kiersten, and Sarah Almukhtar. 2017. "Where Women's Marches Are Happening around the World." *New York Times*, January 20. https://www.nytimes.com/interactive/2017/01/17/us/womens-march.html.

Sullivan, Shannon, and Nancy Tuana. 2007. "Introduction." In *Race and Epistemologies of Ignorance*, ed. Shannon Sullivan and Nancy Tuana, 1–10. Albany: State University of New York Press.

U.S. Congress. 1972. *Federal Election Campaign Act of 1971*. Pub.L. 92–225, 86 Stat. 3, 52 U.S.C.

———. 2002. *Bipartisan Campaign Reform Act* (McCain–Feingold Act). Pub.L. 107–55, 116 Stat. 81, H.R. 2356.

Weigel, David. 2018. "Once-Safe Republican Districts Suddenly in Play as Democrats Expand the Map." *Washington Post*, March 18. https://www.washingtonpost.com/powerpost/once-safe-republican-districts-suddenly-in-play-as-democrats-expand-the-map/2018/03/17/441460ea-2921-11e8-bc72-077aa4dab9ef_story.html?utm_term=.8efeb6f54b49.

Weintraub, Ellen L. 2016. "Taking on Citizens United." *New York Times*, March 30. https://www.nytimes.com/2016/03/30/opinion/taking-n-citizens-united.html.

Wikipedia. 2018a. "Donald Trump Presidential Campaign 2020." https://en.wikipedia.org/wiki/Donald_Trump_presidential_campaign,_2020.

———. 2018b. "MoveOn." https://en.wikipedia.org/wiki/MoveOn.

———. 2018c. "Winning Isn't Everything; It's The Only Thing." https://en.wikipedia.org/wiki/Winning_isn%27t_everything;_it%27s_the_only_thing.

Chapter Two

The Junction of Race

The principle of explosion is a logical rule of inference. According to the rule, from a set of premises in which a sentence A and its negation \neg A are both true (i.e., a contradiction is true), any sentence B may be inferred. It is also known by its Latin name *ex contradictione quodlibet*, meaning from a contradiction anything follows, or ECQ for short. (Rational Wiki 2018)

AFTER A CONTRADICTION

Race is now a separate category of human social status that is on a separate track after a junction, following a contradiction. It was not always so. The racial junction is the result of the contradiction between stated legal equality and attitudes and practices of inequality. The achievement of legal equality as a result of the 1950s and 1960s civil rights movements, from the Supreme Court ruling for integrated education in 1954 to the egalitarian employment, voting rights, and immigration legislation of 1964–1965, was a culmination of applicative justice concerning race. Nonwhites were to have the same employment access, citizen rights, and immigration opportunities as whites. The social contract had thereby been perfected regarding race. Government sanction and instigation of racist exclusion and persecution after that fact and its lack of correction is part of the current breakage of the social contract, as the social contract has been popularly understood.

The racial junction is most sharply evident pertaining to African Americans, although its life-shattering effects are comparable for Latinx and Native Americans, as will become evident in later chapters. During Jim Crow, when there were explicit antiblack laws and policies regarding public facilities, residential location, education, and employment, antiblack treatment was not unpredictable or surprising to either whites or blacks. After the civil rights legislation, there was a period of time with a general consensus that African Americans and other minorities would steadily progress toward equality, so that descriptions of racist treatment could be addressed as anomalous but tractable. It was not difficult to imagine what could be done to correct them. And progressives assumed that their racially egalitarian views represented a broad social consensus. Such assumption conveniently ignored the growing prison system that was largely populated by minorities, persistent poverty in minority communities, and the transformation of affirmative action as a project for the betterment of nonwhites into diversity as a project to benefit organizations that remain predominantly white.

The contradiction between formal equality and reality regarding racial difference has given rise to the small variety of issues considered here: how the junction of race goes beyond an intersection; racial life spoilage and insecurity; race-based insecurity and hermeneutic conflict; whether racism can be reduced to other factors. All of this leads to discussion of the scope of needed change and the contrast between historical trends and individual life.

BEYOND INTERSECTION

Consider in regard to civil rights–era optimism Kimberle Crenshaw's 1989 introduction of the methodological concept of *intersection*, with the example of black women falling through the cracks of discrimination claims in employment terminations, when official policy protected blacks and women separately but not specifically black women. There was no statistical pattern of discrimination against blacks because black men were not discriminated against, or against women because white women were not discriminated against. Therefore, discrimination against black women could not be supported by any of the accepted statistical patterns pertaining to race or gender, which were based on legally protected classifications (Crenshaw 1989). But there was ongoing discrimination against black women! The solution to Crenshaw's legal dead end would have been a new protected class of black women. Crenshaw's analysis of how black women fell through a crack in antidiscrimination employment law identified black women as an *intersection* between identities of race and gender. And that launched the critical theory of intersectionality.

Leaving aside the inertial forces against the creation of a new protected class of black women, the difficulty of proving discrimination for members of racial groups with existing protected class status, and the years it takes to bring any one racial discrimination case through the courts, there is now no reason to be confident that such a new classification of black women would end discrimination against black women in employment situations. This is because law is insufficient to effect real change. Changes in laws have to be applied, and if the changes are progressive, their application requires good-will for changing individual habits and group traditions. A new protected class of black women would require changes in thought and habit, away from assimilating them into existing protected classes of women and blacks to-ward practical recognition of them as members of a new protected class. But even should that happen, insofar as existing protected classes are not pro-tected, why should a new one be?

Concerning black men, formal safeguards against racial discrimination in the criminal justice system have not prevented arbitrary killings of innocent black men by local police officers. Perpetrators of such homicides have usually been immune to indictments and convictions based on the "reason-able officer standard" that a police officer could exonerate himself by claim-ing he believed his life was in danger. Several U.S. Supreme Court rulings about this standard would have to be reversed to create legal accountability for such cases. And even should that occur, there would need to be further changes in individual attitudes and group traditions for juries to indict and convict (Zack 2015).

This present living discrepancy between general formal equality and real inequality provides a lesson that changes in laws and directives are only part of what is necessary to correct racial inequality when racism persists in attitudes and action. When Crenshaw identified the ways that black women fell through the cracks of antidiscrimination law in 1989, she was writing under an assumption that formal changes could be real changes. Many pro-gressive Americans are now being forced to wake up to the reality that written law in itself has no efficacy without a will to obey it, and that forcing the public and government officials to obey just written law is an indepen-dent uphill project. Indeed, even if legal corrections of injustice were effica-cious, as Arthur Bentley emphasized, the process of getting to just legislation is not based on simple recognition of what would be just, but is the result of contending interests (Zack 2016, 24–32, 36–40).

However, a thoroughgoing acceptance of Bentley's perspective is ulti-mately cynical about the possible permanence of anything that is initially intended to be a lasting change. Would we say, for example, that despite constitutional amendments black chattel slavery could still recur, and that if it did, it would just have to be dealt with as a matter of conflicting interests? Scholars and researchers have largely addressed arbitrary post–civil rights era racism through explanations in terms of institutional or structural racism. In practical terms, such explanations amount to concessions that racism is too deeply embedded in habits and practices and the legacies of past injustice, passed on intergenerationally, to be eradicated once and for all. But how do we know this is the case? Has there ever been a national effort in the United States to eradicate racism once and for all?

As a violation of post–civil rights legislation, ongoing racist exclusions and persecutions that go unchecked, and are sometimes even encouraged by government officials, are part of the breakage of the social contract. If government proclaims explicit legal egalitarianism, regardless of race, and some of those governed are not treated equally to others, because of race, then government is not benefiting all of the governed. Many have devoted lifetimes to scholarship about constitutional interpretation, a smaller number to constitutional interpretation regarding race, but very little of any depth is written or spoken about interpretation of the social contract and much less in terms of the social contract and race. Of course, the social contract is not a legal founding document but a set of background assumptions about the purpose of government. It may be that the social contract is therefore irrelevant because it is only an oral or thought tradition. Or it may be that the social contract is the unseen glue holding civil society under government together.

RACIAL LIFE SPOILAGE AND INSECURITY

Whether it is a matter of conforming to the principles of the social contract or an unavoidable part of the process of government, the issue of getting people to behave justly extends into institutions that may have explicit, egalitarian policies, analogous to egalitarian laws from government. Both black men and black women are now free to enter institutions, such as higher education or corporations, and they may even be encouraged to do so; they are also free to move around unobstructed in public spaces and use public facilities, with no official or formal racial barriers. However, within institutions, traditional patterns of power allocation and cronyism often prevent equality with whites of blacks and other people of color in advancement to leadership positions based on merit (Zack 2013, 2016). That is, equal opportunity for access does not extend to equal opportunities to share power for people of color who gain entry. In public spaces, many situations are chaotically arbitrary. Black and brown people are unpredictably vulnerable to interference with their autonomous purposes, through harassment by security guards, violence by police, or both harassment and violence by random members of the public. They may also be subject to individual expressions of race-based devaluation and insult, which because they are not in accord with stated general policy are treated as isolated incidents in terms of correction. In addition, in seemingly egalitarian contexts, people of color may be personally stereotyped by co-workers, supervisors, service personnel, and members of organizations with which they do business. As with overt and incontrovertible aggression, such microaggression is unpredictable.

The result of such macro- and microaggression, for any given black individual, is that life itself and the quality of life in society is precarious, simply based on race. There is always, and perhaps everywhere, overhanging, unpredictable obstruction or danger. For people of color, but especially black people, anything that should happen can fail to happen because of their race, and anything that should not happen could happen because of their race. When events proceed as expected based on merit or unjust events do not occur, it may look as though the system is racially just and equal. But no black individual can know when and where they will be the unjust victim of racism, until after the fact. And after that fact, the racist event will be treated as an isolated anomaly, much like an automobile accident or an episode in a constant ongoing national game of Russian roulette in which, for black people, the bullets are disproportionately in their chambers when triggers are pulled. Any deprivation of life or quality of life resulting from police homicide, racial profiling, suspicion by white people in public spaces, outright harassment, or failure to advance within institutions based on merit can spoil life for any individual black person concerned. The spoilage may be forever, for a day, for a period of time in a residential neighborhood, or over the course of a career.

Black racial appearance in itself can spark suspicion and surveillance, especially when blacks are present in de facto segregated white neighborhoods in cities and suburbs. In predominantly black neighborhoods, whites who enter are fearful of crime and police officers may take preemptive self-protective action. But such danger is not limited to cities or suburbs. Much of the most egregious violence against African Americans after the late nineteenth century took place in rural areas. One of the most poignantly dehumanizing legacies of antiblack racism in rural America is the alienation of African Americans from national parks and other venues for recreation in nature. That alienation is not based merely on folk stories of what happened where, such as local lore or casual remarks about what was once a "lynching tree," but ongoing suspicion by whites of the mere presence of any black people in wilderness areas (Finney 2014). There is a cruel irony here because 90 percent of the African American population lived in rural areas before great migrations to urban areas, both North and South, in the early twentieth century (Pruitt 2013; Wilkerson 2010).

The present racial whiteness of environmental preservation goals and projects is similar to the traditional racial whiteness of high culture, including art, music, theater, and western European literature. Such alienation persists despite curatorial, directorial, and media efforts to introduce diversity. In all likelihood, it is at the root of the well-known problem of rejection of school by even very young poor black children, in that case transmogrified into peer censure of "acting white."

Both this kind of spoilage and its possibility are far more than the results of an intersection. They occur at the *junction of race*, when race goes off on its own track in ways that are not predictable for any given instance but always have some degree of probability beyond mere possibility. Even when diversity is a stated value, people can experience surprising, instantaneous exclusions, for example, as of this writing, allegations that Donald Trump removed women who were "too ethnic" from the group of final contestants in the 2013 Miss Universe Pageant (Williams 2018).

Although such unjust explicitly discriminatory acts are episodic and happen only to individuals here and there, and now and then, because they happen to those individuals as a result of their race and because that race is shared by all members of the same racial group, the psychic aspect of the resulting fear, alienation, and dehumanization extends to all members of the group. Indeed, the arbitrary and unpredictable quality of such harm makes it ominous. That the harm may occur after admission or entry in the name of diversity adds to potential anxiety for all members of the group. If one black person is harmed because she is black, then any black person can and may be harmed, in the same way and at any time, because she is black.

The same ominous structure hangs over members of other racial minority groups, when harm to individuals is based on their racial or ethnic identities. To call this condition "racial stress" in a psychological sense may do it a disservice in adding insult to the initial injuries, by categorizing such psychic effects as matters of mental health or associating them with increased morbidity and mortality (Bulatao and Anderson 2004). They are matters of mental health that affect physical health, but not in a sense that should be relegated to individual subjective pathology and preexisting debility. Racial stress is the result of racism. It is shared by many, and only recognizing and treating the stress does not address its causes. On an individual level, if people are intending to harm you and disrupt your life, concern about such a threat is not paranoia. It is an individual instance of a social problem. It cannot be cured by medication or counseling, although both may alleviate it and minimize symptoms. The cure is justice. In the meantime, individuals who experience or fear racial injustice dedicate differing parts of their life energies to coping with it, in ways dependent on their temperaments and resources: they suffer, sicken, die, talk, support one another, protest, seek treatment, and express their experience in creative and intellectual projects. All of these reactions are part of existential situations (Zack 1996).

The incidental quality of unjust harm to people of color is not a constant condition. Most unarmed young black men are not shot and killed by police. Indeed, the percentage of the whole black population that is killed by police is probably miniscule. Because the numbers may not be significant statistically, the white public can briefly attend to high-profile incidents and then go on its way as though these uncommon but not rare incidents and the attention they demand are not really part of daily life. And the white public is correct about this, from its white racial perspective. But from the perspective of nonwhites, the ominous possibility of such incidents is a constant condition. This disparity can be described as a difference in security, and it is unjust that nonwhite race is the cause of this difference as a constant overhanging aspect of the lives of nonwhite people, especially African Americans. If security is a fundamental human right, *race-based insecurity* is a violation of that right, a breakage of the social contract, insofar as government fails to deter and punish offenders.

RACE-BASED INSECURITY AND HERMENEUTIC CONFLICT

One barrier to effective resistance against race-based insecurity is what Miranda Fricker has called *hermeneutic injustice*, a form of epistemic injustice pertaining to shared interpretation. The *collective* interpretation of race shared by whites and nonwhites in the United States has not provided resources for everyone in that system, that is, both whites and nonwhites, to name or conceptualize race-based insecurity. As a form of injustice that is systematic, part of an overall system, and linked to hierarchy within that system, race-based insecurity is caused by differences in status based on racial identities that are determined by the members of the dominant group in the system. Although Fricker's analysis of hermeneutic injustice primarily relies on examples involving white women and men, her definition of hermeneutic injustice is highly relevant to nonwhite racial injustice. Fricker writes, "Hermeneutical injustice is: the injustice of having some significant area of one's social experience obscured from collective understanding owing to a structural identity prejudice in the collective hermeneutical resource" (2007, 155).

Kristie Dotson (2014) extends Fricker's work on epistemic injustice to distinguish between forms of epistemic oppression that can be reduced to wider systems of political and social oppression, so as to correct them, and those that cannot be reduced because of the strength and resilience of an oppressive system. Alison Bailey (2014) notes that there is some vagueness in how Dotson identifies the nature of such recalcitrance or inertia, on the side of the racist system, and suggests development of earlier work by Jean Bartunek and Michael Moch (1994), who emphasized emotional and spiritual epistemic breakthroughs. Bailey (2014) herself advocates aesthetic and affective additions to purely cognitive approaches to epistemic injustice.

THE REDUCTION OF RACISM TO OTHER FACTORS

To reduce racism to social and political factors is to comprehensively explain it as an effect of them. Before diminishing the importance of such cognitive approaches to the inertia of racist systems or systems of racism, it is important to consider Frantz Fanon's claim that racism is *always* reducible to social and political factors, and to economic gain especially. Fanon fully explored the phenomenological effects of antiblack racism on the oppressed, based on his own psychological experience. But in his more revolutionary mode, he was mindful of the material gains of racists. He wrote:

> The oppressed continues to come up against racism. He finds this sequel illogical, what he has left behind him inexplicable, without motive, incorrect. His knowledge, the appropriation of precise and complicated techniques, sometimes his intellectual superiority as compared to a great number of racists, lead him to qualify the racist world as passion-charged. He perceives that the racist atmosphere impregnates all the elements of the social life. The sense of an overwhelming injustice is correspondingly very strong. Forgetting racism as a consequence, one concentrates on racism as cause. (Fanon 1969, 40)

Still, the deep inertia of racism as an oppressive system with irrational eruptions has not as yet been conclusively or permanently disrupted, not by law, literature, reform, or even public protest. Of all these, public protest has an existential force that may, at least momentarily—activists aim for permanent changes—speak to the existential force of an otherwise inert oppressive racist system. At the same time, protest may soften oppressive structures so as to attack the material aspect of the social and political structure to which it may be reduced. The problem with refusal or failure of those who benefit from and defend the system to allow for criticism or correction is that they live higher-status lives without understanding or imagining what life is like for those who are oppressed in the system—they do not walk in their shoes. The oppressed cannot make their oppressors walk in their shoes—if they could, they would not be oppressed. But the oppressed can literally demonstrate or express their frustration, as recently evident in the Black Lives Matter movement.

#BlackLivesMatter was founded by activists Alicia Garza, Patrisse Cullors, and Opal Tometi after George Zimmerman was acquitted of killing Trayvon Martin in 2013 (Black Lives Matter 2018). Its street presence came to national prominence after the killing of Michael Brown in Ferguson, Missouri, in 2014, although its real public sphere was Twitter, where it was opposed by #AllLivesMatter in contentious discussion over whether police or unarmed black men were the real victims in such incidents (Carney 2016). But apart from those directly involved in discursive, rhetorical struggle over how to present the reality of race and racism in the twenty-first-century

United States, it was the videos of physical protest and reactions against protestors that captured attention in the national auditorium (YouTube 2018). The optics have virtual and real visceral effects, from the bodies of protesters to the bodies of onlookers. People are moved by certain images, sounds, and action sequences.

There has, of course, been vehement reaction against Black Lives Matter, for instance, Blue Lives Matter, with the tagline, "Sometimes there's justice, sometimes there's just us" (Blue Lives Matter 2018). Returning to the importance of politics as discussed in chapter 1, it is not surprising that those who support Blue Lives Matter also emphasize their affiliation with "the Law and Order party"—Trump proudly described himself as the "Law and Order Candidate" during the 2016 presidential campaign (Nelson 2016). But Black Lives Matter continues, with growing national and worldwide resonance, physical protest, and public demonstration, which may be the material needed to effectively dislodge the inertia of those social and political structures that are otherwise resistant to change on cognitive levels. The most resistant forms of hermeneutical injustice could be dislodged by such physical methods that also have aesthetic and affective dimensions, with depiction on both mass and social media.

As opposition to injustice, Black Lives Matter and the opposition to it is a site of *hermeneutic conflict*. Black Lives Matter activists, their supporters among the public, academics, and other intellectuals who agree with their protests do not themselves suffer from hermeneutic injustice because they have plenty of resources to interpret violence against minorities and they handily deploy them. However, the entire collective of this movement, plus those who oppose it, lacks resources for *shared* interpretations. Epistemic conflict is not a problem in a First Amendment sense, but it is disruptive to the social contract premise that government benefits all of those governed. In cases of social injustice perpetrated by government officials, the failure of government to check offenders by privileging the perspective of some police officers constitutes the epistemic nature of the conflict. What minorities call injustice, those in power call the just application of law for social order. Also, the expression of propensities to create crimes against racial minorities are treated as free speech issues, instead of expression of criminal intent. Epistemic conflict politicizes injustice in this case, thereby bringing it into the zero-sum game of racism versus egalitarianism. Still, it may be that to the extent the conflict has been won by Black Lives Matter, some inertial racism has been dislodged.

Not the least of liberatory gains after protests in Ferguson was the revelation that the context of intrusive police surveillance in that city was the tip of an iceberg consisting of city funding by indebtedness through fines and court fees levied against poor black people for typically minor, nonviolent offenses. Under the Obama administration, Department of Justice investigations in multiple cities across the United States revealed similar connections between municipal finances and "crime fighting" (Pinard 2015). Such exposure has led to reform in a number of police departments, with a reemphasis on community involvement to build trust for police work (Reisig and Kane 2014; James 2015). After the protests in Ferguson, there was a wide perception that police officers were demoralized and not as willing to perform regular policing jobs. But it seems that individual officers who believe they are fair are no less motivated to engage with communities (Wolfe and Nix 2016). In addition, there has been widespread discussion about the effectiveness of requiring police to wear body cameras as a deterrence for, and documentation of, crimes they might commit (Simmons 2015).

THE SCOPE OF NEEDED CHANGE

As Black Lives Matter tripped the radar of intellectuals, the discourse of white privilege, conducted by white people, drew fresh breath. But insofar as the lives and quality of life of white people are not precarious as those of black people are, it does not adequately describe or address injustice to black people by saying that there is white privilege. There is white privilege, which is normal, lawful, predictable, human, and humane treatment of white people, with corresponding well-confirmed expectations of such treatment. White privilege is a contrast to the precarious nature of life and quality of life for nonwhite and especially black people because of the track of race. When white people acknowledge their privilege, they are recognizing the discrimination they are free of, by comparison. But this recognition is no more than that—it does nothing to change the underlying system that makes black life and quality of life precarious (Zack 2015, chap. 1). The question naturally arises of what would decisively change this underlying system that is like a rigged game of Russian roulette for black Americans.

To speak of systemic change that would create parity between black and white Americans in life and quality of life is like constructing ideas of utopia or composing wish lists. There is no evidence that such change could occur immediately or in the foreseeable future. In fact, the steps back in progress toward equality that have been evident in contemporary neo–white supremacist activism and expression suggest that before positive change can be undertaken, there will need to be effective measures against these abuses of free speech shading into abusive action (as well as illegitimate acquisition of political power). Nevertheless, it is worthwhile to consider the scope of such systematic change and therein distinguish between big- and small-picture changes.

Big-picture changes range from beatific visions of universal love to critiques of capitalism as the primary system for the production and distribution of material goods and services. We should return to Fanon and put love aside, because viewing a feeling as a cure for racism may lead to mistaking racism as a cause instead of an effect, a justification, or a rationalization for exploitation, ill-gotten gains, or criminal activities that may have begun as race-neutral. Fanon offered a caution to revolutionaries against positing racism as a cause, whereby "campaigns of deintoxication are launched. Appeal is made to the sense of humanity, to love, to respect for the supreme values" (Fanon 1969, 40). In addition, love can result in harm (e.g., "for their own good"), and even benevolent love need not result in the cessation of harm or in positive good.

The problem with supplanting capitalism with a more equitable system is that the great mass of people in the world appear to prefer capitalism over other economic systems, including communism. They prefer capitalism for its opportunities for individual enterprise, as well as its promise of the consumption of more and better products, more services, and general relief from poverty. Moreover, it is not always clear how capitalism itself results in racism within the United States at this time, although global economic empires do exist to the disadvantage of people of color worldwide. Within the United States, the return to a mixed economy with adequate safety nets for the poor and support of education on all levels could be both national and local goals, after their abandonment on a federal level. Education is of particular importance, not only for its instrumental value of making graduates competitive for employment, but because educated people of all races are less easily persuaded by ideologies that ignore problems experienced by people whose identities are connected to lives different from their own.

The public dispute via Twitter between Ta-Nehisi Coates and Cornel West about the causes of racial inequality in the early twenty-first century is instructive about these issues. Coates highlighted white supremacy and white privilege in his 2015 book *Between the World and Me*. In his 2017 collection of essays *We Were Eight Years in Power*, Coates described the transition from President Obama to President Trump as an erasure of the progress toward racial equality that had been made under the Obama administration. West criticized Coates as "fetishizing white supremacy" to the neglect of big-picture global issues. He wrote, "The disagreement between Coates and me is clear. Any analysis or vision of our world that omits the centrality of Wall Street power, US military policies, and the complex dynamics of class, gender, and sexuality in black America is too narrow and dangerously misleading. So it is with Ta-Nehisi Coates' worldview." Coates responded that he had previously criticized monetary interests and global imperialism many times. He then withdrew from the dispute by canceling his Twitter account, which had millions of followers (Rogers et al. 2017).

It is not clear from this public clash precisely where the disagreement lies. West is clearly interested in the position of the United States, globally, as a background condition for internal racism. Coates is more focused on the precarious nature of black life in the United States, as a result and expression of white supremacy and racism. The questions are how the factors of national racism and global imperialism are related, whether one causes the other and whether one can be corrected without the other. We can imagine global egalitarianism coexisting with national racism within the United States. We can also imagine U.S. racial egalitarianism coexisting with ongoing global imperialism. This is not to say that there is no relationship between American white supremacy and American global imperialism but simply that correcting one does not guarantee correction of the other. Which injustice becomes a primary liberatory project is a matter of the interest of the progressive thinker in question. There is also an earlier Fanonian choice of viewing nonwhite racial life within the United States as a form of internal colonial oppression (Staples 1987).

It is difficult to convince people of color that hateful expressions of racism against them are a smokescreen for material exploitation. It is a hard sell because racist aggression hurts beyond physical damage, and reactions of indignation and anger are justified. But racism could still be a smokescreen. Ongoing racism can obscure the antiblack exploitation and real material gains to whites exemplified in Ferguson, as just discussed. Where racism against a minority nonwhite group, such as Native Americans, does not dominate discourse, ongoing settler colonialism may be more visible. (See the discussion of Standing Rock in chapter 7.)

Concerning race and racism within the United States (the subject here), the precarious nature of black life and black quality of life is kept going by racist ideology that motivates segments of the electorate to vote for candidates who may ultimately serve the global interests West describes. But more to the point, it is the racist ideology on a U.S. national level that needs to be addressed in order to address the threats to nonwhite life within this nation.

The Russian roulette nature of dangers to those who bear nonwhite racial identities represents a change in U.S. culture that constitutes the explicit contradiction between formal racial equality in law and stated policy and what can and does happen in reality. From such a contradiction, anything can, and does, happen, as suggested by this chapter's epigraph. That is, when the rights of people of color were explicitly violated under Jim Crow laws, the harm to them was predictable and circumscribed. The harm today is unpredictable and unbounded. (That the logical principle refers to contradictory language does not limit its applicability here because the contradictions can be identified between statements of egalitarian law and policy and descriptions of actions that contradict those statements.) The cultural change resulting from this contradiction is a condition that can be focused and implemented in politics. Politicians can call it forth through coded hate speech and even explicit racist exhortation and vilification, just as a magnifying glass can concentrate sunlight to start a fire. The result is that the dynamic and unpredictable nature of the category of race exceeds identities and spills over into politics. While other progressive categories have also been politicized, there is at this time nothing as arbitrary as the use of nonwhite race in turbocharged politics.

HISTORICAL TRENDS AND INDIVIDUAL LIFE

Given its arbitrary nature and independent track that goes beyond intersection, the reality of race can no longer be contained within a single subject, as will be evident throughout the remaining chapters. But before we do go on, something should be said about the balance between individual tragedy and statistical well-being for the group to which individuals struck by tragedy belong. Steven Pinker has devoted substantial scholarly effort and as a public intellectual has engaged wide professional and intellectual audiences with an optimistic thesis that human life has progressed over centuries in accord with humanistic values made real through the rational application of scientific knowledge (Lavin Agency 2018). Concerning race and the contemporary circumstances of African Americans, in his *Enlightenment Now: The Case for Reason, Science, Humanism, and Progress*, Pinker presents the following evidence of progress: Barack Obama's presidency; declines in prejudice against black and white dating between 1985 and 2010; less racism among millennials (who will be the majority dominant population in the future) than senior citizens; a fall in the black poverty rate from 55 to 17.6 percent between 1960 and 2011; a rise in black life expectancy from age thirty-three in 1900 to 75.6 in 2015, with less of a gap with whites. Pinker also presents statistical evidence that black suspects are not more likely than white suspects to be killed by police (2018, 214–17).

Pinker omits the white racist backlash against Obama's presidency, and his life-span and poverty statistics omit comparison between blacks and whites. But let's say for the sake of argument that there has been substantial progress in the aggregate circumstances of African Americans, over the past century. Is that relevant to arbitrary and life-shattering aspects of bearing black identities at this time? It is not, because people do not live in centuries but in years, months, days, hours, minutes, seconds. Individual life is concrete and immediate, and shared on the basis of racial identity, so that harm to an individual based on race, even if it is statistically insignificant, does affect large numbers of other members of that individual's racial group. Also, any individual who is harmed on the basis of race cannot find real comfort or compensation in optimistic statistical data. In fact, such data may make the individual feel worse about her circumstances. The point here is that racial life (all life) is experienced by specific individuals in limited time spans.

But of course it is a good thing if there is progress in the aggregate, and knowledge of that may help restore perspective in the face of bad news. One of Pinker's reiterated complaints is the failure of many progressive intellectuals to duly acknowledge progress. And he suggests that they are too caught up in events of the moment: "Like other forms of progressophobia, the denial of advances in rights has been abetted by sensational headlines. A string of highly publicized killings by American police officers of unarmed African American suspects, some of them caught on smartphone videos, has led to a sense that the country is suffering an epidemic of racist attacks by police on black men" (2018, 215). Again, granting Pinker his thesis of progress in the long term, part of that progress has been in response to those who protest and complain about the regress emblazoned in the headlines. It may be that the contradiction between regressive events in the moment and long-term progress is all the more bitter against the "arc of progress" and that the intensity of such bitterness is part of what is necessary for there to be long-term progress.

REFERENCES

Bailey, Alison. 2014. "The Unlevel Knowing Field: An Engagement with Dotson's Third-Order Epistemic Oppression." *Social Epistemology Review and Reply Collective* 3 (10): 62–68. https://social-epistemology.com/2014/09/29/the-unlevel-knowing-field-an-engagement-with-dotsons-third-order-epistemic-oppression-alison-bailey/.

Bartunek, Jean M., and Michael K. Moch. 1994. "Third-Order Organizational Change and the Western Mystical Tradition." *Journal of Organizational Change Management* 7 (1): 24–41.

Black Lives Matter. 2018. "About." https://blacklivesmatter.com/about/.

Blue Lives Matter. 2018. https://www.facebook.com/bluematters/.

Bulatao, Rudolfo A., and Norman B. Anderson, eds. 2004. *Understanding Racial and Ethnic Differences in Health in Late Life: A Research Agenda*. National Research Council Panel on Race, Ethnicity, and Health in Later Life. Washington, DC: National Academies Press. https://www.ncbi.nlm.nih.gov/books/NBK24685/.

Carney, Nikita. 2016. "All Lives Matter, but So Does Race: Black Lives Matter and the Evolving Role of Social Media." *Humanity & Society* 40 (2): 1–21. https://www.researchgate.net/publication/301310750_All_Lives_Matter_but_so_Does_Race_Black_Lives_Matter_and_the_Evolving_Role_of_Social_Media.

Crenshaw, Kimberle. 1989. "Demarginalizing the Intersection of Race and Sex: A Black Feminist Critique of Antidiscrimination Doctrine, Feminist Theory and Antiracist Politics." *University of Chicago Legal Forum* 1989 (1): 139–67. http://chicagounbound.uchicago.edu/uclf/vol1989/iss1/8.

Coates, Ta-Nehisi. 2015. *Between the World and Me*. New York: Spiegel and Grau.

Dotson, Kristie. 2014. "Conceptualizing Epistemic Oppression." *Social Epistemology* 28 (2): 115–38. DOI:10.1080/02691728.2013.782585.

Fanon, Frantz. 1969. *Toward the African Revolution: Political Essays*. Trans. Haakon Chevalier. New York: Grove Press.

Finney, Carolyn. 2014. *Black Faces, White Spaces: Reimagining the Relationship of African Americans to the Great Outdoors*. Chapel Hill: University of North Carolina Press.

Fricker, Miranda. 2007. *Epistemic Injustice: Power and the Ethics of Knowing*. Oxford: Oxford University Press.

James, Joy. 2015. "Moving Targets." *Cultural Anthropology* website, June 29. https://culanth.org/fieldsights/689-moving-targets.

Lavin Agency. 2018. "Steven Pinker." March. http://www.thelavinagency.com/speakers/steven-pinker.

Nelson, Louis. 2016. "Trump: 'I Am the Law and Order Candidate.'" *Politico*, July 11. https://www.politico.com/story/2016/07/trump-law-order-candidate-225372.

Pinard, Michael. 2015. "Poor, Black and 'Wanted': Criminal Justice in Ferguson and Baltimore." *Howard Law Journal* 58 (3): 1–16. http://digitalcommons.law.umaryland.edu/fac_pubs/1532/.

Pinker, Stephen. 2018. *Enlightenment Now: The Case for Reason, Science, Humanism, and Progress*. New York: Crown.

Pruitt, Bernadette. 2013. *The Other Great Migration: The Movement of Rural African Americans to Houston, 1900–1941*. College Station: Texas A&M University Press.

Rational Wiki. 2018. "The Principle of Explosion." March. https://rationalwiki.org/wiki/Principle_of_explosion.

Reisig, Michael D., and Robert J. Kane, eds. 2014. *The Oxford Handbook of Police and Policing*. Oxford: Oxford University Press.

Rogers, Melvin, Patrisse Cullors, Carol Anderson, and Shailja Patel. 2017. "Ta-Nehisi Coates v Cornel West: Black Academics and Activists Give Their Verdict." *Guardian*, December 22. https://www.theguardian.com/commentisfree/2017/dec/22/-ta-nehisi-coates-cornel-west-black-academic-activists-debate-equality.

Simmons, K. C. 2015. "Body-Mounted Police Cameras: A Primer on Police Accountability vs. Privacy." *Howard Law Journal* 58 (3): 881–91.

Staples, Robert. 1987. *The Urban Plantation: Racism and Colonialism in the Post Civil Rights Era*. Oakland, CA: Black Scholar Press.

Wilkerson, Isabel. 2010. *The Warmth of Other Suns: The Epic Story of America's Great Migration*. New York: Random House.

Williams, Cara. 2018. "Trump Would Remove Women Deemed 'Too Ethnic' from Miss Universe." *Vibe*, March 9. https://www.vibe.com/2018/03/trump-racial-discrimination-miss-universe-report/.

Wolfe, S. E., and J. Nix. 2016. "The Alleged 'Ferguson Effect' and Police Willingness to Engage in Community Partnership." *Law and Human Behavior* 40 (1): 1–10. http://dx.doi.org/10.1037/lhb0000164.

YouTube. 2018. Black Lives Matter videos. https://video.search.yahoo.com/search/video;_ylt=Awr9DuxmuKVaZjMA6EpXNyoA;_ylu=X3oDMTE0ZXJsN2l2BGNvbG8DZ3Ex BHBvcwMxBHZ0aWQDQjUxOTVfMQRzZWMDc2l2cw--?p=black+lives+matter&fr2=piv-web&fr=mcafee.

Zack, Naomi. 1996. "Race, Life, Death, Identity, Tragedy and Good Faith." In *Existence in Black*, ed. Lewis R. Gordon, 99–110. New York: Routledge.

———. 2013. "Pluralism in 'Academic Politics': The Collateral Damage of Cronyism and Legal Aspects of Common Misconduct." *American Philosophical Association Newsletter* 12 (2): 3–8.

———. 2015. *White Privilege and Black Rights: The Injustice of U.S. Police Racial Profiling and Homicide*. Lanham, MD: Rowman & Littlefield.

———. 2016. *Applicative Justice: A Pragmatic Empirical Approach to Racial Injustice*. Lanham, MD: Rowman & Littlefield.

Chapter Three

The Political Creation of Class

What is your social class? Take our quiz to find out!

How do you feel about gospel music? Pedestrian crosswalks? Humanity in general? Your social class is more complex than your salary or your educational pedigree.

This quiz is based on polling data and peer-reviewed research from an array of academic fields which have explored how socioeconomic status helps shape our inner and social lives. (Tepper 2013)

A majority of Republicans and Republican-leaning independents (58%) now say that colleges and universities have a negative effect on the country, up from 45% last year. By contrast, most Democrats and Democratic leaners (72%) say colleges and universities have a positive effect, which is little changed from recent years. (Pew Research Center 2017)

Obviously Victor Frankenstein meets a tragic end as a result of a tragic character flaw—he dies pursuing the monster that he created out of his own misguided attempt to manipulate nature by endeavoring to do something man was never meant to do—create life. ("How Is Frankenstein a Tragic Hero?" 2018)

The correspondence between the philosophical or theoretical treatments of class and the way people live and understand themselves and others within a class system is very different from the match concerning race. Within systems of race, the philosophical analyses and lived realities resemble one another, and there is agreement between theorists and nontheorists about the existence of a racial system. Moreover, most individuals living within racial systems would say that they knew what race they were. (The viability of the U.S. Census depends on exactly that kind of self-knowledge.) This is not to say that race, both as a taxonomy of human divisions and as a status ranking, is natural or unfiltered by ideologies—the socially constructed nature of

43

human races has always been more like an ideology than a merely false description of reality (Spears and Gilliam 1999). But it does mean that racial systems are mostly transparent. Mixed-race people may be exceptions to this transparency because their self-identities and racial ascriptions do not coincide. But their knowledge of how they do not fit into the dominant racial system occurs in the context of a larger transparent racial context.

The situation is different with class. In democratic societies, the existence of classes is often denied by nontheorists, who look for other characteristics to substitute for what theorists consider their class identities. That is not due to the fact that skin color differences are perceived more dramatically, because the markers of class in dress, speech, possessions, and consumption habits are just as easy to detect as skin color and just as likely to stimulate aversion, attraction, and judgment. Rather, the reason for the difference is that the idea of democracy, in the United States especially, makes people very uncomfortable with class differences and quite comfortable with racial ones, especially among whites. It is important to many people that "no one is better than me." Self- and other-identification by race is explicit and common, whereas explicit identification by class, especially involving factors distinct from wealth and income, is uncommon.

To identify someone else by class, to her face, requires consent, because if the subject doesn't agree she is likely to feel insulted or disrespected. And class self-identification is also delicate because people are aware of class status and may be reluctant to claim a higher status that they aspire to but are not confident they have, or ashamed to explicitly identify with a lower status. Expressions of unapologetic class pride are uncommon. It is more usual for people to describe themselves as generically "middle class" and thereby obscure working- or lower-class existential struggles. Those with affluence and privilege may experience either diffidence about proclaiming their advantages or insecurity about how those advantages compare with those of others with the same income or wealth; for instance, some very rich people may have deficits in cultural components of class. Overall, Americans are diffident about naming a vaguely imagined class hierarchy and claiming their place in it. And as the first epigraph to this chapter implies, many do not know what class they are.

In public discourse, although not private thought, the question arises of whether class is real. Of course, class is real because we know that large groups of people have shared economic and social advantages and disadvantages, and we sense that outside of employment, business, and profession-al–client relationships, people associate mainly with members of their own class. But unless she is (deliberately) constructing an ideology, the theorist has to approach class inquisitively and tentatively. I will attempt that here through an examination of politics and culture.

POLITICAL CLASS

Let us distinguish among economic, cultural, and for our purposes political class. The formation of political classes at a time of turbocharged, hegemonic politics is dynamic and innovative. At such times, it may be more useful to view political class as invented in the process of politics than to view politics as a mobilization of existing economic or social classes. Individuals may come to new class consciousness as they undergo this progress. Indeed, social scientists have distinguished between self- and other-perceptions of class and suggest that as a class is formed, its members may change their subjective perceptions of their class identities (Turner et al. 1994).

During the 2016 U.S. presidential election and the early years of his presidency, Donald J. Trump attacked "elites" on grounds meant to appeal to preexisting members of a neglected social class that constituted his "base." What Trump means by elites is far ranging, including journalists, news organizations, the Washington establishment, the Hollywood establishment, other Republicans, scientists, Democrats, and intellectuals—YouTube has over half a million videos under "Trump Attacks Elites" (Decker 2017; YouTube 2018). As a Republican, Trump's attacks are historically ironic. In October 2000, at the Alfred E. Smith Memorial Foundation Dinner, the Republican presidential candidate George W. Bush called the rich, cultured, East Coast elite audience "my base" (Bush 2006). The irony has been twisted further insofar as President Trump has served economic and political elites that include himself as a billionaire who has not completely divested himself of the financial interests and real estate holdings that predate his presidency. Other Republicans and their financial backers are also part of a real elite in ongoing political campaigns. But Trump's major backers may be unique on a presidential level because their interests seem to be more ideological than financial, as has traditionally been the case. It is not obvious how these backers benefit financially from the success of their political clients (a subject to be revisited in chapter 5). For instance, the billionaire CEO of the hedge fund Renaissance Technologies, who is an anti-Republican libertarian, has been a major backer of Trump and other conservative Republicans on apparently ideological grounds (Mayer 2017). While these ideological grounds may be no more than a baited hook for potential voters, the ideologies put forth and so far implemented in immigration policies are not of obvious financial benefit to such backers.

THE SILENT MAJORITY

Both Bush's avowed base and Trump's patrons are a class or classes that exist independently of politics and antecedently to political campaigns. The class called forth as an electorate in turbocharged political campaigns may be largely imaginary, apart from its uses in politics and created for those uses to get people to vote in certain ways. So that they do vote as desired, the process of the political creation of class requires a starting point, a thin end of the wedge that will leverage the mass of voters necessary for victory; its members have to be engaged, galvanized, and mobilized by the right symbols, buzzwords (dog whistles), emotional appeals, and above all, promises that flatter them with visions of their future vindication against present disrespect.

On November 3, 1969, amid antiwar criticism and protest, President Richard Nixon reaffirmed his administration's "Vietnamization effort." He called for support for "peace with honor" from "the silent majority" (Nixon 1969). Seventy-seven percent of Americans and the majority of Republicans received his speech favorably (This Day in History 2018). Of course, Nixon's Vietnamization effort was soon routed, but the phrase "silent majority" had a spectacular political career, as it became evident that there was more to this political class than support for a contested war. Over the years, the silent majority was to acquire a number of other characteristics: they were against welfare, especially for African Americans; they had an unreflective and exaggerated view of black criminals; they were generally Christian, later "born again fundamentalist or evangelical"; they supported Second Amendment gun rights for individuals; they were not intellectuals; they were patriotic; they were white; they had strong family values; they were fiscal conservatives. The term "silent majority" was used by Ronald Reagan, and political analysts have heard it in the rhetoric favored by noncollege educated white voters among the Reagan Democrats of 1980, the Angry White Men of 1994, and the Tea Party insurgents of 2010 (Edsall 2016). Over the same time period, the former segregationist segment of the Democratic Party became Republicans (Charen 2015).

THE NEO–SILENT MAJORITY

The views and positions of the silent majority were not merely political content to support politicians in power or get them elected. For over fifty years, it was expected, and such expectations were fulfilled, that when politicians were elected as a result of the support of Nixon's silent majority and its successors, they would put government programs into effect that would carry out their views. For example, as Michelle Alexander recounts, the political leaders of the silent majority restructured U.S. society in line with its political content, which disproportionately affected poor African Americans: welfare was cut and the prison system expanded tenfold; Bill Clinton was twice elected because he stuck to fiscal conservatism and slashed entitlement payments (Alexander 2010, 56–57, 157–58, 187–90, 252–53). During the 1970s, the NRA (National Rifle Association) changed its mission from gun regulation to individual gun ownership, and the Second Amendment was reinterpreted to support individual gun ownership in 2008 (*District of Columbia v. Heller*; Elving 2017). There was over this period no effective or sustained political opposition to the silent majority, except perhaps for the national and international protests against income inequality during Occupy Wall Street in 2011 (Chomsky 2012). But the aims of participants in the Occupy movement were vague, as were their connections to contemporary politics. There were no mainstream candidates whom they could support, and they did not put forth new candidates. This is not to diminish the importance of such opposition, intellectually and aspirationally, particularly its bottom-up capacity to inform multitudes by making the public aware of extreme and increasing income inequality (Ruggerio 2012). And it does not mean that Occupy participants were not political activists for their time (less than a decade ago).

Despite these antecedents, although President Trump represents the culmination of the neoconservative ideology of the silent majority, the turbocharged politics that propelled him into office does not seem to represent a preexisting political class so much as an instantly created one. Simplistically, if the class preexisted, vigorous and expensive political campaigns would not be necessary—knowing themselves, members of the class could just be named, reaffirmed through rallies, and thereby mobilized by a candidate seeking to represent them. But recent turbocharged politics uses more elaborate methods than that, deploying surveys and metadata to create electorates. This creation of political class is evident in initial attempts to identify and misinform its members and subsequent support of their political cohesion through control of the news and information to the same targeted group.

The thin end of the wedge for political class creation in the 2016 Trump campaign was the efforts of Kellyanne Conway, a conservative political pollster. Since the 1990s, Conway had worked for groups seeking to reduce immigration, such as the Center for Immigration Studies, the Federation for American Immigration Reform, and NumbersUSA. In the 2012 election, Republican candidate Mitt Romney had received only 27 percent of the Hispanic vote. Following an "autopsy" of this defeat, Republicans were split on the subject of immigration reform: reform favorable to immigrants would bring Hispanics and other minorities into the party, but such reform would also alienate die-hard anti-immigrant voters. Conway had long argued that there was broad voter support for what Romney had called "self-deportation," or tighter border security and stricter immigration laws to encourage immigrants to leave the United States. In 2014, Conway emphasized results from a poll sponsored by NumbersUSA showing strong support for anti-immigrant restrictions on welfare and work access, as well as limiting options to bring family members to the United States. Writing in *Breitbart* and

Politico Pro, she advocated a unifying anti-immigrant Republican issue of "America first" and "fairness to [nativist] blue collar workers."

Also in 2014, Sean Trende, an elections analyst for *RealClearPolitics*, claimed that "downscale, Northern, rural whites" had stayed home from the 2012 election because neither Obama's liberalism nor Romney's big business message appealed to them. Steven Bannon, then CEO of *Breitbart*, who was later to serve as Donald Trump's chief of staff, hypothesized a Republican or populist victory without racial and ethnic minority support, which would bring the nonvoters described by Trende to the polls, based on a "forgotten man," anti-immigration campaign message. It should be noted that Trende had not intended that his analysis be used for political purposes and that NumbersUSA was interested in decreasing immigration to increase jobs for U.S. citizens. But nevertheless, the core anti-immigration stance, as embellished by Trump's vilifications of Mexicans, rallied powerful political support, especially in midwestern working-class areas that had previously voted Democratic (Ball 2017a, 2017b).

However, barriers to immigration, while a rallying cry, were not believed sufficient to create the Trump electorate. Robert Mercer, CEO of Renaissance Technologies, and his daughter Ruth founded an electronic data-mining and -managing firm, Cambridge Analytica. In a 2016 speech, Alexander Nix, the CEO of Cambridge Analytica, announced, "We've rolled out a long-form quantitative instrument to probe the underlying traits that inform personality. If you know the personality of the people you're targeting, you can nuance your messaging to resonate more effectively with those key groups" (Illing 2018). Cambridge Analytica "scraped" social media accounts to gather data on individuals through their Facebook "likes," Twitter, and other sources of preference—involving as many 87 million Facebook users. In 2013, Michal Kosinski, a Cambridge University graduate student, had developed the psychometric algorithms that produced data for Cambridge Analytica. The results: "Seventy 'likes' were enough to outdo what a person's friends knew, 150 what their parents knew, and 300 'likes' what their partner knew. More 'likes' could even surpass what a person thought they knew about themselves." *Das Magazin*, a Zürich-based culture magazine, reported in a 2016 profile of Kosinski that there were five to six thousand data points for each individual. This enabled precision in bots and "fake news" sent to individuals to persuade them to form desired political opinions and voting choices—what Nix presented as getting the message of clients across (Illing 2018).

Cambridge Analytica's information was used to disseminate pro-Trump and anti-Clinton bots and fake news stories, many put together with precision in Russia. The Trump campaign was also able to procure advance information about audiences in areas near stops on his campaign tours (Illing 2018). After Trump was elected, the digital transmission of propaganda was not as individualized. Sinclair Broadcasting Group owns 193 television stations and is now the largest U.S. household TV broadcaster. In 2018, Sinclair will reach seventy million households if its merger with Tribune Media goes through. Sinclair requires that local news broadcasters, who already have the trust of their communities, announce its prepared conservative broadcasts that largely echo Trump campaign propaganda. In April 2018, the following "must read," as in "must be read aloud, on air," was sent to Sinclair's local news anchors: "The sharing of biased and false news has become all too common on social media. Some members of the media use their platforms to push their own personal bias. This is extremely dangerous to our democracy" (Fortin and Bromwich 2018). Taken on face value, this statement seems like a balanced public service announcement. But in the context of conservative news, which has appropriated the term "fake news" to refer to mainstream news, the announcement is partisan, and it has been criticized along those lines, as has Sinclair's infringement on journalistic freedom (Fortin and Bromwich 2018, Guo 2017).

So far in this account of the groups collected to vote for Trump—northern rural whites and midwestern blue-collar workers, as well as other conservatives and reactionaries—the *creation* of a political class, in the old vague meaning of class, has not been fully proved. There is more to class than an electoral group. To understand how the turbocharged politics of the 2016 presidential campaign created a class in a more robust social sense, we need to turn to cultural dimensions of class, which are more enduring and extend into more areas of life than voting.

THE CULTURE WARS AND CLASS

Class has always been integrally associated with culture, as consumption, opinions, values, interests, and hobbies, as well as different lifestyle practices. But in an era of turbocharged politics, such cultural aspects of class become intensely politicized, not in abstract terms about the kind of society we should have, although there is that, but in alignment with party affiliation, especially in support of a specific candidate. Thus, issues of climate change, gun regulation, immigration, abortion, and balanced budgets become part of what used to be called "campaign platforms." Because these aspects of class extend into so many life activities, they politicize ordinary life. The now-political aspects of ordinary life are coextensive with the creation of class, existentially, in ways that go beyond mere voting. At the same time, political sides become more divided and more purist. For example, in previous decades, pro-life and pro-choice abortion advocacy crossed party lines and there were differences in opinion within each party (Fingerhut 2017). However, in April 2018, there was only one pro-life Democrat in Congress, and

Democrats were not projected to run any for the 2018 midterm elections (Bilger 2018). Although there are four pro-choice Republicans in Congress, the Republican Party has become uniformly pro-life (GOP 2018).

A key aspect of the culture of the neo–silent majority is its racial whiteness. White nationalists may freely refer to white supremacist ideologies, but even extreme populist politicians continue the tradition of allowing their audiences to draw racial implications without making white supremacy an explicit part of their political platforms. Here we can see how the race track, discussed in chapter 2, goes off on its own, politically, this time underground, albeit close enough to the surface so that its rumblings and vibrations are audible to all. This race track is the racism track, and while injustice studies tends to focus on its nonwhite casualties, the way it tears through the white population, both incorporating them into new political masses and crushing their humanity in the process, is the other side of nonwhite victimization.

Most members of the neo–silent majority appear to be generically white. Those who are not northern European or members of the Scots-Irish group J. D. Vance eulogized in his 2016 *Hillbilly Elegy* are white enough, in keeping with a long tradition of white supremacy that allows for ethnic variety among racial whites. In the turbocharged political process, white racial identities become proxies for socioeconomic class distinctions, which outside of politics and myth, are real. The substitution of racial or ethnic identities for real class identities preserves the myth of a classless democratic system (e.g., the Scots-Irish of Kentucky and the Midwest are said to have a distinct culture that accounts for their socioeconomic disadvantage). Some "left" critics have claimed that the neo–silent majority fails to identify the system of capitalism as its overriding life obstacle. This misses the intermediate and perhaps even greater obstacle, evident in the "culture wars," namely, the recalcitrant denial of social class insofar as economic and cultural distinctions are relevant to members of that white majority and insofar as they are part of a hierarchy *within the racially white group*.

Social class has economic, social, and cultural components, and almost all observers of contemporary politics focus on the first, resting with the umbrella designation of "blue-collar workers." In fact, this blue-collar designation is inaccurate economically. According to a March 2016 NBC survey, "Only a third of Trump supporters had household incomes at or below the national median of about $50,000. Another third made $50,000 to $100,000, and another third made $100,000 [or more]" (Carnes and Lupu 2017). The affluent Trump supporters may have believed in their solidarity with blue-collar workers. Still, the income statistics do not speak to the cultural aspects of class.

The cultural capital of those classes more advantaged than the neo–silent majority consist of important assets visible through the culture wars, primarily education. Insofar as the cultural capital of a class becomes politicized, such assets may be devalued. For instance, as noted in the second epigraph to this chapter, there was a 13 percent increase over a year in the percentage of Republicans who do not believe that higher education contributes positively to U.S. society. A year is insufficient time for large numbers of people to assess the contribution of higher education, but it is apparently sufficient time for a political class to identify higher education with candidates in the party they oppose, that is, sufficient time to politicize higher education. Additional class-related cultural assets, known as "cultural capital," which are subject to politicization, include knowledge of the arts and sciences, foreign travel, geographical mobility within the United States, contact with members of ethnic groups other than one's own, and advanced lifestyle skills (dietary, exercise, and stress-reduction habits) (Holt 1998).

Members of the neo–silent majority may be likely to regard their own cultural capital as a matter of their distinctive white ethnicities, with an emphasis on family ties. As a result, they are able to view themselves as one distinct racial or ethnic group among others, and that becomes an important part of their political identity, especially if supporters of an opposing party include members of different races. Of course, external to politics, cultural capital as related to social class is part of a system that determines status and who one knows and interacts with, plus access to higher education and desirable employment. This system is intergenerational in ways that predispose quality of life, throughout life. The system is based on the assets of privileged classes, not on what are known as identities. Even though whites throughout society may have more of such assets than nonwhites, it is the assets that constitute cultural capital, not the race of those who have those assets. This is not to say that people of color with high degrees of cultural capital will be treated the same as whites with the same assets—they will not—but simply to distinguish between class assets and race in more normal nonpolitical societal periods.

Concerning the actual blue-collar segment of Trump supporters, while upward mobility is still common, despite a decline over the twentieth century (Chetty et al. 2017), it does not affect the situations of those who remain in the class into which they were born. Those members of the neo–silent majority who substitute ethnic identities with strong family and geographical connections for what would be a concept of social class may be less likely to advance socioeconomically, because their white racial self-identification is a determinist, static identity. To seek socioeconomic advancement might seem like betrayal to those who believe that their class identities are their racial and ethnic identities, which they cannot change. The national embarrassment about admitting the existence of social class also supports the obstruction of upward mobility in this case.

This is not to say that "class" causes "racism" or that "racism" causes "class" or "class position." When white people are ignorant about their own class, which is real in economic, cultural, and social terms, and instead turn to racial taxonomies to better their lot through claims of reverse discrimination that victimize them, it does not make sense to talk about causation in any real sense. The substitution of race for real class difference is an imaginary move, a consensual hallucination. People taking this turn, no matter how violent they may be in reality, have no political power except in large numbers to vote for candidates who convince them that they are victims of injustice as a result of "identity politics" going back to the civil rights movement.

In what sense could poor white people who were politically inert before 2016 be victims of injustice, and what kind of injustice? Present poverty, including inadequate health care, is a humanitarian issue that could have been addressed, but wasn't. That failure could render those who suffer subjects of humanitarian injustice. But the question of political injustice is difficult to substantiate. There may be an undercurrent of jealousy and envy in comparison to nonwhites and nonmales who have been helped, protected, and affirmed by ruling elites (Zack 2017). However, nonwhite and nonmale minorities have histories of discrimination and oppression that were worse than conditions currently experienced by those identifying with, or as, white blue-collar workers. Therefore, to the extent that these groups have been helped or affirmed, even if it has been at the cost of benefits to the white blue-collar group, it does not constitute injustice.

The Marxist idea of class resistance is based on the idea of struggle between different economic groups for their own economic advancement. When groups who should be struggling to advance their interests fail to do so, this Marxist idea cannot be applied to reality and becomes a hypothetical preoccupation of theorists alone: *If* members of the working class realized their economic interests, *then* they *could begin* to struggle to advance them *and* they *should* realize their interests. (That is what the Marxist position amounts to at this time.) There have been no clear and explicit political platforms or policies to address the economic problems of whites who claim disenfranchisement. "More jobs" continues as a very weak rallying call at a time when unemployment is at its lowest rate in decades (United States Department of Labor 2018a, 2018b).

In 1941, the literary theorist Kenneth Burke wrote about the rhetoric used by Adolf Hitler during his rise to power. There was inflation, widespread poverty, and despair among the German population at that time, which had been caused by the ravages of World War I and the Great Depression, resulting in an unemployment rate of 30 percent. We know, of course, that Hitler blamed the Jews and valorized the Germans. But in terms of class analysis, the most important point Burke makes is that Hitler avoided the realities of economics in his ideology for the masses. Burke wrote, "Hitler obviously here had something to sell—and it was but a question of time until he sold it (i.e., got financial backers for his movement). For it provided *a noneconomic interpretation of economic ills*. As such, it served with maximum efficiency in deflecting the attention from the economic facts involved in modern conflict" (Burke 1941, 219; emphasis original). Pre–World War II Germans had severe economic problems. They were to have roles in a historical tragedy. Class warfare is now, for U.S. political purposes, culture warfare. All serious ills are described in rhetoric that assigns noneconomic causes to economic problems, both real and imagined; investigation and evidence of corruption, self-dealing, and collusion with national opponents are dismissed as mere politics or "fake news." Tragedy is thus repeating itself as farce, but farce has its own dangers and harms.

Insofar as the culture wars are the main political subject for a substantial part of the U.S. electorate that is mainly white, largely undereducated, and unashamed to have neo-Nazis and neo–white supremacists among them, racial identities have been substituted for class interests. If this situation lasts, it will change an important component of the category of social class in America. Without at least explicit hypocrisy about racial equality, as a reliable fixture of public discourse, the category of race/racism has expanded into the category of class. This means that race relations have taken over and obscured what were previously viewed as class interests. That it is a false change, mainly on the level of rhetoric, insofar as race is socially constructed and racism is unjustified, does not mitigate the resulting damage to individuals and to civic life in general.

Theoretically, there is either a partial reduction of class to race, or for the time being a linkage of the two, within turbocharged politics. The result is that the politicized class wars have become politicized race wars. And this is a serious problem because, as noted, people may not know what class they belong to in the old sense of class, but they do know what race they are. According to even the most minimal version of social contract theory, government is justified by its ability to keep the peace as an impartial referee over citizen disputes. When government officials encourage racism to stoke the fires of political class warfare, not only is government failing as a referee and thereby not upholding its side of the social contract. It directly attacks the social contract itself, because internal warfare in any form is an ill. Racism as supported by political candidates and elected officials is an extreme, and after the civil rights movement, shocking case of government failing to benefit those governed and instead actively harming them.

WHERE WE ARE NOW

By spring 2018, there is no strong evidence that beyond rhetoric for reelection Trump is willing and able to rule in line with his campaign promises or that Republicans in Congress are able to pass the enabling legislation. For example, the national deficit increases, the border wall with Mexico has not been funded, and many probusiness and antienvironmental presidential edicts and policies have yet to clear state and institutional opposition in the courts. The ban on transgender military service people has been mitigated by the military itself. Lawsuits against Trump, from his alleged violation of the emoluments clause to offenses related to sexual assaults on women, not to mention the Mueller investigation, are paving the road for presidential indictment. That Trump's White House and cabinet are in constant disarray due to firings and resignations is evident on an almost daily basis (Lu and Yourish 2018). Republicans and libertarians have many reasons to be disappointed. Charles and David Koch, who lead the libertarian Koch network, are reported to be frustrated by the lack of Republican action following Trump's election. In an April 2018 interview, James Davis, a senior member of the network, said,

> This is now a time for Republicans to call out Republicans and Democrats to call out Democrats and push them to work for the American people. Otherwise they retreat into their corners and wait out the clock and they're more focused on reelection than they are doing the job. . . . That's where we can play a significant role in turning up the heat. . . . Neither party is really leading with a strong agenda to help the American people here. There's a lot of rhetoric. People pay lip service to the shared concern about government spending, corporate welfare, a solution for dreamers or, more long-term, a solution for immigration. Yet they're largely absent. (Hohmann 2018)

Davis's claims are fascinating as a demand that government function, which sounds very nonpartisan coming from a libertarian. The U.S. legislature is distinct from the executive, and political scientists have differed on the role of presidential popularity for determining president-centered or Congress-centered legislation (Rivers and Rose 1985). However, what appears to be at stake presently is whether government is functional or not, and most observers would expect that government functions most effectively when president and Congress are members of the same party. Democrats and others who criticize and resist the present administration have made good use of their intellectual and ethical disagreements with both Trump and his supporters in academic and popular discourse, as well as well-grounded public spectacles (see chapter 1) that oppose what may turn out to be empty rhetoric. But the issue of government content is distinct from the issue of government function—government officials are expected to govern as part of the implicit social contract.

Based on the U.S. Constitution in a First Amendment society and U.S. Supreme Court interpretations in *Citizens United* as discussed in chapter 1, there is superficially nothing illegal or unconstitutional in what has been described and analyzed so far. But it feels wrong. If the results of pending Federal Trade Commission investigations of Facebook's enablement of Cambridge Analytica's data scraping for eventual political purposes seem not to be more severe than wrist slapping, it will continue to feel wrong (Byers 2018). Of course, investigation will not stop with Facebook as an enabler but should and will move on to the board and CEO of Cambridge Analytica in the United States, as it already has in the United Kingdom (Rosenberg and Confessore 2018). Much energy has already been wasted in trying to determine what Facebook is. It is obvious that Facebook is an interactive digital publishing company that retains all rights to published material and pays no royalties to those who provide content.

The wrong of manipulating people through their unique preferences and invading their privacy for political purposes is more than a moral harm, because it breaks the unspoken consensus about the social contract that government not harm its citizens. It was not the government but those supporting Trump who politically weaponized the scrapings of Facebook data for invasive harm, which furthered their cause. The invasion itself, even if it were for legitimate purposes such as enhanced security through airport searches following 9/11, was a violation of a general right as scholars have interpreted the Third and Fourth Amendments. As Louis D. Brandeis put it, "The makers of the Constitution conferred the most comprehensive of rights and the right most valued by all civilized men—the right to be let alone" (Skousen 2002). A corollary to not harming is punishing those who do harm citizens, and it is a social contract failure of government if it does not punish those who violate the right to be left alone.

The original social contract theorists addressed legitimate and rational grounds for the formation of government. Those same grounds are also part of the justification of ongoing government. Americans and others depend on and trust government to oversee and safeguard free elections. If free elections have been obstructed by manipulation of the votes of individual voters and these actions stand unpunished, that would be further breakage of the social contract.

Returning to the foundations of a free-speech society, there is a difference in terms of class between organically developing political classes and turbocharged political classes. As an effective political movement, despite its potential to identify and call out 99 percent of the U.S. population, Occupy Wall Street was doomed by the limitations of expressiveness on its own. Occupy's lack of organization, funding, polls, and access to what would later be called metadata, as well as its lack of legal defense against dispersion by police, was related to the absence of focused political objectives and visible leadership. But Occupy could in time serve as a precursor to authentic bottom-up constructions of political class. Noam Chomksy thus wrote,

> Well, now the world is indeed splitting into a plutonomy and a precariat—again, in the imagery of the Occupy movement, the 1 percent and the 99 percent. . . . And the Occupy movement is the first real, major popular reaction that could avert this. But, as I said, it's going to be necessary to face the fact that it's a long, hard struggle. You don't win victories tomorrow. You have to go on, have to form the structures that will be sustained, that will go on through hard times and can win major victories. And there are a lot of things that can be done. (2012, 34)

REFERENCES

Alexander, Michelle. 2010. *The New Jim Crow: Mass Incarceration in the Age of Colorblindness*. New York: New Press.

Ball, Molly. 2017a. "The Unsung Architect of Trumpism." *Atlantic*, March 20. https://www.theatlantic.com/politics/archive/2017/03/kellyanne-conway-trumpism/520095/.

———. 2017b. "Kellyanne's Alternative Universe: Will the Truth Ever Catch Up with Trump's Most Skilled Spin Artist?" *Atlantic*, April. https://www.theatlantic.com/magazine/archive/2017/04/kellyannes-alternative-universe/517821/.

Bilger, Micaiah. 2018. "Democrats Are Not Running a Single Pro-Life Candidate in Any Targeted District in 2018." LifeNews.com, February 15. http://www.lifenews.com/2018/02/15/democrats-are-not-running-a-single-pro-life-candidate-in-any-targeted-district-in-2018/.

Burke, Kenneth. 1941. *The Philosophy of Literary Form: Studies in Symbolic Action*. Baton Rouge: Louisiana State University Press.

Bush, George W. 2006. "The Elite My Base." YouTube, June 15. https://www.youtube.com/watch?v=mn4daYJzyls.

Byers, Dylan. 2018. "The U.S. Government Is Officially Investigating Facebook." CNN Tech, March 26. http://money.cnn.com/2018/03/26/technology/facebook-ftc-investigation/index.html.

Carnes, Nicholas, and Noam Lupu. 2017. "It's Time to Bust the Myth: Most Trump Voters Were Not Working Class." *Washington Post*, June 5. https://www.washingtonpost.com/news/monkey-cage/wp/2017/06/05/its-time-to-bust-the-myth-most-trump-voters-were-not-working-class/?utm_term=.b78614412187.

Charen, Mona. 2015. "Whitewashing the Democratic Party's History." *National Review*, June 26. https://www.nationalreview.com/2015/06/democratic-party-racist-history-mona-charen/.

Chetty, Raj, David Grusky, Maximilian Hell, Nathaniel Hendren, Robert Manduca, and Jimmy Narang. 2017. "The Fading American Dream: Declining Mobility and Increasing Inequality." The Equality of Opportunity Project, *Evonomics*, April. http://evonomics.com/the-end-of-upward-mobility-america-concentrated-wealth-chetty/.

Chomsky, Noam. 2012. *Occupy*. Brooklyn, NY: Zuccotti Park Press.

Decker, Cathleen. 2017. "Trump's War against Elites and Expertise." *Los Angeles Times*, July 27. http://www.latimes.com/politics/la-na-pol-trump-elites-20170725-story.html.

District of Columbia v. Heller. 2008. 554 U.S. 570.

Edsall, Thomas B. 2016. "The Not-So-Silent White Majority." *New York Times*, November 17. https://www.nytimes.com/2016/11/17/opinion/the-not-so-silent-white-majority.html.

Elving, Ron. 2017. "The NRA Wasn't Always against Gun Restrictions." National Public Radio, October 10. https://www.npr.org/2017/10/10/556578593/the-nra-wasnt-always-against-gun-restrictions.

Fingerhut, Hannah. 2017. "On Abortion, Persistent Divides between—and within—the Two Parties" Pew Research Center Fact Tank, July 7. http://www.pewresearch.org/fact-tank/2017/07/07/on-abortion-persistent-divides-between-and-within-the-two-parties-2/.

Fortin, Jacey, and Jonah Engel Bromwich. 2018. "Sinclair Made Dozens of Local News Anchors Recite the Same Script." *New York Times*, April 2. https://www.nytimes.com/2018/04/02/business/media/sinclair-news-anchors-script.html.

GOP. 2018. "Pro-Life." April. https://www.gop.com/topic/family-values-pro-life/canonical/.

Guo, Jeff. 2017. "Thanks to Trump, Sinclair Broadcast Group Will Soon Have All It Needs to Be the Next Big Force in Right-Wing News: The Imminent Conservative Takeover of Local TV News, Explained." *Vox*, May 15. https://www.vox.com/2017/5/15/15598270/sinclair-broadcast-imminent-conservative-takeover-of-local-tv-news-explained.

Hohmann, James. 2018. "The Daily 202: Koch Network Growing Frustrated with the GOP's 2018 Agenda." *Washington Post*, April 4. https://www.washingtonpost.com/news/powerpost/paloma/daily-202/2018/04/06/daily-202-koch-network-growing-frustrated-with-the-gop-s-2018-agenda/5ac6d16a30fb043deaded788/?utm_term=.e922bc0f0895.

Holt, Douglas B. 1998. "Does Cultural Capital Structure American Consumption?," *Journal of Consumer Research* 25 (1): 1–25,https://doi.org/10.1086/209523.

"How Is Frankenstein a Tragic Hero?" 2018. eNotes.com. https://www.enotes.com/homework-help/how-frankenstein-tragic-hero-235303.

Illing, Sean. 2018. "Cambridge Analytica, the Shady Data Firm That Might Be a Key Trump–Russia Link, Explained: Why House Investigators Think This Company Might Have Gamed Facebook and Helped Russia Spread Fake News." *Vox*, April 4. https://www.vox.com/policy-and-politics/2017/10/16/15657512/cambridge-analytica-facebook-alexander-nix-christopher-wylie.

Lu, Denise, and Karen Yourish. 2018. "Turnover at a Constant Clip: The Trump Administration's Major Departures." *New York Times*, March 28. https://www.nytimes.com/interactive/2018/03/16/us/politics/all-the-major-firings-and-resignations-in-trump-administration.html.

Mayer, Jane. 2017. "The Reclusive Hedge-Fund Tycoon behind the Trump Presidency: How Robert Mercer Exploited America's Populist Insurgency." *New Yorker*, March 17. https://www.newyorker.com/magazine/2017/03/27/the-reclusive-hedge-fund-tycoon-behind-the-trump-presidency.

Nixon, Richard. 1969. "Nixon's Silent Majority Speech." Watergate.info, November 3. http://watergate.info/1969/11/03/nixons-silent-majority-speech.html.

Pew Research Center. 2017. "Sharp Partisan Divisions in Views of National Institutions." July 10. http://assets.pewresearch.org/wp-content/uploads/sites/5/2017/07/11101505/07-10-17-Institutions-release.pdf.

Rivers, Douglas, and Nancy L. Rose. 1985. "Passing the President's Program: Public Opinion and Presidential Influence in Congress." *American Journal of Political Science* 29 (2): 183–96. http://www.jstor.org/stable/2111162.

Rosenberg, Matthew, and Nicholas Confessore. 2018. "Justice Department and F.B.I. Are Investigating Cambridge Analytica." *New York Times*, May 15. https://www.nytimes.com/2018/05/15/us/cambridge-analytica-federal-investigation.html.

Ruggerio, Greg. 2012. "Editor's Note." In *Occupy*, by Noam Chomsky, 9–19. Brooklyn, NY: Zuccotti Park Press.

Skousen, Mark. 2002. "The Right to Be Left Alone." Foundation for Economic Education, May 1. https://fee.org/articles/the-right-to-be-left-alone/.

Spears, Arthur K., and Angela Gilliam, eds. 1999. *Race and Ideology: Language, Symbolism and Popular Culture*. Detroit: Wayne State University Press.

Tepper, Fabien. 2013. "What Is Your Social Class? Take Our Quiz to Find Out!" *Christian Science Monitor*, October 17. https://www.csmonitor.com/USA/Society/2013/1017/What-is-your-social-class-Take-our-quiz-to-find-out/dream-vehicle.

This Day in History. 2018. "Nixon Calls on the Silent Majority." History.com, November 3. https://www.history.com/this-day-in-history/nixon-calls-on-the-silent-majority.

Turner, J. C., P. J. Oakes, S. A. Haslam, and C. McGarty. 1994. "Self and Collective: Cognition and Social Context." *Personality and Social Psychology Bulletin* 20 (5): 454–63.

United States Department of Labor. 2018a. "Local Area Unemployment Statistics." Bureau of Labor Statistics, March 12. https://www.bls.gov/web/laus/laumstch.htm.

———. 2018b. "Databases, Tables & Calculators by Subject," April 7. https://data.bls.gov/timeseries/LNU04000000?years_option=all_years&periods_option=specific_periods&periods=Annual+Data.

Vance, J. D. 2016. *Hillbilly Elegy: A Memoir of a Family and Culture in Crisis*. New York: Harper Press.

YouTube. 2018. "Trump Attacks Elites." https://www.youtube.com/results?search_query=trump%27s+attacks+on+elites.

Zack, Naomi. 2017. "Contemporary Claims of Political Injustice: History and the Race to the Bottom." *Res Philosophica*, October 18. https://doi.org/10.11612/resphil.1613 and https://www.pdcnet.org/resphilosophica/content/resphilosophica_2017_0999_10_16_70.

Chapter Four

The Amazing Success of Feminism

In several leisurely conversations over dinner she admitted that the woman's movement was making a noticeable and helpful difference in the behavior of her female students: for the first time they were beginning to speak in class. And she did listen with interest to the arguments that I and other women offered on the validity of feminism and the need for a woman's movement. (Virginia Held on Hannah Arendt; Held 1982)

"It's a Cromwell moment!" Bannon said. "It's even more powerful than populism. It's deeper. It's primal. It's elemental. The long black dresses and all that—this is the Puritans. It's anti-patriarchy." (Steve Bannon while watching the 2018 Golden Globe Awards; Green 2018)

It is hard to put into words the intense anxiety, stress and sense of oppression our community is currently experiencing. Right now, thousands of individuals are wondering where they are going to go to earn money they need to pay rent, buy their family's clothes and food and fill their metro card or gas tank. (Sex Workers Outreach Project, on the removal of Backpage.com; Kutner 2017)

U.S. feminism has been amazingly successful over the past one hundred years! This includes intellectual feminism as advocacy for the rights and well-being of women and real-life progress for those who identify as women in reality. The success is palpable: massive entry of women into higher education and the workforce, the professions, business; reproductive autonomy; political presence and the U.S. Supreme Court ruling on the rights of same-sex couples to marry; general support in progressive communities for transgender people. Where they are not yet fully represented at the top, for instance, as corporate CEOs or U.S. senators, the heights are nevertheless clearly in view for some women. Part of this success may be the result of a broad feminist perspective about who can be a woman and a sense of inclusiveness regarding race and gender, which is to say that part of the success is socially metaphysical in a philosophical sense. Consonant with that success and the preexisting communities that were shocked by the 2016 U.S. presidential election, the spectacles of hypermasculine turbocharged politics have been met by women's spectacles: the 2017 Women's March on Washington, #MeToo, #TimesUp, and the teachers' strikes and walkouts in West Virginia, Kentucky, and Oklahoma—76 percent of preschool through middle school teachers are women (National Center for Education Statistics 2017).

Another part of U.S. women's success is the necessity that women either support themselves or contribute to family income through work outside the home, as rising prices and stagnating wages have made it too difficult for a working- or middle-class man to support a family and household on his salary only. Women are now the sole breadwinners in 40 percent of U.S. households (Wang, Parker, and Taylor 2013). Consider these statistics: from 1948 to 2016, the percentage of women in the labor force increased from 32.7 to 56.8 percent; 40 percent of working women had college degrees in 2016, compared to 11 percent in 1970; 70 percent of women with children under eighteen now work outside the home, and 75 percent of that 70 percent work full-time (DeWolf 2017). Along with this success of feminism is a broad shared sense that women are valuable, worthy of respect, and capable. On individual levels, compared to their mothers and grandmothers, women have more self-confidence and greater ability to make their wishes known, assert what they are entitled to, and confront men.

However, it is a great problem that the vision of the 1912 Bread and Roses Strike demanding fair pay and dignity for laboring women has not been realized (Ross 2013). There has not yet been full inclusion of nonwhite women in feminist success, and the distribution of gains taken for granted among the middle class has not extended to working-class and poor women, nor to gender minorities such as sex workers and transgender people. There is also a seemingly minor issue of who is willing to be called a feminist, which is related to the nature of feminist inclusion.

This chapter presents the metaphysical underpinnings of the category of women, the history and present concerning U.S. women's rights and movements, the multiplicity of women's identities, and an analysis of how feminism as a progressive movement remains a *top-rest* project, which is strikingly evident in the cases of sex workers, transgender people, and the #MeToo movement. There have been opportunities for bottom-up intervention, as happened with Anita Hill's U.S. Senate testimony against Clarence Thomas in 1991 and Stormy Daniels's recent *60 Minutes* interview by Anderson Cooper about her claims of sexual foreplay and intercourse with President Donald Trump (Hill and Jordan 1995; Cooper 2018). But these interventions have a backdrop of a more general condition that depends on prior privileges and favors well-established members of society within progressive movements.

However, before beginning the core observations of the chapter, we should note that the success of feminism and some feminists is a matter of traction against oppression rather than overthrow of oppression, particularly the misogynistic rule over women by men. Kate Manne (2017) in *Down Girl: The Logic of Misogyny* explains how misogyny is a set of practices by men that keep women subordinate to them, through surveillance, criticism, punishment, insult, and shame if they get out of line. Those successful women who have the heights of male power in sight, while successful as women and part of the success of feminism, are nevertheless subject to vilification and obstruction simply because they are women. To see how misogyny still operates in politics, we need only remember how Hillary Clinton was mocked and disrespectfully objectified in both the 2008 Democratic primary and her 2016 presidential candidacy, followed by defeat to less experienced men in both cases. Attempts were also made to disarm her from defending herself through vitriolic attacks on *What Happened*, her memoir about the 2016 election (Freeman 2017).

Misogyny operates in the background of feminist struggle, just as racism operates in the background of racial liberation. Both are always ready to be mobilized if a woman or a nonwhite is perceived to be too successful for who they are, the seemingly gratuitous backlash against Barack Obama providing an example of the latter. Therefore, to speak of the success of feminism and inequalities within feminism is not to minimize ongoing structural oppression and opposition.

THE SOCIAL METAPHYSICS OF FEMINISM AND ITS SUBJECTS

We saw in chapter 3 that scholarly work may not match individual self-ascriptions of class, while for race this match is reliable (except for mixed-race identities that derive their meaning from the dominant reliable match). In this sense of a match between what experts and ordinary people perceive and believe, the social epistemology of feminism is more like race than class. Women are those who identify as women. Controversy concerning transgender and nonbinary identities is disagreement between those who affirm them and those who are prejudicial and discriminatory against them, rather than contestations over identities. Overall, there is a match between those who identify as women within a multiplicity of identities and the external recognition of those identities (insofar as feminism has enabled such external recognition).

However, there is an important metaphysical difference between nonwhites as the subjects of progressive theories of race and women as the subjects of feminism, which difference may be related to the social success of feminism compared to race. In a word, racial identities remain *essentialist* and feminist identities are *nominalist*. Social racial differences and distinctions are based on substantive identities, essences, or the legacy of essences. For instance, racial whites have an imagined purity if they and others believe that they have no nonwhite ancestors. By contrast, nonwhites have known nonwhite ancestry. In addition, nonwhites are objects of racism, which consists of myriad relations that differ according to context, and nonwhites have developed practices and theories of resistance against racism, as well as aspirations for life beyond racism. Both whites and nonwhites believe that physical appearance expresses racial identities, a correspondence that is expected of individuals so that they will look like what they are racially. The effect of ancestry and appearance in constituting racial identity is that people literally imagine that they and others *are* the race they identify as or others perceive them to be.

The metaphysics of racial identity is, of course, imaginary, because physical race does not have the foundation in independent biological taxonomy that it is presumed to have in society (Templeton 1998; Relethford 2017). And even in society, racial identities vary from place to place and historically, depending on external criteria, such as the Nazi designation of a Jew as anyone with three or four Jewish grandparents (United States Holocaust Memorial Museum 2018), or the U.S. change from whites being permitted some degree of black ancestry before the one-drop rule became the custom of the land in about 1900 (Lemelle 2007). But the imagined metaphysics has nothing whimsical or poetic about it when black identities can be an arbitrary death sentence and white identities confer unearned status and privilege.

In contrast to race, women's gender is an identity category based on a shared psychic relation. Members of large groups with little in common identify with, or as, a core imagined identity. Women are those who share a relation to female designation at birth, motherhood, and being preferred objects of male heterosexual desire (FMP—female, mothers, preferred) (Zack 2005, 8–11, 23–25, 42–44, 61, 113–14, 124, 135, 165). To say that a person is a woman is to say that she identifies as a member of the group that contains FMPs, not that she is all of those things herself or even any one of them. Thus, transgender people as well as lesbians and women who are not mothers are women. This flexibility in identification has made it theoretically possible for feminism to contain multiplicities within the group of women. In activist terms, within popular culture, while elite white heterosexual women, many women of color, and poor women have not all embraced the causes or label of white middle-class feminism, their reactions to crises and immediate oppression have not been to reject feminism. Rather, they insist that they are women, too, and use the tools of feminist advocacy for themselves. Feminism is advocacy for women. Being a woman is an identity. There is no (logical) contradiction in women not being feminists, even if they are bene-fiting from feminism, as we will see in the section below on feminist identity.

While there have at times been acrid disagreements based on race and class, among feminists, feminists as advocates for the rights and well-being of women have not generally moved to exclude any adversaries on the grounds that they are not women or feminists. Those who participate in social movements need some grounding organizational identity for support, and the labels *women* and *feminism* have been readily available to anyone who needs them, including disagreeing factions, splinter groups, and critics. Individuals or small groups may be doctrinally rigid feminists, but the overall critical theory and movements of feminism have been heterodox and flexible. Intellectual feminism is a critical theory insofar as it has progressive goals for women, which are supported by analyses of culture as oppressive to women. Reality as described in feminist cultural analysis might not be recog-nized or accepted as accurate descriptions of their lives and circumstances by nonfeminists (Zack 2005, 66–67, 114; Caputi 2013).

The strength of feminism in pushing back against oppression may not depend on its unity or cohesion but rather on the utility of its transactional role in allowing new groups to touch base, find that the feminists whom they encounter do not speak for them, and then go off on their own toward the construction of feminism(s) that fit them better. WeRise.com describes just these few feminisms in an introductory toolkit: liberal feminism, radical feminism, black feminism, Marxist and socialist feminism, cultural femi-nism, eco-feminism, transnational or global feminism, visionary feminism (WeRise 2018). There are as well myriad feminist strains and themes in every academic subject and segment of society, every racial and ethnic group. The expression of concern about gender bias or oppression is thereby highly varied and dependent on context. In this regard, feminism is like a traffic circle (roundabout or rotary). One arrives at the circle and takes the turn leading to one's destination in leaving the circle. But the circle itself remains as a named destination on the map and route. If one has chosen the wrong exit or changes one's mind about a destination, it's easy to return to the circle and get off somewhere else.

U.S. HISTORY OF FEMINIST RIGHTS

Historical timelines of women's rights and LBGT movements are readily available from mass media. Past gains provide the context for present prob-lems and concerns, so tables 4.1, 4.2, and 4.3 are useful for background information in considering key issues in the present. It should be noted that although LGBT issues are part of feminism as an intellectual project, in the mass media, women's, gay and lesbian, and transgender milestones are separately presented. The inclusive nature of intellectual feminism has not yet diffused through popular U.S. culture, a stagnation that, as we shall see, also allows for some whom intellectual feminists would call feminists to deny that they are feminists.

Table 4.1.   U.S. Women's Rights Timeline

1769	The colonies adopt the English system, in which women cannot own property in their own name or keep their own earnings.
1777	All states pass laws that take away women's right to vote.
1839	Mississippi is the first state to grant women the right to hold property in their own names, with permission from their husbands.
1848	At Seneca Falls, New York, three hundred women and men sign the Declaration of Sentiments, a plea for the end of discrimination against women.
1866	The Fourteenth Amendment is passed by Congress, with "citizens" and "voters" defined as male.
1872	Victoria Claflin Woodhull becomes the first female presidential candidate in the United States, nominated by the National Radical Reformers. After Susan B. Anthony votes, she is convicted of "unlawful voting." Female federal employees (but not private-sector workers) are guaranteed equal pay for equal work under the law.
1873	The Supreme Court rules that a state has the right to exclude a married woman from practicing law.
1887	Susanna Madora Salter becomes the first woman elected mayor of an American town, in Argonia, Kansas.
1890	Wyoming grants women the right to vote in all elections.
1900	Every state has legislation granting married women the right to keep their own wages and to own property in their own name.
1916	Jeannette Rankin of Montana is the first woman to be elected to the U.S. House of Representatives
1918	Margaret Sanger wins her suit in New York to allow doctors to advise their married patients about birth control for health purposes. Her clinic and others become Planned Parenthood in 1942.
1920	The Nineteenth Amendment is ratified, giving women the right to vote.
1923	The first version of an equal rights amendment is introduced. It says, "Men and women shall have equal rights throughout the United States and every place subject to its jurisdiction."
1932	Hattie Wyatt Caraway of Arkansas becomes the first woman elected to the U.S. Senate.
1933	Frances Perkins becomes the first female cabinet member, appointed secretary of labor by President Franklin D. Roosevelt.

1963   The Equal Pay Act is passed by Congress, promising equitable wages for the same work, regardless of the race, color, religion, national origin, or sex of the worker.

1964   Title VII of the Civil Rights Act passes, prohibiting sex discrimination in employment. The Equal Employment Opportunity Commission is created.

1965   The Supreme Court establishes the right of married couples to use contraception.

1968   President Lyndon B. Johnson signs an executive order prohibiting sex discrimination by government contractors and requiring affirmative action plans for hiring women.

1969   California adopts the nation's first "no fault" divorce law, allowing divorce by mutual consent.

1972   Title IX of the Education Amendments prohibits sex discrimination in all aspects of education programs that receive federal support. The Supreme Court upholds the right to use birth control by unmarried couples.

1973   *Roe v. Wade* makes abortion legal. The Supreme Court also bans sex-segregated "help wanted" advertising.

1974   Housing discrimination on the basis of sex and credit discrimination against women are outlawed by Congress.

1978   The Pregnancy Discrimination Act bans employment discrimination against pregnant women.

1981   Sandra Day O'Connor becomes the first woman to serve on the Supreme Court. The court overturns state laws designating a husband "head and master" with unilateral control of property owned jointly with his wife.

1982   The ERA (Equal Rights Amendment) falls short of ratification.

1983   Dr. Sally K. Ride is the first American woman to be sent into space.

1984   Geraldine Ferraro is the first woman nominated vice president on a major party ticket. The U.S. Supreme Court bans sex discrimination in membership for onetime all-male groups like the Jaycees, Kiwanis, and Rotary Clubs. The state of Mississippi belatedly ratifies the Nineteenth Amendment, granting women the vote.

1985   Emily's List is founded, with a mission to elect Democratic pro-choice women to office.

1986   The U.S. Supreme Court holds that a work environment can be declared hostile or abusive because of discrimination based on sex.

1989   The Supreme Court affirms the right of states to deny public funding for abortions and to prohibit public hospitals from performing abortions.

1992   The Year of the Woman: Following 1991 hearings in which lawyer Anita Hill accused Supreme Court nominee Clarence Thomas of sexual harassment, four women win Senate elections and two dozen women are elected to first terms in the House. The Supreme Court upholds *Roe v. Wade* but allows states to impose restrictions such as a waiting period and parental consent for minors seeking abortions.

1994	The Violence Against Women Act funds services for victims of rape and domestic violence and allows women to seek civil rights remedies for gender-related crimes. In 2000, the Supreme Court invalidates those parts of the law permitting victims of rape, domestic violence, and the like to sue their attackers in federal court.
1997	Madeleine Albright become the first female U.S. Secretary of State.
2005	Congress passes the Partial-Birth Abortion Ban Act, and the Supreme Court upholds the ban in 2006.
2007	Nancy Pelosi becomes the first female speaker of the U.S. House of Representatives.
2009	The Lilly Ledbetter Fair Pay Restoration Act allows victims, usually women, of pay discrimination to file a complaint with the government against their employer within 180 days of their last paycheck.
2012	The Paycheck Fairness Act, meant to fight gender discrimination in the workplace, fails in the Senate on a party-line vote. Two years later, Republicans filibuster the bill (twice).
2013	The ban against women in military combat positions is removed, overturning a 1994 Pentagon decision restricting women from combat roles.
2016	Hillary Rodham Clinton secures the Democratic presidential nomination, becoming the first U.S. woman to lead the ticket of a major party. She loses to Republican Donald Trump in the fall. The Supreme Court strikes down onerous abortion clinic regulations that were forcing women's clinics to close.
2017	Congress has a record number of women, with 104 female House members and 21 female senators, including the chamber's first Latina, Nevada Sen. Catherine Cortez Masto.

From Milligan (2017).

Table 4.2. LGB Rights Timeline

1924	Henry Gerber founds the Society for Human Rights, the first documented gay rights organization in the United States, in Illinois, but it is soon disbanded.
1928	Radclyffe Hall's lesbian novel *The Well of Loneliness* is published, and homosexuality becomes a topic of public conversation in the United States and England.
1948	Alfred Kinsey's *Sexual Behavior in the Human Male* is published, reporting that 37 percent of men he interviewed had participated in homosexual behavior at least once.
1950	Harry Hay founds the Mattachine Society, with goals to organize and advocate for homosexual rights and reduce the feelings of isolation that many gays and lesbians of the time were experiencing.
1953	Executive Order 10450 is signed by President Dwight Eisenhower, ordering the dismissal of government workers who engage in "sexual perversion"

and other "immoral acts." Although the order does not explicitly mention homosexuality, hundreds of gays and lesbians lose their jobs as a result.

1955 In San Francisco, Del Martin and Phyllis Lyon found the Daughters of Bilitis, a lesbian civil and political rights organization.

1956 At the meeting of the American Psychological Association, Evelyn Hooker presents research comparing the psychological health of homosexual and heterosexual men, finding no differences in the mental health of these two groups.

1962 Illinois is the first state to decriminalize homosexual acts between two consenting adults in private.

1966 The oldest collegiate student organization for gays, the Student Homophile League, is founded at Columbia University.

1969 The Stonewall Riots, named after the historically gay-frequented bar the Stonewall Inn, take place in Greenwich Village in New York City. Police forces had unjustly raided the establishment in the past, but gays protest the raids and the event becomes a pivotal, defining moment in the movement for LGB rights.

1970 The first gay pride marches are held in multiple cities in the United States on the first anniversary of the Stonewall Riots.

1973 The American Psychiatric Association removes homosexuality from the *Diagnostic and Statistical Manual of Mental Disorders* II, concluding that it is not a mental illness.

1974 Elaine Noble becomes the first openly gay person to be elected as a state legislator, serving twice in the Massachusetts State House of Representatives.

1975 The Bisexual Forum is founded in New York City, and the Gay American Indians Organization is founded in San Francisco.

1977 Harvey Milk is elected city-county supervisor in San Francisco and becomes the third "out" elected public official in the United States. Quebec, Canada, passes laws to prohibit discrimination based on sexual orientation in both the private and public sectors.

1978 Harvey Milk is assassinated along with San Francisco's Mayor George Moscone. Supervisor Dan White is convicted of voluntary manslaughter and sentenced to seven years in prison. In San Francisco, the rainbow flag is first flown.

1979 Over one hundred thousand people participate in the National March on Washington for Lesbian and Gay Rights. Chapters of the national organization of Parents and Friends of Lesbians and Gays (PFLAG) are founded across the United States.

1980 David McReynolds appears on the Socialist Party ballot, becoming the first openly gay individual to run for president of the United States.

1981 A lethal virus is noticed spreading through the gay community. It is first reported in the *New York Times* as a rare pneumonia and skin cancer and is initially referred to by the Centers for Disease Control (CDC) as gay-related immunodeficiency (GRID). When it is recognized that the virus is found in other populations, it is renamed the Acquired Immune Deficiency Syndrome (AIDS).

1982   The National Gay and Lesbian Task Force initiates a project aimed to counter the rise in violence related to homophobia in the United States.

1983   The first National Lesbians of Color Conference is organized in Los Angeles.

1984   After an eight-year legal battle, Duncan Donovan, a Los Angeles gay activist, wins the right to receive the death benefits of his life partner.

1986   The Supreme Court ruling in *Bowers v. Hardwick* upholds the right of each state to criminalize private same-sex acts.

1987   ACT UP is formed in order to protest inaction in response to the AIDS epidemic in the United States. Old Lesbians Organizing for Change (OLOC) is founded with the goal of fighting against ageism and for lesbian rights.

1988   The brochure "Understanding AIDS" is mailed by the CDC to every American household. The World Health Organization organizes the first World AIDS Day.

1992   Homosexuality is removed from the *International Statistical Classification of Diseases* by the World Health Organization.

1993   The Department of Defense issues the "Don't Ask, Don't Tell" policy; applicants to the U.S. armed forces would not be asked about nor required to disclose their sexual orientation.

1996   In *Romer v. Evans*, the Supreme Court rules that Colorado's second amendment, which denies gays and lesbians protections against discrimination, is unconstitutional. President Clinton signs the Defense of Marriage Act (DOMA) into law, which defines marriage as a union between one man and one woman.

1998   The widow of the late Martin Luther King Jr., Coretta Scott King, speaks out against homophobia in America, despite criticism for comparing black civil rights to gay rights.

1999   California adopts a domestic partner law, allowing same-sex couples equal rights, responsibilities, benefits, and protections as married couples.

2000   Vermont becomes the first state to legalize civil unions, a unity similar to domestic partnerships. Israel begins recognizing same-sex relationships for foreign partners of Israeli residents.

2004   Massachusetts legalizes same-sex marriage, and New Jersey legalizes domestic partnerships; eleven other states ban such legal recognitions.

2009   President Obama signs the Matthew Shepard and James Byrd Jr. Hate Crimes Prevention Act, which expands the Federal Hate Crime Law to include crimes motivated by a victim's actual or perceived gender, sexual orientation, gender identity, or disability.

2010   The "Don't Ask, Don't Tell" policy is repealed following a U.S. Senate vote; gays and lesbians can now serve openly in the U.S. armed forces.

2013   The Supreme Court rules that the key parts of DOMA are unconstitutional and that gay couples are entitled to federal benefits such as Social Security survivor benefits and family leave. The court's ruling on California's Proposition 8 results in gay marriages being resumed in that state.

From Breaking Prejudice (2013).

Table 4.3.   U.S. Transgender Rights Timeline

1952	Christine Jorgensen completes sex-reassignment surgery in Denmark; she is the first American known for undergoing such a transition.
1966	San Francisco's Compton's Cafeteria riot of drag queens and transgender women against police occurs in August and is not reported by mainstream media (Broverman 2016).
1969	Transgender people are at the forefront of the Stonewall Riots in New York City, which help spark the U.S. gay rights movement.
1977	The New York Supreme Court rules in favor of transgender physician/athlete Renée Richards in her bid to play pro tennis as a woman.
1993	Transgender man Brandon Teena is raped and murdered in Nebraska; his story is later made into the film *Boys Don't Cry*. Minnesota becomes the first state to ban antitransgender discrimination in employment, housing, and public accommodations.
1999	Observance is held of the first International Day of Remembrance, an annual event honoring victims of antitransgender violence.
2005	A pioneering California law bars health insurance companies from discriminating against transgender people.
2008	Isis King becomes the first transgender model featured in the reality TV show *America's Next Top Model*.
2009	President Obama signs a federal hate-crimes law that covers crimes motivated by antitransgender bias.
2010	In response to a lawsuit, players of the Ladies Professional Golf Association vote to allow transgender players to compete on tour.
2012	Miss Universe opens its competition to transgender contestants. The Equal Employment Opportunity Commission rules that discrimination based on transgender status is sex discrimination in violation of the Civil Rights Act.
2013	The American Psychiatric Association updates its diagnostic manual to stipulate that being transgender is no longer considered a mental disorder.
2014	Actress Laverne Cox becomes the first transgender person featured on the cover of *Time*. Maine's highest court rules that a transgender fifth-grader should have been allowed to use the girls' bathroom at her school.
2015	Caitlyn Jenner completes her gender transition and appears on the cover of *Vanity Fair*. Voters in Houston defeat an ordinance that would have extended nondiscrimination protections to transgender people.
2016	The U.S. military lifts its ban on transgender service members. The Supreme Court agrees to hear a Virginia case involving Gavin Grimm, a transgender boy seeking the right to use the boys' restroom at his high

school. The Obama administration advises public schools that transgender students should be allowed to use restrooms and locker rooms of their choice.

2017   The Trump administration revokes the Obama-era directive, saying policies for transgender students' bathroom access should be set at the state and local level. The Supreme Court sends Grimm's case back to lower courts.

From Associated Press (2017).

The trajectories of the rights of all three groups are clearly trending toward more positive recognition. However, the recognition of LGB and transgender rights has been more of a struggle against violence and attempts at outright legal discrimination. All three groups are subjects for applicative justice—they share the goal of securing the same fundamental rights protections that heterosexual men already experience. In terms of the social contract, this looks like a straightforward matter of government benefiting all of those governed, as well as punishing those who would interfere with benefits to others. But structural inequalities not only exist in society as a whole, but function as obstacles within feminist progressive movements themselves.

It is evident from these three timelines that heterosexual women and lesbian, gay, bisexual, and transgender people have a range of formal equality in the United States. The women's timeline of formal progress has the longest successful history, followed by lesbian, gay, and bisexual people. The remaining contested identities of transgender and nonbinary (apparently too new to have a popular timeline) have been less successful. Both of these identities reject traditional gender categories, as well as heteronormativity. They will probably be the most innovative gender categories in years to come, because they go beyond attacks on patriarchy to destabilize the entire sex/gender taxonomy. The cost of the project is the suffering of individuals who are discriminated against, shunned, maimed, and killed for their transgressive gender identities.

Some scholars and observers divide the history of feminism into "waves." The first wave began with Mary Wollstonecraft's *Vindication of the Rights of Women*, followed by John Stuart Mill's 1865 *The Subjection of Women*. Both of these classic texts argued for women's civil rights on the grounds that their access to education and inclusion in public life would make them better wives and mothers (Wollstonecraft [1792] 1996; Mill [1869] 1997). The culmination of the first wave was the 1920 Nineteenth Amendment to the U.S. Constitution, granting women the right to vote. The second wave occurred in the late 1960s and 1970s, constituted by equal rights to education and employment access and culminating with the reproductive rights gained through *Roe v. Wade*. The third wave is the aftermath of *Roe v. Wade* and extends into the present. During the early part of the third wave, in the 1980s, the subject of feminism began to enter the academy, while a new generation of women became adults in the aftermath of the liberatory legislation and U.S. Supreme Court rulings of the two decades before (see table 4.1). But in the 1990s, problems began to emerge within feminism—despite the continued success of the movement and its intellectual products. In the rest of this chapter, we will consider issues of feminist identity and how fame and obscurity intersect with sex work and transgender identity. It will also be evident how racial difference is relevant to contemporary third-wave feminism(s).

FEMINIST IDENTITY

Mary Caputi begins her *Feminism and Power: The Need for Critical Theory* with this reflection:

> Somewhere in the 1990s, things started to change for women in their understanding of feminism. It was especially among younger women that I perceived a shift in how they understood the term whose meanings seemed to have changed from the 1980s when I had studied it in graduate school. . . . There was a certain complacency, but also a thrill—a thrilled complacency— at returning to and indeed endorsing an older version of femininity and male- female relations. A regressive attitude seemingly prevailed among younger women as witnessed in their highly sexualized clothing, their extravagant, expensive weddings, their eagerness to take their husbands' last names, and their unapologetic desire to undergo cosmetic surgery and Botox infusions. They deliberately distanced themselves from feminism, and often identified with backlash efforts aimed at undermining its impact on American culture and society. Even as they entered professional and graduate schools in record numbers, and began to outlearn their spouses, they often began sentences with the disclaimer, "I am not a feminist, but . . ." (2013, ix)

Also in 2013 and updated in 2017, *Huffpost* chronicled ten celebrities who proudly proclaimed that they were not feminists: Kelly Clarkson, Taylor Swift, Lady Gaga, Bjork, Katy Perry, Carrie Underwood, Susan Sarandon, Sarah Jessica Parker, Demi Moore, and Madonna. Their reasons for repudiating a feminist label included commitments to humanism, gender fairness, the strength of women, and a desire not to alienate people. The net effect is that these elite women did not want to call themselves feminists because they believed that doing so would unnecessarily politicize their public personae and damage their popularity (*Huffpost* 2017).

One wonders if such successful women who take feminism lightly are not in reality feminists. It is ironic that when celebrities deny feminism to protect themselves as brands they seem not to realize that such self-brands could not have arisen without feminist gains. Although many famous women who came forward under the #MeToo movement drew on core feminist principles of women's right to bodily autonomy, they did not generally claim feminist identities in that process. The sixty-eight actresses who had come forward by January 2018 did not generally credit feminism for their victories in bringing down scores of prestigious and powerful men in show business, a process that is still ongoing (Pasquini and Pearl 2018; *Glamour* 2018). Perhaps another type of feminism should be added to introductory toolkits: Have My Cake and Eat It Too feminism. Nevertheless, it remains an effective strategy for feminism to include all those identifying as women as part of their constituency, without requiring explicit commitment to feminism by that name. And it is no small matter that a hyperconservative or reactionary such as Steve Bannon is disconcerted by the spectacle of Have My Cake and Eat It Too feminism, as indicated in the second epigraph to this chapter.

For Bannon, women standing up for their rights to respect for their bodily sexual autonomy is a puritanical attack on the patriarchy. Disregarding fashion, he interpreted the black dresses as the garb of ascetic religious Puritans who were attacking men. It follows that Bannon's idea of rule by men includes what many cynics have suspected, a universal *droit de seigneur* that includes unrestricted sexual access to individuals under male "rule." Or, Bannon thinks with ideas from the U.S. colonial era and imagines property ownership to be restricted to men and entails that anything and everyone can be owned by them, without usufruct or an obligation to preserve and protect their possessions.

However, theorists ought not to be too fastidious in interpreting life. It may be that Have My Cake and Eat It Too feminists are the most effective opponents against those who share Bannon's view of the world and his place in it as a certain kind of male subject. Famous, beautiful, sexually attractive, and professionally successful, Have My Cake and Eat It Too feminists may have a hook into the desires of men like Steve Bannon, an ability to get under their skin, which obscure intellectuals with more modest heterosexually attractive attributes simply lack. Bannon and his ilk are probably not disconcerted when threats to the patriarchy are expressed by feminist theorists.

TRANSGRESSION, FAME, AND OBSCURITY

Feminism and its labels remain elite in three ways: already privileged women have benefited in educational and career opportunities from formal equality and legally stipulated access; feminist discourse is an intellectual occupation in which not all women can or are willing to participate; fame sweetens transgression by individuals. Famous sex workers and transgender people, who already have socioeconomic resources before they become famous, are not punished or despised for even radically nonconforming gender identities, while at the same time members of the obscure mass in each of these categories may be severely oppressed.

The implicit feminism of elite, powerful women is a great boon to feminism in theoretical terms, as is the activism itself of #MeToo. However, problems among the mass of nonelite women and women of color, some of them existentially crushing, are a major dimension in which feminist success is not yet complete. If elite women go on to their envisioned heights of what have been male bastions, but the nonelite mass does not share in this success, feminism will remain incomplete. It will not be as incomplete as in European historical periods when female monarchs ruled over men and women who had no civil rights, but it will be incomplete as a twenty-first-century progressive movement. The women who have benefited from the success of feminism have tended to be established people. They tend to have wealth, at least middle-class incomes, white racial status, and social respectability. At present, except for Hillary Clinton's defeat, they have been able to press their advantages without antimisogynism in plain view as a motivating factor.

Turbocharged politics may be led by sexual predators, but the ideology of its creation of class has been white racist, rather than explicitly misogynistic, even though, as indicated earlier, misogyny was mobilized to keep Hillary Clinton in her place. There are single issues that have been politicized along party lines, such as transgender bathrooms and abortion rights, but no wholesale turning against women. This may be why 52 percent of white women voted for Donald Trump in 2016, including 44 percent of women who were college educated (Scott 2017). Although liberals assumed that a majority of women would vote for Hillary Clinton—because she was a woman and because she more strongly represented women's values such as universal health care and education—the white supremacist element of Trump's campaign enabled the race track to block gender for white women (see chapter 2). That over 90 percent of black women voted for Clinton suggests that those who do not benefit from white racism may still recognize the importance of gender-related issues (Scott 2017). There is implicit racial exclusion among famous progressive white women who have spoken up within the #MeToo movement, and some have complained that LGBTQ women and strippers have also been left out (Scott 2018). The fact that #MeToo was started by Tarana Burke, an African American woman, seems to be easily overlooked (Burke 2017)!

The elitist nature of the visibility of progressive feminist representatives is evident in the occasional celebrity of sex workers and isolated successes of transgender people. When Stormy Daniels/Stephanie Clifford was interviewed by Anderson Cooper and considered credible by the majority of the audience (62 percent versus 21 percent), she was treated respectfully. Cooper accepted her work as an adult film actor and her stated willingness to prostitute herself for a possible role in Trump's *The Apprentice* as legitimate employment and reasonable motivation (Gerson 2018). But within weeks of Daniels's *60 Minutes* interview, complaints were voiced about the dislocation in work and life among sex workers caused by the federal government's shutdown of Backpage.com, following Craigslist and Reddit's terminations of their personal ad sections (Savage and Williams 2018). Sex workers who had depended on such electronic postings for livelihood were faced with the dangers and economic disruption of going back on the street to find clients. The importance of the ability to screen clients enabled by electronic postings was emphasized by those in favor of decriminalizing prostitution before SESTA (Stop Enabling Sex Trafficking Act) was passed. The rationale for SESTA was that it would limit sex trafficking of children, and no distinction was made between that crime and voluntary sex work by adults (Mitchell 2018). However, only two senators voted against FOSTA (Fight Online Sex Trafficking Act), the earlier version of SESTA (Brown 2018), suggesting that damage to sex workers was not even worthy of consideration by federal legislators. Although this was not an issue that divided on party political lines, it points to parts of the U.S. population whose well-being is easily ignored by those in power, that is, sex workers who are not celebrities or otherwise elite.

Transgender celebrities have been well received since Christine Jorgensen, a U.S. Army veteran, became world famous for undergoing hormone therapy and sex reassignment surgery in 1952 (Zack 2009, 71–74). At this time, Caitlyn Jenner and Chaz Bono are close to household names. On November 7, 2017, Danica Roem of Virginia became the first openly transgender person elected to the Virginia House of Delegates. Roem was part of a group of nine transgender people who achieved electoral success that year, including Andrea Jenkins (Minneapolis City Council), Phillipe Cunningham (Minneapolis City Council), Lisa Middleton (Palm Springs City Council), Stephe Koontz (Doraville City Council), Gerri Cannon (Doraville City Council), Tyler Titus (Erie School Board), Raven Matherne (Stamford Board of Representatives), Jacquelyn Ryan (Southbridge School Board) (Sopelsa 2017).

Despite such public success, Sarah McBride, national press secretary for the LGBTQ advocacy group Human Right Campaign, points out throughout *Tomorrow Will Be Different* (which bears a foreword by former vice president Joe Biden) how a 2011 report from the National Center for Transgender Equality and the National Gay and Lesbian Task Force reveals the precarious quality of transgender life. The executive summary of this report provides the following results from their survey of 6,450 transgender respondents: discrimination is pervasive and especially severe for transgender people of color; an income of less than $10,000 a year was four times more likely than for the general population; 41 percent had attempted suicide; over 60 percent were victims of physical assault and sexual assault; 15 percent left K–12 educational settings because of harassment (Grant et al. 2011). (According to the Williams Institute of UCLA Law, in 2016, 0.6 percent of the U.S. population, or about 2.6 million adults, are transgender (Flores et al. 2016), which is double the estimate from the same entity in 2011.

Recent transgender successes in politics may also be part of a resistance to the Republican Party line signaled by the Trump administration's reversal of Obama administration guidelines that schools allow transgender students to use the bathrooms of their choice (Peters, Becker, and Davis 2017). The political nature of Trump's attempts to ban recruitment of transgender people in the U.S. military is not in doubt (Diamond 2017). But again, people have to have a living wage and support in traditional communities in order to seek political office.

WHERE TO GO FROM HERE

Successful progressive movements tend to have three components—intellectual or theoretical, activist, and the mass of subjects whom theorists and activists literally or symbolically represent. It would be unrealistic to expect that these three components be aligned at the same time. Alignments in mass consciousness and discourse with activism probably have to reach a critical point for there to be lasting historical change. But there is as yet no science beyond the study of history, always after the fact, that can determine what that critical point is. The numerical majority consisting of nonaffluent white women, nonwhite women, and transgender people have not shared in the benefits of their elite and famous representatives. The same can probably be said of members of other socially disadvantaged groups with famous spokespersons, such as disabled people, addicts, and the white poor. When numerical majorities fall through the cracks, it is not an anomaly or even a problem, but a broad social structure. Such unevenness in progressive success is not in violation of existing state and federal law or the U.S. Constitution. Part of the gap is supported by the inertia of tradition and conservative public attitudes. Little can be done about that apart from slow processes of education and persuasion. But intellectually and theoretically, this may be a situation calling for an intervention in terms of social contract reinterpretation. Chapter 5, which is devoted to that reinterpretation, may thus be relevant to this top-rest aspect of progressive success.

REFERENCES

Associated Press. 2017. "Key Dates for Transgender Rights in the US." *Seattle Times*, February 23. https://www.seattletimes.com/nation-world/key-dates-for-transgender-rights-in-the-us/.

Breaking Prejudice. 2013. "LGBQ Timeline." http://www.breakingprejudice.org/assets/ AHAA/Activities/Gay%20Rights%20Movement%20Timeline%20Activity/ LGBT%20Rights%20Timeline.pdf.

Broverman, Neal. 2016. "We Can Still Hear the 'Screaming Queens' of the Compton's Cafeteria Riot." *Advocate*, August 8. https://www.advocate.com/transgender/2016/8/08/we-can-still-hear-screaming-queens-comptons-cafeteria-riot.

Brown, Elizabeth Nolan. 2018. "FOSTA Passes Senate, Making Prostitution Ads a Federal Crime against Objections from DOJ and Trafficking Victims." Reason.com, March 21. https://reason.com/blog/2018/03/21/senate-passes-fosta-sex-trafficking-bill.

Burke, Tarana. 2017. "#MeToo Was Started for Black and Brown Women and Girls. They're Still Being Ignored." *Washington Post*, November 9. https://www.washingtonpost.com/ news/post-nation/wp/2017/11/09/the-waitress-who-works-in-the-diner-needs-to-know-that-the-issue-of-sexual-harassment-is-about-her-too/?utm_term=.4db0ee4c849f.

Caputi, Mary. 2013. *Feminism and Power: The Need for Critical Theory*. Lanham, MD: Lexington Books, 2013.

Clinton, Hillary Rodham. 2017. *What Happened*. New York: Simon and Schuster.

Cooper, Anderson. 2018. "Stormy Daniels Describes Her Alleged Affair with Donald Trump," *60 Minutes*, March 28. https://www.cbsnews.com/news/stormy-daniels-describes-her-alleged-affair-with-donald-trump-60-minutes-interview/.

DeWolf, Mark. 2017. "12 Stats about Working Women." US Department of Labor blog, March 1. https://blog.dol.gov/2017/03/01/12-stats-about-working-women.

Diamond, Jeremy. 2017. "Trump Signs Directive Banning Transgender Military Recruits." CNN, August 25. https://www.cnn.com/2017/08/25/politics/trump-transgender-military/ index.html.

Flores, Andrew, Jody L. Herman, Gary J. Gates, and Taylor N. T. Brown. 2016. "How Many Adults Identify as Transgender in the United States?" Williams Institute, UCLA Law. https:/ /williamsinstitute.law.ucla.edu/wp-content/uploads/How-Many-Adults-Identify-as-Transgender-in-the-United-States.pdf.

Freeman, Hadley. 2017. "America's Vitriol towards Clinton Reveals a Nation Mired in Misogyny." *Guardian*, September 15. https://www.theguardian.com/commentisfree/2017/sep/15/ america-hillary-clinton-misogyny.

Gerson, Michael. 2018. "The Strange, Unexpected Public Contribution of Stormy Daniels." *Washington Post*, March 26. https://www.washingtonpost.com/opinions/the-strange-unexpected-public-contribution-of-stormy-daniels/2018/03/26/2c2bce4e-312a-11e8-8abc-22a366b72f2d_story.html?noredirect=on&utm_term=.88f067750a7b.

Glamour. 2018. "Post-Weinstein, These Are the Powerful Men Facing Sexual Harassment Allegations." February 26. https://www.glamour.com/gallery/post-weinstein-these-are-the-powerful-men-facing-sexual-harassment-allegations.

Grant, Jaime M., Lisa A. Mottet, Justin Tanis, Jack Harrison, Jody L. Herman, and Mara Keisling. 2011. *Injustice at Every Turn: A Report of the National Transgender Discrimination Survey*. Washington, DC: National Center for Transgender Equality and National Gay and Lesbian Task Force.

Green, Joshua. 2018. *The Devil's Bargain: Steve Bannon, Donald Trump, and the National Uprising*. New York: Penguin.

Held, Virginia. 1982. "Feminism and Hannah Arendt." *New York Review of Books*, October 21. http://www.nybooks.com/articles/1982/10/21/feminism-hannah-arendt/.

Hill, Anita, and E. C. Jordan. 1995. *Race, Gender, and Power in America: The Legacy of the Hill–Thomas Hearings*. New York: Oxford University Press.

Huffpost. 2017. "10 Celebrities Who Say They Aren't Feminists." December 6. https://www. huffingtonpost.com/2013/12/17/feminist-celebrities_n_4460416.html.

Kutner, Max. 2017. "Backpage.com Removes Adult Ads Hours before Senate Hearing." *Newsweek*, January 9. http://www.newsweek.com/backpage-adult-section-shut-down-540774.

Lemelle, Anthony. 2007. "One Drop Rule." In *The Blackwell Encyclopedia of Sociology*, ed. G. Ritzer. DOI:10.1002/9781405165518.wbeoso011.

Manne, Kate. 2016. *Down Girl: The Logic of Misogyny*. New York: Oxford University Press.

Markus, Maria. 1987. "The 'Anti-Feminism' of Hannah Arendt.'" *Thesis Eleven* 17 (1): 76-87. https://doi.org/10.1177/072551368701700106.

McBride, Sarah, and Joe Biden. 2018. *Tomorrow Will Be Different: Love, Loss, and the Fight for Trans Equality*. New York: Crown.

Mill, John Stuart. [1869] 1997. *The Subjection of Women*. Ed. Susan L. Rattiner. Mineola, NY: Dover.

Milligan, Susan. 2017. "Timeline: The Women's Rights Movement in the US." AOL.com, January 21. https://www.aol.com/article/news/2017/01/21/timeline-the-womens-rights-movement-in-the-us/21659519/.

Mitchell, Ty. 2018. "If Lawmakers Want to Protect Sex Workers, They Must Listen to Us." *HuffPost*, March 8. https://www.huffingtonpost.com/entry/sex-workers-bill-fosta-sesta_us_5aa1924fe4b04c33cb6cecb2.

National Center for Education Statistics. 2017. "Teacher Trends." Fast Facts. https://nces.ed.gov/fastfacts/display.asp?id=28.

Pasquini, Maria, and Diana Pearl. 2018. "All of the Hollywood Figures Who Have Spoken Out against Harvey Weinstein." *People*, January 25. http://people.com/celebrity/harvey-weinstein-scandal-gallery/.

Peters, Jeremy W., Jo Becker, and Julie Hirschfeld Davis. 2017. "Trump Rescinds Rules on Bathrooms for Transgender Students." *New York Times*, February 22. https://www.nytimes.com/2017/02/22/us/politics/devos-sessions-transgender-students-rights.html.

Relethford, John H. 2017. "Biological Anthropology, Population Genetics, and Race." In *The Oxford Handbook of Philosophy and Race*, ed. Naomi Zack, 160–69. New York: Oxford University Press.

Ross, R. J. 2013. "Bread and Roses: Women Workers and the Struggle for Dignity and Respect. *WorkingUSA* 16:59–68. DOI:10.1111/wusa.12023.

Savage, Charlie, and Timothy Williams. 2018. "U.S. Seizes Backpage.com, a Site Accused of Enabling Prostitution." *New York Times*, April 4. https://www.nytimes.com/2018/04/07/us/politics/backpage-prostitution-classified.html.

Scott, Eugene. 2017. "The Democratic Party Owes Black Female Voters a Big 'Thank You.'" *Washington Post*, November 9. https://www.washingtonpost.com/news/the-fix/wp/2017/11/09/the-democratic-party-owes-black-women-voters-a-big-thank-you/?utm_term=.1bb481843656.

Scott, Sidney. 2018. "Amber Rose Believes Black Women and the LGBTQ Community Are Being Left Out of the #MeToo Movement." *Essence*, March 15. https://www.essence.com/celebrity/amber-rose-black-women-lgbtq-community-metoo-movement.

Sopelsa, Brooke. 2017. "Meet 2017's Newly Elected Transgender Officials." NBCNews.com, December 28. https://www.nbcnews.com/feature/nbc-out/meet-2017-s-newly-elected-transgender-officials-n832826.

Templeton, Alan R. 1998. "Human Races: A Genetic and Evolutionary Perspective." *American Anthropologist* 100 (3): 632–51.

United States Holocaust Memorial Museum. 2018. "Nuremberg Race Laws." Holocaust Encyclopedia. https://www.ushmm.org/outreach/en/article.php?ModuleId=10007695.

Wang, Wendy, Kim Parker, and Paul Taylor. 2013. "Breadwinner Moms." *Social and Demographic Trends*, Pew Research Center, May 29. http://www.pewsocialtrends.org/2013/05/29/breadwinner-moms/.

WeRise. 2018. "Different Kinds of Feminism." April. https://werise-toolkit.org/en/system/tdf/pdf/tools/Different-Kinds-of-Feminism.pdf?file=1&force=.

Wollstonecraft, Mary. [1792] 1996. *Vindication of the Rights of Women*. Ed. Candace Ward. Mineola, NY: Dover.

Zack, Naomi. 2005. *Inclusive Feminism: A Third Wave Theory of Women's Commonality*. Lanham, MD: Rowman & Littlefield.

———. 2009. "Transsexuality and Daseia Y. Cavers-Huff." In *You've Changed: Sex Reassignment and Personal Identity*, ed. Laurie J. Shrage, 103–22. Oxford: Oxford University Press.

Part II

The Need for the Social Compact

Chapter Five

The Social Contract and the
Social Compact

To ask how you may be guarded from harm coming from the direction where the strongest hand is available to do it is to use the voice of faction and rebellion; as if when men left the state of nature and entered into society they agreed that all but one of them should be under the restraint of laws, and that that one should keep all the liberty of the state of nature, increased by power, and made licentious by impunity. This implies that men are so foolish that they would take care to avoid harms from polecats or foxes, but think it is safety to be eaten by lions. (Locke [1689] 2017, chap. 7, sec. 93)

The mutual transferring of right is that which men call contract. (Hobbes [1651] 1999, pt. 2, chap. 14, p. 114)

Governments are instituted among Men, deriving their just Powers from the Consent of the Governed, that whenever any form of Government becomes destructive of these Ends, it is the Right of the People to alter or to abolish it, and to institute new Government, laying its Foundation on such Principles, and organizing its Powers in such form, as to them shall seem most likely to effect their Safety and Happiness. (Declaration of Independence; Jefferson 1776)

Chapter 4 ended with the observation that the inequality in status, wealth, and treatment between celebrity and obscure sex workers and transgender people pointed to structural issues that create a division between the top and the rest within progressive movements. The same top-rest situation was identified between elite women and the mass of women experiencing sexual harassment. In chapter 2, racial differences were posited as a junction, leading to an unpredictable track that could disrupt the lives of people of color, instantly and over time, both in public and within institutions. The obscure members of disadvantaged groups have higher levels of poverty in all cases, but poverty does not cause female gender, nonwhite race, or transgender identity. Poverty may contribute to sex work, but that is because sex work is a low-status occupation that is not usually the first career choice of sex workers. The inequalities within progressive movements suggests that prior socioeconomic resources determine who can succeed from within such movements or within the categories of disadvantaged citizens and residents that the movements represent. However, that does not address the inertia preventing the obscure masses from escaping oppression after they have been progressively represented. There are likely more poor and disadvantaged masses than successful leaders within feminist groups, racial groups, and all other disadvantaged groups. These masses are "the rest." The top, people who speak up for members of the disadvantaged groups, seem mainly able to help only themselves. There is no evidence of ill will or corruption in this situation, so the top-rest division therefore must have a deeper social component, or perhaps the absence of a structure yet to be formed, which constitutes this inertia.

The social aspect of inequality within progressive movements and organizations is not illegal or unconstitutional, and it is therefore difficult to say how such inequality is unjust. Insofar as justice is a matter of rights in law, we cannot say that the obscure masses in disadvantaged groups suffer from applicative injustice because we cannot point to enough people in each of the disadvantaged categories who are treated justly. We could say that those in the obscure masses should be treated as justly as those at the top in the same disadvantaged category are treated, but nonviolent social discrimination, which creates the social, economic, and status differences between members of the same disadvantaged category, are not matters of justice in a legal or political sense, which is what we have been talking about so far. This raises the question of whether there is a higher or deeper or more fundamental kind of law that might apply, which is why it might be worthwhile to consider the social contract here. For consistency, we should remain in the discourse of politics and law instead of turning to religion, humanitarianism, or even morality.

The scholarship and terminology surrounding the social contract is dense, complicated, at times confusing. Although I am here delving into several relevant parts of this field, it is important to begin with the popular notion that the social contract is an agreement between citizens and government. That is not the original historical or philosophical meaning of the social contract, but it sums up a shared intuition that citizen expect to benefit from government. I will call agreements among citizens, before, during, and after any particular government, the *social compact*. We will see that historically this concept of the social compact was the meaning of the term *social contract* as imputed to Thomas Hobbes and John Locke, who were the main social contract theorists in the Anglo-American tradition. We will also see that the idea that the people are sovereign, with the abiding right to change as well as set up a government, appealed to the framers of the U.S. Declaration of Independence, but that the Civil War resulted in retiring this social compact notion from public discourse. (The aim of this book is to revive that notion.)

With these preliminary considerations in mind, this chapter begins with a discussion of the nature of the social contract and contracts within governed society, followed by a brief examination of the invocation of the social contract in U.S. history. Then an interpretation of Locke's meaning of property, in comparison to its historical and contemporary meaning, will be offered in order to reintroduce an idea of the *social compact*. Finally, some light may be shed on the top-rest phenomenon within progressive movements, and, beyond that, the idea of the social compact will be useful on its own for considering other subjects in the chapters ahead.

THE SOCIAL CONTRACT AND CONTRACTS WITHIN SOCIETY

The social contract is a sacred existential legal doctrine, and we don't know what it is. This allows for a certain degree of freedom in explicating it. Let's imagine that the social contract is an agreement between citizens concerning their government that is prior in time and logic to any particular body of law, founding document, or existing government. Because it is prior in logic, the social contract does not end with the formation or dissolution of government. Let's also stipulate that the social contract requires that citizens consent to their government because it benefits them by providing for order in society. The idea of consent is supported by the fact that even the most totalitarian, tyrannical, and authoritarian regimes think it is necessary to construct ideologies that justify and even elevate the oppressions they perpetrate—they not only need to prevent revolution to stay in power but require at least the appearance of approval to maintain their legitimacy. And if the consent of those ruled is necessary for even oppressive rulers, then the people must be able to consent—they must be free in some fundamental political sense that even oppressive governments must reckon with. This is to say that the people are sovereign.

Beyond this inference of freedom of the people on their side of the social contract, we still don't know much about it. People tend to invoke the social contract when they believe that it has been violated or broken. This supports the claim that no one knows what it is in a positive sense, justifying the use of imagination in specifying what it is. The lack of a positive explication of the social contract is not unusual if the idea of the social contract is compared to the idea of justice. Nonacademic people are not ordinarily concerned with what justice is in a positive sense. But they care a great deal about injustice, which somehow they are able to recognize without a prior idea of justice (Zack 2016, 9–65).

The role of creativity in explicating the social contract is evident through the varied use made of it by the classical social contract theories—it allows for social contract theory, in a general sense. First, the classical social contract theorists posited a "state of nature" in which government did not exist. Then they described a social contract that would result in government, specifically the kind of government they already favored. Thus, Hobbes, whose patron believed in absolute monarchy, posited a social contract that led to authoritarian government. By contrast, Locke, whose patron was part of the rising seventeenth-century aristocracy of landowners and traders, posited a social contract that led to representative government, for members of that class. In U.S. history, Hobbes's vision is the state of affairs most feared, authoritarian government as irrevocable salvation from warlike anarchy. Locke, who is widely believed to have influenced the founders of the U.S. Constitution, especially Jefferson, posited representative government as a convenience for members of a preexisting peaceful, cooperative society in the state of nature or before government. Hobbes did not think that enforceable or real rights existed until the ruler created them; Locke believed that rights existed before, during, and, should it happen, after the duration of government. Clearly, Locke remains more in accord with contemporary progressive sensibilities and activism.

However, Hobbes is useful for his explicit use of the term *compact* or *contract* as a fundamental organizing principle for peaceful civil society. He believed that government was necessary to enforce contracts when one side had not fulfilled their contractual obligations and the other side had. Hobbes defined contracts as a transfer of rights, but it is likely that he also had experience of contracts within his society and intended to draw on similar experience from readers. Locke did not use the term *contract* in his discussion of what came to be known as his theory of the social contract. Locke's use of the term occurs in his discussion of marriage, where he distinguishes "natural right" from agreed-upon contract (Locke [1689] 2017, secs. 83 and 85). That is, Locke also reserved the term *contract* for agreements occurring within society under government, not prior to it.

Here it is not of particular interest exactly what Hobbes and Locke and their readers would have thought contracts were before reading their definitions and how they put them to use. But it might be useful for explicating the social contract to begin with looking at what contracts are in our society. There is a substantial body of law involving contracts, in both the common law tradition and according to contemporary North American statute. This has resulted in agreement about the elements of a valid contract: (1) offer, (2) acceptance, (3) consideration, (4) mutuality of obligation, (5) competency and capacity, and in certain circumstances, (6) a written instrument.

The offer element of the social contract is difficult to pin down because the social contract is not coincident with the founding of governments or benefits after governments are established. For instance, both the U.S. Declaration of Independence and Constitution are proclamations rather than offers. In the process of their formulation, different drafts and negotiations about their revisions may have been offers and acceptances, but they were about what the final form of the proclamation would be, rather than agreements between government and all who were qualified to have a say among those to be governed. Not only were slaves, women, and those without property (who therefore could not vote) excluded from the formulation, but even all who could eventually vote did not participate in constructing these proclamations. Although representatives from the colonies and states did ratify each document, ratification is a process of giving formal consent to a preformed agreement, rather than acting as a party in the creation of a contract or performing in accordance with a contract.

To continue with the legal consensus about the nature of contracts within society, a written instrument is required for certain kinds of contract only, such as real estate agreements and promises to perform an act that cannot possibly be performed within a year from the date of the promise. A contract is breached if one party does not live up to its terms, which causes the other party to suffer damages (loss) (USLegal.com 2018a). A contract is fulfilled if both parties have performed their obligations (Law Dictionary 2018). A contract is complete if it specifies how it applies in all possible instances (Bolton and Dewatripont 2005, 4–20). Another element of contracts within society is that the parties to the contract must be identified. It is difficult to determine who all the parties to the social contract are. We could say that the people of an established society is one party, and that this party always retains the power to specify a government. The situation is similar to the idea behind the British practice of the monarch asking the newly elected prime minister to form a government, or the power of an organization's board of directors or trustees to select a president or CEO.

Twentieth-century politicians such as Bill Clinton and Newt Gingrich have presented Locke's social contract as a contract between the people and their government (Pease 2009, 97). But others have described the social contract as expectations that citizens have about their employment opportunities, job security, and purchasing power, that is, in terms of their expectations about the economy (Freedman and Lind 2013). These formulations are present neither in Hobbes's nor Locke's political philosophy, but they reflect popular understandings of citizen–government relationships. Hobbes is explicit that the social contract is an agreement among the people to transfer their rights to a ruler (Hobbes [1651] 1999, pt. 2, chap. 18, pp. 151–52). Locke, as noted, does not speak of a contract at all. Historian Mark Hulliung writes:

> Locke explicitly disallowed the notion of a contract between government and people. The sovereign people owe nothing to the rulers; the rulers owe everything to the governed. . . .There is a social contract by which the people bind themselves to one another, but no subsequent political contract. The rulers hold power temporarily, as mere "trustees" of the people. A second contract [between the people and the government] must be disallowed on the grounds that it contradicts the sovereignty of the people. What the people give they can take away whenever they please, because they are bound by no contract between governors and governed. (2007, 2)

The social contract is not written down anywhere as a contract, which would be required if it is like contracts within society, because it takes longer than a year to perform. But if it has been performed—which it has, because we can see or make plausible claims that it has been broken, then this prior performance would be what validates it as an *implied-in-fact contract*. An implied-in-fact contract is a contract agreed on by nonverbal conduct rather than by explicit words. Such contracts are automatically created when a party tacitly accepts a benefit at a time when it is possible to reject it (USLegal.com 2018b). But the issue of contract benefits is complicated in terms of the social contract. Either the people or government officials might accept or reject any given benefit, without this having an effect on the social contract (e.g., government officials may accept or decline their pay and citizens accept or decline government funds due them). But because the social contract is neither explicit nor written down, it is not clear what the contractual benefits are. This allows for a built-in vagueness or indeterminacy in the social contract, but it also provides for flexibility in social contract theory. Finally, the social contract is not a *complete contract* because we do not know and cannot describe all of the situations and events to which it applies.

To summarize thus far: The social contract requires that the people consent to government because they are free. They consent to government to have order in society, which is one of the benefits they expect to receive from government, but these benefits are not part of a contract with government, because government is not part of the contract. If the government or any particular government is not part of the social contract, then the social contract has a very large number of parties, including all of the adult members of society, and it might be better to call it a *compact* than a contract. A contract is enforceable by law within nations, whereas a compact may occur among sovereign entities, such as states, nations, or in the case of the social contract, understood as a compact, free individuals. The social contract or compact is neither written down nor explicit. Its specific provisions are best known when they are violated or the contract is believed to be broken. We cannot describe everything to which the social compact applies, but it may be a good rule of thumb that when unfairness spoils people's lives in important ways and there is no legal recourse, the social contract may be invoked.

EVOCATIONS OF THE SOCIAL CONTRACT AND SOCIAL COMPACT IN U.S. HISTORY

To distinguish between society and government, let's refer to the "social compact" as an agreement among individuals outside of government and the "social contract" as an agreement between the parties to the social compact and any government that they select or find themselves under. As noted, the social contract has been invoked throughout U.S. history in political contexts to express dissatisfactions with or preferences concerning government, usually the federal government. However, the social compact has been envisioned as prior to government—for example, in the 1780 Constitution of the Commonwealth of Massachusetts (Peters 1978, 66–81), which drew from John Adams in its preamble: "The body politic is formed by a voluntary association of individuals. It is a social compact, by which the whole people covenants with each citizen, and each citizen with the whole people" (Massachusetts [1780] 2018).

There is ongoing ambiguity and confusion between the ideas of the social compact as within society, to which government is external, and the social contract as an agreement between society and government. Popular thought and usage, as well as philosophical understanding, tend to focus on the social contract, positing a direct connection between people and government. However, when former FBI director James Comey was asked if President Trump should be impeached, given that he is morally unfit for office, his response was, "I hope not. . . . Because I think impeaching and removing Donald Trump from office would let the American people off the hook and have something happen indirectly that I believe they're duty bound to do directly. People in this country need to stand up and go to the voting booth and vote their values. And so impeachment, in a way, would short circuit that" (Stracqualursi 2018). If Comey was here referring to Aristotle, as Judith Shklar did in 1989, being a good citizen is not the same thing as being a good person. The goodness of persons is a private, moral matter, whereas the goodness of citizens, including those who serve in government, belongs to the area of the social compact, which although political is outside of any given government (Shklar 1991, 6; Aristotle 1985, bk. 3, chap. 4, 1276b–77b, pp. 90–92.) Citizens thereby have duties to themselves and other citizens that arise from the social compact.

We could say that the ability of the people to vote Trump out of office belongs to the people as parties in the social compact. On this construction, voting candidates in or out of office is a social compact activity, which although regulated by government is not ruled by government—the government cannot tell the people how to vote. However, if government officials have an obligation to reflect the people's values, then failing to do so would be a violation of the social contract. That is, on this construction, the social compact is an agreement within society, whereas the social contract is an agreement between society and government.

Some Americans believe that the morality of their elected officials is part of their legitimacy as officeholders; others believe that morality is distinct from political legitimacy. Philosophers do not agree on the nature of moral character or what the virtues are. However the connection with morality and government may be resolved, both the social compact and the social contract are necessary concepts. So long as the people are able to respond to violations of the social contract by government officials, and government officials in turn respond to them, their social contract is intact. However, in terms of the kinds of organic resistance discussed in chapter 3, we can see now that such activities occur on the basis of, or from within, the social compact. Hulliung's claim that a second contract after the social contract would violate the sovereignty of the people is not a foregone conclusion. When a board of directors fires the CEO of a company and appoints a new one, the sovereignty of the board has not been violated because at no point has the CEO usurped the power of the board. Something analogous can be imagined to obtain in the relationship between the electorate and any government in power. Of course, if the people lose their power to change the government by voting, then, in Locke's words in the first chapter epigraph, they will have been so foolish as to exchange the annoyance of polecats and foxes for the danger of lions.

In *The Social Contract in America*, Hulliung tracks the focal point of social contract discourse over U.S. history. From the Revolutionary War until the end of the Civil War, there was a burning question of whether, in accord with Locke's *Second Treatise of Government* and Jefferson's 1789 assertion in a letter to James Madison that "the earth belongs to the living," the people retain a right to rebel against government. While Southern secessionists affirmed that right before and during the Civil War, there was the more politically conservative legacy of Edmund Burke concerning duty extending across generations. By the time of the Gettysburg Address, Lincoln was able both to enshrine a Jeffersonian doctrine that individual liberty was more important than property rights (affirming the abolition of slavery) and to call for the present generation "to be dedicated here to the unfinished work which they who fought here have thus far so nobly advanced" (i.e., discouraging future rebellion) (Hulliung 2007, 178; Tate 1965).

Hulliung recounts how, after the Civil War, the inspirational and justificatory subject of national discourse shifted from the Declaration of Independence to the U.S. Constitution as the primary sacred founding document. The creation of new and more powerful federal institutions strengthened government in its mission of westward expansion. Imperialism during the 1898 Spanish-American War was based on ignoring the doctrine that legitimate government required the consent of those governed, when the United States acquired Cuba, Guam, Puerto Rico, and the Philippines. During the same time, the National American Woman Suffrage Association removed references to rights, consent, and equality from its discourse, partly in deference to racist women in the South. Politically, agrarians and progressives were opposed in their valorization of independent farmers versus ill-paid wage laborers. But they agreed in moving beyond the U.S. Constitution to attack the institution of private property and criticize the idea that individuals made society, in favor of ideas that society made individuals, and for both movements talk of rights fell out of favor. As Hulliung concludes his account of the history of the social contract in U.S. public discourse, he notes that even though twentieth-century political discourse largely dispensed with the social contract, the invocation of natural rights was useful to Franklin Roosevelt in describing his New Deal social security program in 1932 and for 1970s Democrats and activists in demanding justice for women and racial minorities (2007, 184–205).

LOCKE'S MEANING OF PROPERTY AND INTERPRETATIONS

The claim that the United States is a materialistic society with high values placed on private property does not need argument. It is understandable that many believe that the protection of private property by government derives from Locke's conception of natural rights and civil society. However, this attribution is not quite accurate, and we should take a closer look at what Locke thought about property.

Locke's conception of property was close to a seventeenth-century concept of *propriety* that emphasized the importance of individual ownership of rights, especially the right to exist. Richard Overton wrote in 1646,

> To every individual in nature is given an individual property by nature, not to be invaded or usurped by any; for everyone as he is himselfe, so he hath a selfe propriety, else he could not be himself, and on this no second may presume to deprive any of, without manifest violation and affront to the very principles of nature and of the Rules of equity and justice between man and man; mine and thine cannot be, except this be: No man hath power over my rights and liberties and I over no man's. (cited in Larkin 1930, 42–43)

According to Overton, everyone owns himself, including his or her rights and liberties. The result is that self-ownership is the foundation for the individual ownership of other things (mine and thine). Overton did not invent this conception of ownership. An anonymous pamphleteer had written two years earlier, "[Let us] who are English subjects . . . blesse God for His goodness who hath . . . made us absolute proprietors of who, so that our lives, liberties and estates, do not depend, nor are subject to, the sole breath or arbitrary will of our Soveraigne" (Larkin 1930, 52). Going further back, Conal Condren refers to the association of the status of rulers with the absolute rights of owners during the 1300s in Italy (1988, 98–100).

Locke was not a radical egalitarian. He lived through a time when political representation in the House of Lords was based on amounts of land owned (Larkin 1930, 50–51) and himself thought that suffrage should depend on ownership of at least some property. But he shared a view with those more radical, that individuals other than the sovereign or ruling monarch could be owners.

Locke carves out his theory of private property in chapter 5 of the *Second Treatise*. He begins with the question of how private property is possible after God originally gave the earth and all of its fruits to mankind in common. These fruits require labor to be usable. Locke derived the ownership of material possessions from labor and what someone who labored, or his servants, mixed his labor with. But this labor theory of possessions was based on the deeper idea of self-ownership that derived from Overton and his predecessors. Here is Locke's theory of ownership that makes what one owns part of one: "The Fruit or Venison, which nourishes the wild Indian, who knows no Inclosure, and is still a Tenant in common, must be his, and so his—*i.e.*, a part of him, that another can no longer have any right to it, before it can do him any good for the support of his Life" ([1689] 2017, chap. 5, sec. 26). And here is Locke's theory of ownership of material possessions that derives from self-ownership:

> Every man has a *Property* in his own Person. This no Body has any Right to but himself. The *Labour* of his Body, and the Work of his hands, we may say, are properly his. Whatsoever then he removes out of the State that Nature hath provided, and left it in, he hath mixed his *Labour* with, and joined to it something that it is own, and thereby makes it his Property. ([1689] 2017, chap. 5, sec. 27)

These passages point to two different meanings of *property* for Locke: things owned in the ordinary way in which we still speak of ownership; a person's life and liberty, as well as protection of their property, which later became widely discussed as rights. To put it more precisely, for Locke, a person owned their life, liberty, and estate or material possessions, while for us a person has a right to her life and liberty and a right to own material possessions. If one thinks of ownership in the ordinary way, it is almost shocking to think that life and liberty can be owned, but if one thinks of ownership as Overton and Locke did, then, as Overton asserted, there is no "mine and thine," no individual ownership of property or what we would call property rights, without ownership in that first sense.

When Locke wrote about the purpose of government, in addition to impartial judges and police and military protection, which do not exist without government, its main purpose was to protect property in the broad sense consisting of life, liberty, and estate (material possession):

> As I have shown, man was born with a right to perfect freedom, and with an uncontrolled enjoyment of all the rights and privileges of the law of nature, equally with any other man or men in the world. So he has by nature a power not only to preserve his property, his life, liberty and possessions, against harm from other men, but to judge and punish breaches of the law of nature by others—punishing in the manner he thinks the offence deserves, even punishing with death crimes that he thinks are so dreadful as to deserve it. But no political society can exist or survive without having in itself the power to preserve the property—and therefore to punish the offences—of all the members of that society; and so there can't be a political society except where every one of the members has given up this natural power, passing it into the hands of the community in all cases. . . . With all private judgments of every particular member of the society being excluded, the community comes to be the umpire. (Locke [1689] 2017, chap. 7, sec. 87)

And because people without government give up their natural rights to protect themselves and their property, and to punish offenders, government takes over these functions when they consent to a government. Thus, Locke concluded, "So the great and chief purpose of men's uniting into commonwealths and putting themselves under government is the preservation of their property" (Locke [1689] 2017, chap. 9, sec. 124).

The Declaration of Independence begins with truths held to be self-evident: "That all Men are created equal, that they are endowed by their Creator with certain unalienable Rights, that among these are Life, Liberty, and the Pursuit of Happiness—That to secure these Rights, Governments are instituted among Men" (Jefferson 1776). Property is not mentioned in the declaration.

In the U.S. Constitution, property is mentioned in Articles 5 and 14.1, with the phrase "life, liberty, or property." Article 5 refers to the federal government and Article 14 to states, in both cases stipulating that government cannot deprive individuals of property without due process of law and compensation (ConstitutionUS.com [1787/1788] 2018). It's evident in both articles that rights to life and liberty are separate from property rights. In the Constitution, *property* has come to mean what it means today, possessions. However, the historical and contemporary importance placed on property rights, especially private property as belonging to individuals, has connotations of the importance accorded to life and liberty. John Adams wrote in 1787:

> The moment the idea is admitted into society, that property is not as sacred as the laws of God, and that there is not a force of law and public justice to protect it, anarchy and tyranny commence. If "Thou shalt not covet," and

"Thou shalt not steal," were not commandments of Heaven, they must be made inviolable precepts in every society, before it can be civilized or made free. ([1787] 2018)

The American Dream is intricately bound up with yearly income in an economy that is mainly consumer driven. Aspirations for higher education are closely tied to earnings and purchasing ability, including college education for children, who are expected to make as much or more money than their parents. Money is not the same as possession, but most Americans would not want more money if they could not buy anything with it. President George W. Bush famously referred to the United States as an "ownership society," and President Donald Trump is continually lauded for being a successful businessman.

THE SOCIAL CONTRACT/COMPACT, TOP-REST, AND COMMONWEALTH

When the classical social contract theorists sought to justify the creation of government, they called the human condition without government a *state of nature*. Without the problematic connotations of what is meant by the state of nature in historical terms, we have so far referred simply to conditions without government. Such conditions need not occur in the historical past. They can serve for a thought experiment in ongoing criticism and justification of any particular form of government. The state of nature for us, or life and freedom outside of obligations to government, is the realm of the social compact. Our state of nature is not an imaginary life in the woods or off the grid but our life within society, apart from rule by government. It is all that takes place in the realm of actions that democratic government does not prohibit. Those inhabiting this realm mentally and emotionally can be imagined to constitute a commonwealth whereby each individual has an agreement with the whole and the whole has an agreement with each individual. The U.S. nation may be too large to constitute a commonwealth, except when there are national elections. But smaller units within the nation, whose members are not all fully benefiting from the social contract, can be imagined as commonwealths. This would convert or expand the idea of property to propriety—property is separate from life and liberty, but propriety encompasses all three. All members of a commonwealth have propriety.

If we image a progressive movement or organization as a commonwealth, we can say that what stabilizes structural inequality in such movements is an acceptance of material inequality in combination with a belief in human equality. Those who enter progressive movements with prior material resources and become famous are accepted by the rest as higher in status. The rest become fans of their celebrities without strong envy or resentment because they believe in human equality—everyone in the rest is just as good as the celebrity leaders. It is virtuous that they do not become consumed by envy of those at the top, but that generosity does not help make the distribution of power within the movement or organization more egalitarian.

The distinction between the social compact and contract has an analogous structure in inegalitarian progressive groups. The top in progressive movements can make all sorts of contracts for themselves, or as representatives of the entire group, without real influence from, or interaction with, the rest. They often make these arrangements according to contract law within governed society, while neglecting the full commonwealth that they are representing. And in that process they may lose contact or fail to establish contact with the rest in their organizations, who continue to experience severe harassment, discrimination, or deprivation.

The commonwealth structure requires that everyone except an individual makes an agreement with that individual and the individual makes an agreement with everyone. This interaction applies to all individuals in the commonwealth. If progressive movements and organizations are viewed as having constituents with a common cause or goals, it is important that those at the top constantly interact with the rest, instead of devoting most of their energy to powerful people and entities outside of their movements and organizations, such as media and courts. If all members of disadvantaged groups, drawing on their shared principle of human equality, can communicate more fully within themselves, the top-rest stratification might shift toward greater equality. Contemporary progressives are inherently resistant to the real status quo and conservative political structures and opinions. They are not revolutionary groups because they generally seek to change government rather than overthrow it, but their resistance issuing from the realm of the social compact is evident in expressive demonstrations that can be very impressive and lead to effective political organization.

Free elections are a bridge between the social compact and the social contract. That the people have the power to change their government on all levels amounts to the power to make a revolution during extremely divisive periods of party politics, such as the present. Voter turnout is a pivotal issue because less than 60 percent of those eligible vote in presidential elections and about 40 percent in local elections. Non-Hispanic whites have the highest turnout, followed by non-Hispanic blacks. Other high turnout rates include those over age forty-five and those with college education (United States Elections Project 2018). A number of cultural observers have long believed that people do not vote because they do not think that the outcome of elections will affect their lives. It is assumed that those who do not vote are younger, less educated, less white, and more poor than those who do, and it is further assumed that progressive groups and the Democratic Party are better able to formulate, and if victorious implement, policies that would improve the lives of large numbers of nonvoters. More energetic communication within the commonwealths of already-formed progressive groups could increase voter turnout. Again, this is not merely an issue of good citizenship but, in strongly party-partisan times, an opportunity for a revolution, because Democrats and Republicans now have such opposed ideas and values that to change the balance of power from one party to the other is tantamount to overthrowing and replacing the government. When there has been less difference between parties, it made sense to many, including those recently enfranchised, not to bother voting, because even if their votes conferred benefits on their groups, they would not significantly change individual lives (Shklar 1991, 25–62). Other views concerning low voter turnout cite discriminatory voter registration requirements and inertia within parties about addressing that issue because wealthy backers may not share inclusive political ideas about the passive electorate (Piven and Cloward 1989).

Race and ethnicity are also factors in party identification leading to voter turnout. Democratic voter turnout increased by five million in the 2008 presidential election won by Barack Obama, but as Zoltan Hajnal and Taeku Lee (2011) point out, except for six hundred thousand, the increased turnout was the result of African Americans and Latinx Americans going to the polls. At the same time, 90 percent of those who voted for John McCain were white (Hajnal and Lee 2011, 2–4). This easily overlooked factor of race in voter turnout may not only be relevant to any partisan election effort but may play a role in inertial inequalities within progressive movements and organizations. If minority citizens are not informed about candidates, their failure to vote may be lost opportunities to concretely change their lives. This is especially the case regarding the disproportionate number of minorities in prison. For example, liberal billionaire George Soros, through a fifty-million-dollar grant to the American Civil Liberties Union, has been funding progressive candidates for the office of prosecutor throughout the United States (Schoffstall 2018). Prosecutors have vast local power in lobbying state government, charging defendants with crimes, sentencing, and probation. If successful, this initiative could reduce the numbers of minorities arrested, convicted, and incarcerated (Pugh 2018).

SUMMING UP

The concepts analyzed is this chapter—social contract, social compact, property and propriety, and the top-rest dynamic within progressive movements, added to the concepts of turbocharged politics and the junction of race—will be useful in considering further subjects where suffering, violence, and injustice persist, either in defiance of law or with the support of law. The remaining chapters in part II are about disaster for humans and the environment, homelessness, and immigration. Not all of the new concepts developed so far will apply, but where there are applications new insights can be developed.

REFERENCES

Adams, John. [1787] 2018. "Defence of the Constitutions of Government of the United States." In *The Founders' Constitution*, vol. 1, chap. 16, doc. 15. http://press-pubs.uchicago.edu/founders/documents/v1ch16s15.html.

Aristotle. 1985. *The Politics*. Trans. and ed. Carns Lord. Chicago: University of Chicago Press.

Bolton, Patrick, and Dewatripont, Matthias. 2005. *Contract Theory*. Cambridge, MA: MIT Press.

Condren, Conal. 1988. *George Lawson's Politica and the English Revolution.* Cambridge: Cambridge University Press.

ConstitutionUS.com. [1787/1788] 2018. "The Constitution of the United States." http://constitutionus.com/.

Freedman, Josh, and Michael Lind. 2013. "The Past and Future of America's Social Contract." *Atlantic*, December 19. https://www.theatlantic.com/business/archive/2013/12/the-past-and-future-of-americas-social-contract/282511/.

Hajnal, Zoltan L., and Taeku Lee. 2011. *Why Americans Don't Join the Party: Race, Immigration, and the Failure (of Political Parties) to Engage the Electorate.* Princeton, NJ: Princeton University Press.

Hobbes, Thomas. [1651] 1999. *Leviathan*. University of Oregon. https://scholarsbank.uoregon.edu/xmlui/bitstream/handle/1794/748/leviathan.pdf.

Hulliung, Mark. 2007. *The Social Contract in America*. Lawrence: University of Kansas Press.

Jefferson, Thomas. 1776. "Declaration of Independence." https://www.constitutionfacts.com/content/declaration/files/Declaration_ReadTheDeclaration.pdf.

Larkin, Paschal. 1930. *Property in the Eighteenth Century*. London: Longmans Green.

Law Dictionary. 2018. "What Is Fulfillment of Contract?" April. https://thelawdictionary.org/fulfillment-of-contract/.

Locke, John. [1689] 2017. *Second Treatise of Government*. Ed. Jonathan Bennett. Early Modern Texts. http://www.earlymoderntexts.com/assets/pdfs/locke1689a.pdf.

Massachusetts. [1780] 2018. "A Constitution or Form of Government for the Commonwealth of Massachusetts, Preamble." TeachingAmericanHistory.org. http://teachingamericanhistory.org/library/document/massachusetts-declaration-of-rights/.

Pease, Donald E. 2009. *The New American Exceptionalism*. Minneapolis: University Minnesota Press.

Peters, Ronald M., Jr. 1978. *The Massachusetts Commonwealth of 1780: A Social Compact.* Amherst: University of Massachusetts Press.

Piven, Frances Fox, and Richard A. Cloward. 1989. *Why Americans Don't Vote*. New York: Pantheon Books.

Pugh, Tony. 2018. "Progressive Groups Investing in District Attorney Races as Path to Criminal Justice Reform." McClatchy DC Bureau, March 6. http://www.mcclatchydc.com/news/politics-government/article203622774.html.

Schoffstall, Joel. 2018. "George Soros Notches Another District Attorney Primary Victory, Soros Poured Nearly $1 Million into Bexar County Race." *Free Beacon*, March 7, http://freebeacon.com/politics/george-soros-notches-another-district-attorney-primary-victory/.

Shklar, Judith N. 1991. *American Citizenship: The Quest for Inclusion*. Cambridge, MA: Harvard University Press.

Stracqualursi, Veronica. 2018. "'I Hope Not': Comey on Whether Trump Should Be Impeached." CNN, April 15. https://www.cnn.com/2018/04/15/politics/trump-comey-abc-impeachment/index.html.

Tate, Thad W. 1965. "The Social Contract in America, 1774–1787: Revolutionary Theory as a Conservative Instrument." *William and Mary Quarterly* 22 (3): 376–91. https://www.jstor.org/stable/1920452.

United States Elections Project. 2018. "Voter Demographics." http://www.electproject.org/home/voter-turnout/demographics.

USLegal.com. 2018a. "Contracts." April. https://contracts.uslegal.com/.

———. 2018b. "Implied-in-Fact Contract Law and Legal Definition." April. https://definitions.uslegal.com/i/implied-in-fact-contract/.

Zack, Naomi. 2016. *Applicative Justice: A Pragmatic Empirical Approach to Racial Injustice.* Lanham, MD: Rowman & Littlefield.

Chapter Six

Natural Disaster in Society

Royal Caribbean Cruises takes passengers to the San Juan community of La
Perla for projects like soap making and tree planting. Some enterprising passengers have suggested and helped build a hydroponic garden.

When they visit San Juan, Celebrity Cruises ships also offer trips to La
Perla for passengers interested in volunteering in the soup kitchen or the community garden or working with children or the elderly.

Princess Cruises has announced a new series of service-focused cruises,
called Travel Deep sailings, that will participate in volunteer activities on
hurricane-impacted islands including Puerto Rico, St. Thomas and St. Maart-
en. Past trips have included building furniture on St. Thomas and removing
over a ton of trash from Guana Bay on St. Maarten. (Glusac 2018)

Contemporary disasters tend to be measured in cost for replacement, although the public does not get a line-item invoice. Kendra Pierre-Louis
(2018) reported in the *New York Times* that for 2017 the National Oceanic
and Atmospheric Administration tallied the cost of extreme weather in the
United States at $306 billion. The events included Hurricanes Harvey, Irma,
and Maria; damage to fruit crops from a freeze in the Southeast; hailstorms in
the West; and tornadoes in the Midwest. Sixteen natural disasters cost over
one billion dollars each, compared to three in 1980 (adjusted for inflation).
This exceeded the 2005 record of $215 billion due to Hurricane Katrina. The
average temperature in 2017 was 2.6 degrees Fahrenheit over the average for
the twentieth century, resulting in the third-warmest year on record (Pierre-
Louis 2018). There appears to be a trend in these events, but attributing them
to climate change has now been politicized, and the situation is complicated
by the fact that scientists cannot proclaim 100 percent certainty that the
global climate is changing. This uncertainty is built into the nature of empirical science in a way that a large proportion of the American public is unable
or unwilling to accept (Oreskes 2018).

The subject here is natural disaster, although in the twenty-first century all natural disasters are human made if we consider what happens before and after them. Also at this time, it is difficult to draw the line between natural disasters and extreme natural disasters that may be the result of climate change. Climate change and public policy regarding its causes are part of the environmental issues that will be the subject of chapter 7. In that context, it will be worth considering whether it still makes sense to discuss natural disasters in the ways they have been discussed prior to the recent scientific consensus regarding climate change and related events of unprecedented devastation and frequency (Zack 2006, 2009a, and 2009b). But in this chapter, perhaps straining a dying paradigm, natural disasters as they are traditionally considered will be discussed.

The sudden, frightening, and uncontrollable occurrence of natural disasters strikes humankind as a brute fact that we have to accept. We do have to respond to the immediate reality of hurricanes and earthquakes, but neither the causes of natural disasters nor how we respond to them are the same as their nature and effects. How we think about those causes has shifted from punishment by deities to human activities. For those directly affected, there is an element of being in the wrong place at the wrong time. But before the disaster occurs, construction in disaster-vulnerable areas and lack of preparation for difficult-to-predict, low-probability but high-impact events (such as a storm that is predicted to occur once in a hundred years) affect the impact of the disaster itself. The quality of response, by those immediately on the scene and helpers from afar, is a further aspect of rescue and recovery. There are also totally unexpected events that cannot be prepared for, such as megastorms that exceed prior categorization, earthquakes that turn out to be more devastating than seismologists could have known, or floods and tornadoes in unprecedented places.

The first part of this chapter will briefly consider government's role and accountability in natural disasters through a focus on Japan's "3/11." Comparative discussion of Hurricane Katrina and the 2010 earthquakes in Haiti and Chile follow. Hurricanes Sandy in the U.S. Northeast, Harvey in Houston, and Maria in Puerto Rico will then be considered in the context of preexisting infrastructure. The chapter ends with tentative conclusions about the roles of the social contract and the social compact in natural disasters, which lead into chapter 7.

THE ROLE OF GOVERNMENT IN DISASTER PREPARATION AND ACCOUNTABILITY

In the United States, disaster preparation outside of government remains only partially regulated by government, and the government has only partially fulfilled its own obligations. If government is the overriding disaster manager, such regulation and fulfillment requires improvement, according to social contract theory.

When government preparation has been inadequate, government accountability can follow naturally from unforeseen disasters. The reaction to Japan's 3/11 is an interesting example. On March 11, 2011, Japan experienced a triple disaster in Fukushima prefecture. A 9.0-magnitude offshore earthquake and a twenty-three-foot tsunami resulted in a series of nuclear accidents in which three out of six reactors failed at the Fukushima Daiichi Nuclear Plant. There were twenty-three thousand immediate deaths from the tsunami. Officials had to consider the possibility of evacuating Tokyo, a city of thirty-five million. The effects of nuclear contamination may be permanent. Despite emergency response efforts, the damage seemed irreversible by 2017. Six years after the disaster, not even robots could succeed in nuclear cleanup at the Fukushima Daiichi plant, and three hundred square miles around it remained uninhabitable (Pignataro 2017).

The political and civic process of demands for accountability following the disaster are instructive. There was intense public and official inquiry. Some concluded that the major utility, TEPCO (Tokyo Electric Power Company), had failed in disaster preparation in a culture that was complacent about nuclear risk; others criticized a cozy relationship between government regulation and inspection officials and TEPCO; the lack of prior emergency protocols was also emphasized (Kingston 2014).

In 2012, Japan announced that it would abandon nuclear energy by the 2030s, a reversal of its plans to have half the country served by nuclear energy by that time. Also in 2012, the Japanese government's Fukushima Nuclear Accident Independent Investigation Commission issued a 641-page report stating that the March 11, 2011, nuclear incident was a "profoundly man-made disaster." The commission had spent nine hundred hours on hearings and interviewed 1,167 people. The chairman of the U.S. Nuclear Regulatory Commission stated that no American safety standards had been violated by the Fukushima incident (Horowitz 2012), implying that the same disaster could occur in the United States. It should be noted that there was a Democratic U.S. presidential administration in 2012, indicating that disaster complacency may be as likely among U.S. Democrats as Republicans.

SOCIAL CONTRACT AND SOCIAL COMPACT DISASTERS

Contemporary natural disasters rarely have fully satisfactory government preparation and response. There is at least a short period of time in which survivors are left on their own, without necessities such as shelter, water, utilities, and basic physical security. During that time, there is a return to conditions without government and social organization, a kind of "second state of nature," but worse than the picture Locke drew, where there was organization and cooperation, and not as bad as the picture Hobbes drew, which was a war of everyone against everyone else. There is a growing body of literature to the effect that most people want to help victims in the immediate aftermath of disaster, with many volunteers and few criminal exploiters, as well as abundant generous pledges for future aid (Whittaker, McLennan, and Handmer 2015). First responders are often neighbors and others close by, and they tend to remain after professional responders leave. Informational volunteerism is also on the rise, especially via social media (Boulianne, Minaker, and Haney 2018). Earlier theorists claimed that while people are averse to conflict situations, they are drawn to emergencies and disasters. But while this may be true in developed countries, there is also evidence that in poorer countries conditions of disaster can themselves quickly lead to conflict (Nel and Righarts 2008). If there is no conflict, volunteer civilian disaster rescue and response occurs in the social compact realm.

The main difference between social contract and social compact disasters is that in the social contract scenarios government entities are willing and able to respond with rescue, assistance, and reconstruction, whereas in social compact scenarios government response is either still forthcoming or experienced as fundamentally inadequate. However, in successful social compact situations, there is social cohesion, volunteerism, resiliency, and general optimism. We should now consider recent disasters to further draw out the differences between social contract and social compact disaster situations.

HURRICANE KATRINA RECOVERY

The devastation of lives and property in New Orleans in 2005 had lasting consequences. As of 2016, the final death toll of Katrina was 1,833, with 353,000 homes lost and damages estimated at $180 billion. Over one million people were displaced in the Gulf region. In "A Preliminary Assessment of Social and Economic Impacts Associated with Hurricane Katrina," written in 2006, John Petterson, Laura Stanley, Edward Glazier, and James Philipp presented a grim portrait of long-term recovery prospects for New Orleans. For the African American poor hit hardest by the storm and forced to relocate to other parts of the country, there were inadequate resources to bring them back, rebuild their homes, or provide jobs upon their return. In 2006, reconstruction in the Gulf area was already taking the form of a boom unlikely to leave money in the area as wealthy and insured investors acquired distressed properties. Gentrification and "casinofication" had already expanded by the summer of 2006, and workers from Central America were employed in newly created jobs. Not enough was planned for levy fortification or new building specifications to protect against another Katrina, much less a more powerful storm (Petterson et al. 2006).

In April 2010, Amnesty International reported that the U.S. government had violated human rights to permanently alter the demographics of New Orleans. Public housing complexes were demolished, affordable replacement housing was not built, and many schools and hospitals had not been repaired or reopened. The United Nations Guiding Principles on Internal Displacement, which the U.S. endorsed, requires that government fulfill a duty to help internally displaced people return voluntarily to their former homes and receive compensation for lost property (Amnesty International 2010). In this regard, the U.S. federal government, the State of Louisiana, and the City of New Orleans breached the social contract, but here according to the standards of international law rather than failures in internal disaster preparation according to U.S. law.

During Katrina, it is salient that almost all of the evacuees and residents of the Lower Ninth Ward were African American (Statistic Brain 2016). Aside from a history of structural inadequacy associated with poor black neighborhoods throughout the United States and traditions of residential racial segregation, at the time of the storm natural disaster intersected with race as it was already in place. There has been considerable speculation that rescue would have been faster and replacement of infrastructure more comprehensive had a middle-class white neighborhood been hit hardest, but descriptions of prior institutional racism and subtle bias have grounded the preferred explanations of scholars (Henkel, Dovidio, and Gaertner 2006; Stivers 2007). (The difference in analysis is a focus on antecedent structural racism instead of a focus on racist response.) Nevertheless, the perception of racism among African Americans in New Orleans regarding the Katrina response may not have been given its due in terms of history and existential experience (Adams, O'Brien, and Nelson 2006). Five years later, adults who survived Katrina had not fully recovered psychologically. Half met criteria for posttraumatic stress disorder, and most suffered from depression and anxiety. Ten years after Katrina, the mayor of New Orleans reminded residents that Katrina was not an "act of God" but an "infrastructure disaster" from which healing was not complete (LaJoie, Sprang, and McKinney 2010; White 2015). Katrina is mentioned as a comparator and reference point for later storms, but recovery from the 2005 storm is not a live news item in 2018. In 2015, the *Atlantic* published haunting photographs of shipping containers in marshes, abandoned houses within overgrown vegetation, and ruins of foundations (Taylor 2015).

Even though the U.S. Coast Guard rescued 33,500 Katrina victims (Schleifstein 2015), most observers have agreed that the City of New Orleans and the Army Corps of Engineers should and could have better prepared for the storm. In a deep sense that is difficult to document or make a convincing popular case about, there was a slow social contract failure in inadequate preparation for the Category 1 storm, which was all that Katrina turned out to be. At the same time, those affected had neither the resources nor the time to organize in a social compact framework. One important exception was a community of Vietnamese immigrants who both survived the storm and returned to rebuild later (Assefa 2015). Their resilience was based on shared histories of relocations, multigenerational community ties, and cultural knowledge of endurance through floods. However, the African Americans who were forced to relocate and thereby became internal American refugees did not have an opportunity or the immediate resources for a successful return and reconstruction. Their communities were broken up as they were dispersed throughout the United States, perhaps contributing to another shameful chapter in the history of American antiblack racism, which is yet to be written down. Comparison of Katrina with the 2010 earthquakes in Haiti and Chile may yield further insight concerning disaster resilience.

THE 2010 EARTHQUAKE IN HAITI

The 2010 earthquake in Haiti and its aftermath were unambiguously horrendous, as print details were at the time illuminated by videos (BBC News 2011). On January 12, 2010, an earthquake measuring 7 on the moment magnitude scale (which has replaced the Richter scale as a more accurate measure), with an epicenter 6.2 miles below the surface, struck ten miles southwest of Port-au-Prince. By January 24, there were fifty-two aftershocks greater than 4.5. The Haitian population was at that time still recovering from a 2008 earthquake that had left one million homeless. The 2010 earthquake was finally estimated to have killed 250,000 and left another one million homeless.

Billions of dollars in aid was committed to Haiti from almost every country and humanitarian entity in the world, totaling over $13 billion committed for 2010–2020. But that aid did not translate into immediate relief because of the chaos within Haiti following the quake. Much of Haiti's already inadequate infrastructure had been destroyed, including hospitals, schools, roads, and electronic communications equipment. Destruction to an air traffic control tower and a major port, as well as obstacles from rubble on the ground, further hindered relief efforts. There were shortages of food and water, followed by rioting and looting. Many of the one million who had lost their homes were afraid to go back inside buildings, and flimsy tents were the only available shelter for many. Bodies were disposed of in mass graves holding thousands or tens of thousands. The neighboring Dominican Republic was the first source of outside medical aid, as well as a destination for refugees, although time limits had to be placed on their stay after their numbers and needs became overwhelming. There was an international effort to relocate many orphans, although it was interrupted by objections that some of the orphans had living family members.

By July 2010, six months later, only 2 percent of the $1.1 billion collected for relief had been distributed within Haiti. Almost four billion dollars was pledged for aid to build and supply field hospitals and maintain relief workers. CBS reported that by May 2010 international aid amounted to $37,000 for each displaced family. However, it was also at that time estimated that only 2 percent of earthquake rubble had been cleared, so that Port-au-Prince remained largely impassable. No transitional housing had been built, and the tent camps, estimated to hold 1.6 million, often lacked electricity, water, sewage disposal, and security for individuals, especially women. It was predicted that should there occur another earthquake, a cyclone, or even heavy rain, thousands more would die (Wikipedia 2018a).

By 2017, Haitian recovery from the 2010 earthquake was still unaccomplished. According to the United Nations, 2.5 million were still in need of "humanitarian aid," many remained traumatized, cholera was a threat, and fifty-five thousand resided in tent camps. More than half of the population remained in poverty, and the Dominican Republic was speeding up expulsions of Haitian refugees. In the seven years after the 2010 quake, Haiti was hit by Hurricane Sandy in 2012, followed by a three-year drought. In October 2016, Hurricane Matthew resulted in one thousand deaths and collapsed buildings and downed trees that thwarted rescue efforts. Diarrhea and cholera recurred at that time (Cook 2017).

THE 2010 EARTHQUAKE IN CHILE

The 2010 earthquake in Chile was a more extreme seismological event than the one in Haiti. On February 27, a quake off the coast of the Maule Region registered 8.8 on the moment magnitude scale and was felt throughout the country and by over 80 percent of its population. Seismologists estimated that 1.26 microseconds were shortened from that day's length and that the Earth's figure axis was moved by eight centimeters. Concepción, Chile's second largest city, was most affected, although seiches from the quake occurred almost five thousand miles away in Lake Pontchartrain, near New Orleans; by March 6, there had been 130 aftershocks. The earthquake was followed by a tsunami on February 28 and two more later, which were preceded by coastal warnings throughout the world. Air travel was interrupted from Santiago, and there were food shortages and rioting over several weeks. Deaths were initially estimated at about eight hundred, later revised to under five hundred, with five hundred thousand buildings destroyed. International aid equaled $220,000 in the first two days (compared to $3.9 billion for Haiti).

Clearly, the devastation in Chile could not result in immediate recovery. But as of August, 2010, Chile's unemployment rate had dropped to under 9 percent and its currency was said to be holding its own against the dollar. Life was difficult throughout the country, and the cost of the damage was estimated to be thirty to sixty billion dollars (Long 2011; Wikipedia 2018b). Chile was much harder hit than Haiti but sustained far less loss of life and social and economic disruption. Soon after the quake, the government in partnership with Elemental, a social housing firm, created a "sustainable reconstruction plan," known by its Spanish acronym PRES. Parts of Concepción were rebuilt with sustainable housing, and an expropriated swath of vulnerable land was converted into a forest floor (Long 2015).

KEY DIFFERENCES BETWEEN HAITI AND CHILE

The difference between Chile and Haiti in responding to and recovering from their 2010 earthquakes is a stark example of the ways preexisting poverty and disadvantage increase disaster vulnerability (perhaps exponentially, given the difference in intensity of almost one hundred times for the Chilean earthquake). Chile had a well-developed economy with modern infrastructure when its quake hit, whereas there were not even building codes in Haiti. That is, Haiti was physically more vulnerable to the violence of disaster than Chile. Chile's president made a postquake address within two hours, while it took Haiti's president 168 hours. That is, the Haitian government was either less willing to respond to a disaster or less able.

Other disaster-resilient comparisons between Haiti and Chile concern material well-being. In 2010, life expectancy in Chile was seventy-seven compared to sixty-one in Haiti. In Chile's population of sixteen million, with an average annual income of $14,600, 18 percent lived below the poverty line. In Haiti, the average annual income was $1,300, and 80 percent of the population lived below the poverty line. Also, in 2012, Chile ranked lowest on the *Christian Science Monitor*'s corruption scale for Latin America, whereas Haiti ranked highest (most corrupt) (Villagran 2012).

The comparison between Haiti and Chile is not difficult to draw in terms of disaster recovery. Corruption within leadership suggests that no matter how much aid is available financially, it will not be spent in ways that benefit the people who need it most. Furthermore, if a system is corrupt, those already benefiting or hoping to benefit have financial incentive to welcome natural disaster because money flows after disaster and they can siphon some of it off. The difference between inadequate and adequate infrastructure and predisaster resources is a further factor that requires analysis. Why should prior infrastructure facilitate disaster recovery and its absence work to obstruct it? If there is less infrastructure beforehand, why isn't it easier and cheaper to rebuild from scratch than to replace or repair complicated and expensive infrastructure? Perhaps a comparison among the recent U.S. disasters of Hurricane Sandy in the U.S. Northeast, Hurricane Harvey in Houston, and Hurricane Maria in Puerto Rico will help answer that question.

HURRICANE SANDY

Here is the National Hurricane Center's description of Hurricane Sandy, which occurred on October 22–29, 2012:

> Sandy was a classic late-season hurricane in the southwestern Caribbean Sea. . . . Sandy underwent a complex evolution and grew considerably in size while over the Bahamas, and continued to grow despite weakening into a tropical storm north of those islands. The system restrengthened into a hurricane while it moved northeastward, parallel to the coast of the southeastern United States, and reached a secondary peak intensity of 85 kt [knots] while it turned northwestward toward the mid-Atlantic states. Sandy weakened somewhat and then made landfall as a post-tropical cyclone near Brigantine, New Jersey with 70 kt maximum sustained winds. Because of its tremendous size, however, Sandy drove a catastrophic storm surge into the New Jersey and New York coastlines. Preliminary U.S. damage estimates are near $50 billion, making Sandy the second-costliest cyclone to hit the United States since 1900. There were at least 147 direct deaths recorded across the Atlantic basin due to Sandy, with 72 of these fatalities occurring in the mid-Atlantic and northeastern United States. This is the greatest number of U.S. direct fatalities related to a tropical cyclone outside of the southern states since Hurricane Agnes in 1972. (Blake et al. 2013)

Damage from Sandy was estimated at $71.5 billion. Three hundred homes were destroyed and 1,400 were elevated, requiring complex construction. Although technically a tropical storm when it hit, Sandy obliterated areas of the Jersey shore and caused a storm surge in New York Harbor, with fourteen-foot water levels flooding subway stations and the foundations of the 9/11 memorial, which was under construction at the time. On Staten Island, 495 out of 659 eligible households accepted buyouts. There were power outages in the financial center. Five years later, survivors claimed to still be "haunted." Although preparations were made to protect against flooding in the same places, as well as against power outages, there was widespread skepticism about long-term safety in future storms (Milman 2017; Amadeo 2018).

HURRICANE HARVEY

According to the U.S. National Weather Service, Hurricane Harvey was the first hurricane to hit the Texas coast since 2008, when Hurricane Ike came through the Houston area, and it was the first major (Category 3 or higher) hurricane to hit Texas since Bret in 1999. Here is the official description of Hurricane Harvey:

> Hurricane Harvey started as a tropical wave off the African coast on Sunday, August 13th and tracked westward across the Atlantic and on August 17th become a tropical storm which moved into the Caribbean Sea where Harvey became disorganized. Harvey was then downgraded to a tropical wave which entered the Gulf of Mexico on the 22nd. On the morning of the 23rd, Harvey was upgraded again to tropical depression as the Bay of Campeche and the Western Gulf of Mexico had very warm waters. Over the next 48 hours Harvey would undergo a period of rapid intensification from a tropical depression to a category 4 hurricane. Harvey made landfall along the Texas coast near Port Aransas around 10:00 p.m. on August 25th as a cat 4 and brought devastating impacts. As Harvey moved inland, it's forward motion slowed to near 5mph after landfall and then meandered just north of Victoria, TX by the 26th. Rain bands on the eastern side of the circulation of Harvey moved into southeast Texas on the morning of the 25th and continued through much of the night and into the 26th. A strong rainband developed over Fort Bend and Brazoria Counties during the evening hours of the 26th and spread into Harris County and slowed while training from south to north. This resulted in a rapid development of flash flooding between 10:00 p.m. and 1:00 a.m. as tremendous rainfall rates occurred across much of Harris County. The morning of the 27th saw additional rain bands continue to develop and production of additional excessive rainfall amounts. As the center of Harvey slowly moved east-southeast and back offshore heavy rainfall continued to spread through much of the 29th and the 30th exacerbating the ongoing widespread and devastating flooding. All of this rainfall caused catastrophic drainage issues and made rivers rise greatly. Only around 10 percent of the river forecast points in southeast Texas remained below flood stage due to the event, and approximately 46 percent of the river forecast points reached new record levels. Harvey maintained tropical storm intensity the entire time while inland over the Texas coastal bend and southeast Texas. (National Weather Service 2017a)

The city of Houston, with a population close to seven million, is particularly vulnerable to floods. Urban sprawl has favored road construction over preservation of marshlands and prairies that would otherwise absorb floodwaters and canals that would redirect them (Berke 2017). During Harvey, roads, houses, and municipal buildings were unusable for a while. The initial death toll was seventy, later raised to eighty-eight (NOLA 2017; Afiune 2017). Compared to over 1,800 deaths from Katrina, these figures occasioned self-congratulation about preparation and immediate response—

Houston's mayor had told people the storm was coming and that they should not retreat to their attics unless they took an ax with them. About twenty-four thousand residents were initially displaced, but most or all found housing within months. Harvey was estimated to cost $121 billion, although the federal government initially provided only five billion dollars (Harmon 2018).

However, the economic analysis was rosy from the beginning. On August 28, before the storm was quite over, the *New York Times* reported, "Ellen Zentner, chief United States economist at Morgan Stanley, said that although Hurricane Harvey's impact on national gross domestic product in the third quarter might be fairly neutral, 'the lagged effects of rebuilding homes and replacing motor vehicles can last longer, providing a lift to gross domestic product in the fourth quarter and beyond'" (Dougherty and Schwartz 2017). This almost celebratory response to Harvey not only overlooked the finality of those lives that were lost, but it absorbed the storm into ongoing business profitability in an already booming economy. On this model of disaster response, natural disaster is no more than opportunity for further growth, neither extensively invoking the social contract nor calling for social compact arrangements beyond very immediate civilian response. Houston may have to deal with its infrastructure's vulnerability to flooding at some later date because by the time Harvey hit it was not in the category of a hurricane but a tropical storm. However, the overall civic triumph involving Harvey does not indicate great enthusiasm for disaster preparation for a real hurricane of any category.

HURRICANE MARIA

Hurricane Maria hit Puerto Rico on September 20, 2017, as part of an extended storm system. Here is the National Weather Service's description:

> Maria formed from an African easterly wave that moved across the tropical Atlantic Ocean during the week of September 10th to September 17th, 2017. It was not until 200 PM AST (1800 UTC) on September 16th, that its convective organization improved that the NHC classified the system as a tropical depression about 700 miles east-southeast of the Lesser Antilles. At the 500 PM AST (2100 UTC) advisory, just three hours later, the depression was upgraded to Tropical Storm Maria with maximum sustained winds of 50 mph. Thereafter, Maria gradually intensified and became the 8th hurricane of the 2017 Atlantic hurricane season, with 75 mph maximum sustained winds at 500 PM AST (2100 UTC) on September 17th.
>
> Within the next 24 to 30 hours and within an 18 hour period, Maria underwent rapid intensification, strengthening from a category 1 to an extremely dangerous category 5 hurricane. At the time, environmental conditions were favorable for intensification to occur due to sea surface temperatures greater than 28 degrees Celsius, light vertical wind shear, and moist air. Ma-

ria's first landfall was in Dominica, part of the Windward Islands, as a category 5 hurricane at around 915 PM AST on the 18th (0115 UTC on the 19th). Maria maintained Category 5 strength as it continued its path towards the U.S. Virgin Islands and Puerto Rico. Rain bands first approached Saint Croix, as well as portions of Saint Thomas and Saint John, during the morning hours on the 19th. Throughout the afternoon and early evening hours, rain bands generating tropical storm conditions reached Vieques, Culebra, and Puerto Rico.

As the center of Maria approached the US Virgin Islands and Puerto Rico, the frequency of the rain bands as well as the strength or intensity of the winds increased. Between 12 AM and 1 AM AST (0400-0500 UTC) on September 20th, hurricane force winds were first reported in St. Croix as Maria's eyewall moved over that island. Based on observations from the Hurricane Hunters, the intensity of Maria was lowered from Category 5 hurricane with 175 MPH just southeast of St. Croix, to Category 4 hurricane with 155 MPH south of Vieques. Around 5 AM AST (0900 UTC), hurricane force winds were reported in Vieques and the eastern half of mainland Puerto Rico. At approximately 615 AM AST (1015 UTC), Maria made landfall in Yabucoa, Puerto Rico as a strong category 4 hurricane with maximum sustained winds of 155 mph. As the center of the storm moved west-northwestward over southeastern PR into the interior and northwestern PR, widespread hurricane force winds spread all over mainland PR along with extremely heavy rainfall that produced major to catastrophic flooding and flash flooding, especially across the northern half of Puerto Rico. Maria's center moved over the coastal waters off northwestern Puerto Rico early that afternoon. Even though hurricane force winds started to diminish once the system moved offshore, tropical storm force winds continued well into the evening and overnight hours across mainland Puerto Rico. (National Weather Service 2017b)

Hurricane Maria was a Category 4 storm when it hit Puerto Rico, affecting its 3.5 million residents. Damages were officially estimated at ninety billion dollars. The death toll was officially tallied at sixty-four, but more comprehensive analyses placed it over one thousand. Cell phone towers were felled, and the whole island lost power. A weakened dam led to the evacuation of seventy thousand people, and fifteen thousand needed government shelters. (Amadeo 2018). With the 2018 hurricane season just ahead, in April 2018 Puerto Rico is said to still be "haunted" by Hurricane Maria. Power outages have continued, and the two Federal Aviation Administration radars are not yet functional again, so that Puerto Rico is flying "weather blind," except for satellite information (Shepherd 2018).

TENTATIVE CONCLUSIONS

For all of the storms discussed here, and others, those already sick or disabled, as well as the elderly, are most likely to perish (O'Brien 2017). For those with credit and cash, self-evacuation may be a great inconvenience, but it saves their lives. The poor and disabled, however, do not share such mobility. When the poor and elderly are not middle-class white people, it often looks as though how they fare in natural disasters is a new form of opportunistic racial discrimination. The general problem is that natural disasters are increasingly more intense and by their nature unpredictable. And along with that, all who directly experience them are probably traumatized to some extent.

In reflecting upon the seven disasters considered in this chapter, there is no simple answer to the question of why preexisting infrastructure or the lack thereof determines outcomes. Because Hurricane Katrina was devastating out of proportion to its intensity and there was woefully inadequate flood preparation in New Orleans at the time, a model of disaster response and preparation that prioritizes infrastructure has become the dominant tool for analysis. The difference between Haiti and Chile in recovery from their 2010 earthquakes seems to support that priority. But infrastructure is connected to functionality. It is probably a good bet that locales with highly functional transportation systems, hospitals, and power systems will have the tools and personnel to respond well to disaster. Still, that failed to happen in the Tokyo earthquake and tsunami with its subsequent nuclear meltdown—there was probably good preexisting infrastructure, but it was not maintained through adequate regulation.

Despite urban expansion without adequate flood relief structures, Houston did all right through Harvey because it was a booming area with excellent infrastructure and response lessons learned from Katrina. But although Puerto Rico's recovery has been related to poor prior infrastructure, as well as inadequate response from Washington, it is not comparable to Houston. A Category 4 hurricane hit Puerto Rico, but Houston sustained a tropical storm. Hurricane Sandy was also a tropical storm by the time it hit, and the damage there was greater than in Houston, not least in lives lost. The coastal areas of Sandy's impact were more vulnerable to destruction than Houston's roadways.

Returning to the issue of at this time only partial government regulation of disaster preparation in society and partial fulfillment of government's own obligations, there are specific questions to consider: Should property owners be permitted to repeatedly insure dwellings on coastlines liable to flood, and repeatedly collect money for futile rebuilding? Should construction in general be permitted in areas that have previously been hit by disasters and have a known likelihood of the same events recurring? Should households and communities that cannot afford to adequately prepare for disaster receive government subsidies for preparation? Should elderly and disabled people who have disproportionately numbered among disaster victims be provided with special assistance with preparation and evacuation plans? What penalties ought to be incurred for failure of adequate preparation, in both society and government?

In addition to such specific questions, there is a general question of how the government's role in the regulation of disaster preparation can be improved, a difficult question that also applies to disasters affecting natural environments. The question is difficult because at this time any increase in government regulation is an extreme partisan issue. If health care becomes turbocharged, as it did during the 2016 election, then disaster preparations affecting health in the future could be even more contentious.

The prevailing mode of response to disasters has evolved historically within a range of just deserts, humanitarian sympathy and aid, and the exploitation of new opportunities for profit that are not unlike war profiteering. Indeed, in *The Shock Doctrine: The Rise of Disaster Capitalism*, Naomi Klein identifies the same companies who profited from war in Iraq as profiting from disaster contract work in New Orleans after Hurricane Katrina (2007, 389, 517–29, 534). Disaster exploitation for profit is not the worst response to disaster, although moralists may abhor it. The worst response to disaster occurs where there is insufficient infrastructure for capitalistic exploitation to be possible and people are left in their own immiseration, without apparent wherewithal to help themselves and little incentive for others to intervene, as in Haiti.

As described in the chapter epigraph, disaster tourism also has profit incentives, but where recovery is ongoing it is a form of soft and indirect profit. The opportunities for vacationers to help and for cruise ship companies to profit should not be disparaged, because they are enterprising on both sides and likely to benefit those who are still recovering from recent disasters. As with much else that happens after disasters without comprehensive and timely government response, volunteering occurs in the realm of the social compact, within a kind of free zone of cultural and economic exchange that does not require disaster-related government regulation. But we should not be lulled into thinking that this is all right in situations where government is obligated to do something in ways that are still recognizable under the social contract. There is good reason to resist the social compact realm of disaster and insist on the social contract response, when disaster occurs in parts of the United States and other countries where, before disaster, in normal times, government already performs beneficial functions for those governed. In those situations, government should be held accountable for inadequate disaster preparation and response, because government has material, organizational, and managerial (administrative) resources that are still unrivaled by other institutions in society.

BEYOND NATURAL DISASTERS IN SOCIETY

All of the natural disasters described in this chapter were managed on a social contract model. Government entities were the main responders and performed as best they could with available resources and know-how. There may be future disasters that exceed effective government response and that will be a complete breakdown of the social contract for disaster. If that happens generally, we will be in the realm of the social compact regarding natural disaster in society. Insofar as natural disasters are increasingly the effects of what we humans view as disasters in nature, there is a high probability of that coming to pass. Chapter 7 will focus on disasters in nature and that shared causality.

REFERENCES

Adams, G., L. T. O'Brien, and J. C. Nelson. 2006. "Perceptions of Racism in Hurricane Katrina: A Liberation Psychology Analysis." *Analyses of Social Issues and Public Policy* 6:215–35. DOI:10.1111/j.1530-2415.2006.00112.x.

Afiune, Giulia. 2017. "State Says Harvey's Death Toll Has Reached 88." *Texas Tribune*, October 13. https://www.texastribune.org/2017/10/13/harveys-death-toll-reaches-93-peo ple/.

Amadeo, Kimberly. 2018. "How Hurricanes Damage the Economy." *Balance*, March 20. https://www.thebalance.com/hurricane-damage-economic-costs-4150369.

Amnesty International. 2010. "Un-Natural Disaster: Human Rights in the Gulf Coast." https:// www.amnestyusa.org/files/pdfs/unnaturaldisaster.pdf.

Assefa, Haimy. 2015. "How Louisiana's Vietnamese Community Started Over—Twice." CNN.com, August 8. https://www.cnn.com/2015/08/19/us/vietnamese-community-louisi ana-katrina-anniversary/index.html.

BBC News. 2011. "Haiti Earthquake." http://news.bbc.co.uk/2/hi/in_depth/americas/2010/ haiti_earthquake/default.stm.

Berke, Philip R. 2017. "Why Is Houston So Vulnerable to Devastating Floods?" BBC News, August 31. http://www.bbc.com/news/world-us-canada-41107049.

Blake, Eric S., Todd B. Kimberlain, Robert J., Berg, John P. Cangialosi, and John L. Beven II. 2013. "Tropical Cyclone Report: Hurricane Sandy." National Hurricane Center, February 12. https://www.nhc.noaa.gov/data/tcr/AL182012_Sandy.pdf.

Boulianne, Shelley, Joanne Minaker, and Timothy J. Haney. 2018. "Does Compassion Go Viral? Social Media, Caring, and the Fort McMurray Wildfire." *Information, Communication & Society* 21 (5): 697–711. DOI:10.1080/1369118X.2018.1428651.

Cook, Jesslyn. 2017. "7 Years after Haiti's Earthquake, Millions Still Need Aid: The Resilience of the Haitian People Has Endured through Years of Natural Disasters." *HuffPost*, January 13. https://www.huffingtonpost.com/entry/haiti-earthquake-anniversary_us_5875108de4 b02b5f858b3f9c.

Dougherty, Conor, and Nelson D. Schwartz. 2017. "Hurricane to Cost Tens of Billions, but a Quick Recovery Is Expected." *New York Times*, August 28. https://www.nytimes.com/2017/ 08/28/business/economy/texas-hurricane-harvey-economic-impact.html.

Glusac, Elaine. 2018. "How Travelers Can Help Hurricane-Damaged Islands." *New York Times*, April 3. https://www.nytimes.com/2018/04/03/travel/volunteer-vacations-caribbean. html.

Harmon, Dave. 2018. "Four Months after Hurricane Harvey, Four Major Questions about Recovery for 2018." *Texas Tribune*, January 4. https://www.texastribune.org/2018/01/04/ four-months-after-hurricane-harvey-four-major-questions-about-recovery/.

Henkel, K. E., J. F. Dovidio, and S. L. Gaertner. 2006. "Institutional Discrimination, Individual Racism, and Hurricane Katrina." *Analyses of Social Issues and Public Policy* 6:99–124. DOI:10.1111/j.1530-2415.2006.00106.x.

Horowitz, Andy. 2012. "Official Fukushima Report Blames Japanese Culture, Not Nuclear Power." *Atlantic*, July 11. https://www.theatlantic.com/international/archive/2012/07/official-fukushima-report-blames-japanese-culture-not-nuclear-power/259665/.

Kingston, Jeff. 2014. "Mismanaging Risk and the Fukushima Nuclear Crisis." In *Human Security and Japan's Triple Disaster: Responding to the 2011 Earthquake, Tsunami, and Fukushima Nuclear Crisis*, ed. Paul Bacon and Christopher Hobson, 39–48. London: Routledge.

Klein, Naomi. 2007. *The Shock Doctrine: The Rise of Disaster Capitalism*. New York: Henry Holt.

LaJoie, A. S., G. Sprang, and W. P. McKinney. 2010. "Long-Term Effects of Hurricane Katrina on the Psychological Well-Being of Evacuees." *Disasters* 34:1031–44. DOI:10.1111/j.1467-7717.2010.01181.x.

Long, Gideon. 2011. "Chile Quake Recovery: Back to Normal or Long Way to Go?" BBC News, February 27. http://www.bbc.com/news/world-latin-america-12534552.

———. 2015. "The Rebuilding of Chile's Constitución: How a 'Dead City' Was Brought Back to Life." *Guardian*, February 23. https://www.theguardian.com/cities/2015/feb/23/rebuilding-chile-constitucion-earthquake-tsunami.

Milman, Oliver. 2017. "Hurricane Sandy, Five Years Later: 'No One Was Ready for What Happened After." *Guardian*, October 27. https://www.theguardian.com/us-news/2017/oct/27/hurricane-sandy-five-years-later-climate-change.

National Weather Service. 2017a. "Hurricane Harvey and Its Impacts on Southeast Texas from August 25th to 29th, 2017." https://www.weather.gov/hgx/hurricaneharvey.

———. 2017b. "Major Hurricane Maria—September 20, 2017." https://www.weather.gov/sju/maria2017.

Nel, Philip, and Marjolein Righarts. 2008. "Natural Disasters and the Risk of Violent Civil Conflict." *International Studies Quarterly* 52 (1): 159–85. http://dx.doi.org/10.1111/j.1468-2478.2007.00495.x.

NOLA. 2017. "Relatively Low Harvey Death Toll Is 'Astounding' to Experts." September 6. http://www.nola.com/hurricane/index.ssf/2017/09/harvey_death_toll_relatively_l.html.

O'Brien, Kelley. 2017. "What Happens to the Sick, Disabled and Elderly during Hurricanes." *Bustle*, September 11. https://www.bustle.com/p/what-happens-to-the-sick-disabled-elderly-during-hurricanes-2312012.

Oreskes, Naomi. 2018. "The Scientific Consensus on Climate Change: How Do We Know We're Not Wrong?" In *Climate Modelling*, ed E. Lloyd and E. Winsberg, 31–64. London: Palgrave Macmillan.

Petterson, John S., Laura D. Stanley, Edward Glazier, and James Philipp. 2006. "A Preliminary Assessment of Social and Economic Impacts Associated with Hurricane Katrina." *American Anthropologist* 108 (4): 643–70.

Pierre-Louis, Kendra. 2018. "These Billion-Dollar Natural Disasters Set a U.S. Record in 2017." *New York Times*, January 8. https://www.nytimes.com/2018/01/08/climate/2017-weather-disasters.html.

Pignataro, Juliana Rose. 2017. "What Is Fukushima? Everything to Know about Nuclear Disaster at Daiichi Power Plant." *International Business Times*, February 13. http://www.ibtimes.com/what-fukushima-everything-know-about-nuclear-disaster-daiichi-power-plant-2491158.

Schleifstein, Mark. 2015. "Coast Guard Remembers Their Hurricane Katrina Rescue Efforts." NOLA.com, August 29. http://www.nola.com/katrina/index.ssf/2015/08/coast_guard_remembers_their_hu.html.

Shepherd, Marshall. 2018. "The 2018 Hurricane Season Looms but Hurricane Maria Still Haunts Puerto Rico." *Forbes*, April 20. https://www.forbes.com/sites/marshallshepherd/2018/04/20/the-2018-hurricane-season-looms-but-hurricane-maria-still-haunts-puerto-rico/#28cd9dcc33a4.

Statistic Brain. 2016. "Hurricane Katrina Disaster Statistics." September 6. https://www.statisticbrain.com/hurricane-katrina-disaster-statistics/.

Stivers, C. 2007. "'So Poor and So Black': Hurricane Katrina, Public Administration, and the Issue of Race." *Public Administration Review* 67:48–56. DOI:10.1111/j.1540-6210.2007.00812.x.

Taylor, Alan. 2015. "New Orleans, 10 Years After Katrina." *Atlantic*, August 8. https://www.theatlantic.com/photo/2015/08/new-orleans-10-years-after-katrina/402277/.

Villagran, Lauren. 2012. "Latin America: Region One of Worst for Corruption." *Christian Science Monitor*, December 5. https://www.csmonitor.com/World/Americas/Latin-America-Monitor/2012/1205/Latin-America-Region-one-of-worst-for-corruption.

White, Gillian B. 2015. "10 Years after Katrina, New Orleans Is Far from Healed." *Atlantic*, August 24. https://www.theatlantic.com/business/archive/2015/08/10-years-after-katrina-new-orleans-is-far-from-healed/402169/.

Whittaker, Joshua, Blythe McLennan, and John Handmer. 2015. "A Review of Informal Volunteerism in Emergencies and Disasters: Definition, Opportunities and Challenges." *International Journal of Disaster Risk Reduction* 13:358–68. https://doi.org/10.1016/j.ijdrr.2015.07.010.

Wikipedia. 2018a. "2010 Haiti Earthquake." April 12. https://en.wikipedia.org/wiki/2010_Haiti_earthquake.

———. 2018b. "2010 Chile Earthquake." April 5. https://en.wikipedia.org/wiki/2010_Chile_earthquake.

Zack, Naomi. 2006. "Philosophy and Disaster." *Homeland Security Affairs Journal* 2, Article 5, April. https://www.hsaj.org/articles/176.

———. 2009a. *Ethics for Disaster*. Lanham, MD: Rowman & Littlefield.

———. 2009b. "Ethics of Disaster Planning." In "Ethics of Crisis," ed. Per Sandin, special issue, *Philosophy of Management* 8 (2): 53–64.

Chapter Seven

Environmental Disaster

Today, our Nation commemorates Earth Day, a celebration of the blessings given to us by our Creator. Among them, we cherish our magnificent land and waterways, abundant natural resources, and unique wildlife. As a Nation, it is our duty to recognize the importance of these life-sustaining gifts, and it is our responsibility to protect them for our own benefit and that of generations to come.

A healthy environment and a strong economy go hand in hand. We know that it is impossible for humans to flourish without clean air, land, and water. We also know that a strong, market-driven economy is essential to protecting these resources. For this reason, my Administration is dedicated to removing unnecessary and harmful regulations that restrain economic growth and make it more difficult for local communities to prosper and to choose the best solutions for their environment. Already, we are making great economic progress in concert with—not in opposition to—protecting our environment.

Americans embrace the idea of enjoying nature in a responsible fashion, while preserving the blessings of the land for future generations. My Administration is committed to furthering this rich legacy of conservation.

This Earth Day, I hope all Americans will give thanks for the environment we share, protect, and call home. (Presidential Message on Earth Day; White House 2018)

There's a lot of different components that all lead up to one, and it is a pipeline that is threatening the lives of people, lives of my tribe, as well as millions down the river. It threatens the ancestral sites that are significant to our tribe. And we never had an opportunity to express our concerns. This is a corporation that is coming forward and just bulldozing through without any concern for tribes. And the things that have happened to tribal nations across this nation have been unjust and unfair, and this has come to a point where we can no longer pay the costs for this nation's well-being. We pay for economic development, we pay for national security, and we pay for energy independence. It is at our expense that this nation reaps those benefits. And all too often we share similar concerns, similar wrongdoings to us, so we are uniting, and we're standing up, and we're saying, "No more." (Archambault 2016)

A sperm whale that washed up on a beach in Spain had 64 pounds of plastic and waste in its stomach. (Diaz 2018)

There is a difference in impact between natural disasters that occur within society and human-made disasters that occur within nature, such as oil spills. But we need to keep in mind that natural disasters affecting human society may share causes with disasters occurring in nature and also have effects on natural habitats. We can trace these connections in a recent storm. Hurricane Irma occurred during the 2017 North Atlantic hurricane season (June 1–November 30). It was a Category 5 hurricane that hit Barbuda, the U.S. Florida Keys, the British Virgin Islands, Puerto Rico, the Dominican Republic, and Haiti after September 5. Irma then hit the U.S. mainland as a Category 3. Before reaching its disaster strength, Hurricane Irma had developed from a tropical wave off the coast of West Africa on August 30, 2017. As the strongest hurricane the National Hurricane Center had ever recorded in the Atlantic outside of the Caribbean Sea and Gulf of Mexico, Irma moved with wind speeds greater than 157 miles per hour. As the fifth-costliest hurricane to hit the mainland United States, Irma caused an estimated fifty billion dollars in damage, so the focus within the United States was on that cost rather than its meteorological history or wider environmental impact (World Vision 2017). In Miami, Irma eroded a large swath of the shoreline that had recently been renourished at a cost of over eleven million dollars in order to absorb such storm surges (Flechas 2017). In the Florida Keys after Hurricane Irma, there was a call for volunteers to clean debris from Deer Refuge, a U.S. Fish and Wildlife Refuge that provides vital habitat for endangered Key deer (Glusac 2018).

Our focus here is on environmental disasters that are related to natural disasters in society. Given that natural disasters within society may have the same causes or be part of the same larger weather events that primarily affect the nonhuman environment, it may be necessary at some point to merge discussion of natural disaster in society with disasters affecting nature. However, as people imagine a border between urban/suburban areas and nature and do not fully value the life and well-being of animals and plants, or even of the planet as a whole, the "civilization–nature" bifurcation is likely to continue for some time.

Preparation and prevention seem to be deficient for both natural disasters and disasters in nature that are directly or indirectly human made. Government reaction remains sluggish and perhaps likely to come to a standstill insofar as party politics divides ideas on what is happening and what should be done. Thus, in the first epigraph, President Trump's official announcement for Earth Day 2018 abdicates the role of the federal government in preserving the environment by relegating protection to local communities. However, the environment itself is not divided into local communities, and local communities may yield to corporate pressures at the expense of residents' rights, especially those of indigenous people. Dave Archambault II, chair of the Standing Rock Sioux Tribe, has expressed protest against such rights violations, as indicated by the second epigraph. In addition, the destruction and despoliation of the natural world proceeds with the pace of consumer society, as described in the third epigraph about a sperm whale with sixty-four pounds of plastic and waste in its stomach. The waste products of consumer society also have deliberate global distribution, such as electronic waste that flows from rich to poor societies, without proper recycling or safety measures (Perkins et al. 2014).

The complexities of environmental issues are obviously vast at this time, and one chapter by a philosopher cannot even begin to do them justice. What we can do here is consider the role of government in environmental preservation and protection in the United States, attempt to understand the dominant traditional perspective on the natural environment that has developed in the modern western period, and, keeping examples in mind, offer a sketch of a current holistic view of weather and climate.

GOVERNMENT, DEMOCRACY, AND MONEY CONCERNING NATURAL ENVIRONMENTS

There are two main ways human beings now affect the natural environment. The first is the human contribution to climate change, about which it is disputed that the global climate is changing and that human beings are causing it. Second, there are human contributions to environmental changes that are evident and indisputable, although their effects may take a long time to emerge, so that subsequent argument and litigation is focused on whether initial human-made incidents caused those effects. We know that the reality and causes of climate change have become politicized. Donald Trump called the threat of climate change a "Chinese hoax" during his 2016 presidential campaign. This charge clearly implied that nothing should be done to forestall climate change. But Trump later said, before withdrawing from the Paris Accord, that it would be too expensive for the United States to remain, which implies that he does recognize the value of the accord (Baker 2017).

Even evident and indisputable human contributions to environmental destruction seem not to motivate responsible government policies due to corporate fossil fuel interests that have influenced both Democrats and Republicans. The 2010 British Petroleum oil spill and the early years of the Environmental Protection Agency were related to strong economic interests in ways that do not resemble the Republican–Democratic lineup today. The strength and embeddedness of these economic interests help explain contemporary political resistance to the scientific consensus regarding climate change. Even when or if the scientific consensus regarding climate change were accepted by Democratic politicians, they might still not craft and implement corrective environmental policies given external economic pressures. These external economic interests are a source of supercharged politics. Climate change denial results from turbocharged politics that has made the issue part of a slate of issues for current Republicans.

THE 2010 BRITISH PETROLEUM OIL SPILL

After the 2016 election, it was evident that climate change had become uniquely politicized, with Republicans denying its existence and repudiating scientific assessment of it and Democrats insisting on its reality and the need for central regulation. But the refusal of the U.S. federal government to aggressively counteract even direct and known human causes of environmental despoliation was bipartisan as recently as 2010. On April 20, 2010, Transocean Ltd.'s Deepwater Horizon drilling rig exploded and sank. Eleven men were killed and 115 injured. Over the next four months, 4.5 million barrels or 206 million gallons of oil spilled into the Gulf of Mexico from a drilling well. Some of the oil sank, there were tar balls on beaches, birds and fish died, and the tourism industry dried up. President Obama reacted slowly to the British Petroleum (BP) oil disaster. Except for demanding that a twenty-billion-dollar escrow account be set up by BP, he did not order a freeze on BP's assets for compensation for public and private damage.

Five years later, the dead wildlife had been removed, the oil spill was no longer blatantly visible, and Louisiana seafood was again edible. An Associated Press survey of scientists was inconclusive about long-term effects of the BP spill, which was the world's largest environmental disaster to date (Pope 2017). The damage to 1,300 miles of coastline from Florida to Texas as well as effects further offshore have not yet been fully assessed. Lax government oversight and regulation, as well as the absence of emergency plans on BP's part, continues to raise concern about future offshore oil drilling as demand increases. Especially worrisome are areas such as the North Shore of Alaska, where emergency and cleanup help is difficult to get to the scene of accidents (Ebinger 2016).

THE ENVIRONMENTAL PROTECTION AGENCY

Republican President Richard M. Nixon inaugurated the Environmental Protection Agency (EPA). On April 22, 1970, the First U.S. Earth Day, millions of Americans demonstrated, demanding that air, water, and land be cleaned up and protected. There had been oil spills off the California coast, the Cuyahoga River caught fire, many lakes were too polluted for fishing or swimming, smog blocked horizons and had killed four hundred New Yorkers in 1963, and there were news stories linking automobile exhaust fumes to birth defects. Nixon had been elected president in 1968, and in 1969 he set up a cabinet-level advisory group to address environmental decay, create new pollution control proposals, and foresee problems. A bipartisan Congress passed the Environmental Policy Act of 1969, creating the Council on Environmental Policy, which was "empowered to review all federal activities that affect the quality of life and make reports directly to the President." The Clean Air Act (1970), the Clean Water Act (1972), and the Endangered Species Act (1973) followed (Allen 2014; Rothman 2017; Albeck-Ripka and Pierre-Louis 2018).

William D. Ruckelshaus, the first EPA head, shaped the early course of the agency. He had been counselor to Indiana's Board of Health and was effective in curtailing waterway pollution in that state, as well as helping to draft the 1961 Indiana Air Pollution Control Act. Ruckelshaus's efforts in Indiana were successful without frightening industry out of the state, because business practices causing pollution were large scale and blatant. As EPA head, Ruckelshaus concentrated first on organizational structure, and he sought to establish a central plan for the agency in three divisions: planning and management; standards, enforcement, and general counsel; and research and monitoring. Commissioners of water quality, solid waste, pesticides, and radiation would head central programs. However, enforcement soon became a major preoccupation for the agency. Because the Nixon administration was generally moving away from centralization, Ruckelshaus decided to leave implementation of environmental rules to local authorities and begin with warnings about noncompliance if they were not making progress. He was accused of political motivation in interaction with Democratic city officials. A standoff with Armco Steel Company involving the dumping of chemicals into waterways was resolved in the EPA's favor after it was revealed that Armco had been a major contributor to Nixon's campaign.

Clean air policies were more complicated than clean water ones because it emerged that, despite demands for clean air and strong environmental advocacy, the public itself was unwilling to give up its sources of pollution. Economist Paul Samuelson supported "freedom to drive" initiatives against the EPA's proposed parking regulations. Still, automobile companies began to manufacture cleaner cars, and industrial pollutants substantially decreased. During the Nixon administration's collapse, Ruckelshaus left to become FBI director. His successor, Russell Train, had to change EPA priorities, as inflation, unemployment, and the energy crisis became more pressing (Williams 1993).

This snapshot of the early EPA as an embattled agency within an embattled administration shows the administrative difficulties in implementing federal environmental programs. From the beginning, the EPA was opposed to short-term corporate interests and depended on public support for its success. This is not surprising insofar as it was the American public that spurred the agency's creation. However, the opposition from business, which was perhaps in the long run victorious, suggests that effective environmental regulation by the federal government has slim chances of success, especially as government roles in caretaking generally are shrinking.

Scott Pruitt, head of the EPA in the Trump administration, sued the EPA fourteen times while attorney general of Oklahoma. Pruitt made no secret of his disdain for the agency or his closeness to oil and coal corporate interests. He accepted a budget cut of 25 percent for the agency and rarely met with representatives of environmental groups, devoting his attention to CEOs of fossil fuel companies (Talbot 2018). In addition, a number of Republican congressmen, backed by fossil fuel companies, have signaled support for abolishing the EPA (Kotch 2017).

In the first year and a half of President Trump's administration, with Pruitt as head of the EPA, there were announced rollbacks of sixty-seven environmental rules and regulations, including endangered species protections, clean air and water regulations, and national preserves (Popovich, Albeck-Ripka, and Pierre-Louis 2018). However, announcements of rollbacks are not yet rollbacks in reality but merely signal intent. In most cases it will take years of regulatory administrative work to undo environmental protections in place, and each rollback is likely to be delayed while litigation against it develops; each rollback also requires a period for public comment before it can submitted, and some rollback directives have had to be redone when that procedure was omitted. Washington appellate lawyer David Rivkin, who represented Pruitt in his legal challenges to Obama-era EPA rules while he was in Oklahoma, commented, "The regulatory apparatus is like a super-tanker; it can take a long time to turn around. . . . If you want durable results, you can't be sloppy or rushed." It could be reasonably inferred that so far the Trump–Pruitt environmental rollbacks mainly have been matters of turbocharged political discourse. Also, Pruitt's effectiveness in administrative matters was limited by a series of disclosures concerning the ethics of his use of agency finances for expensive personal security and first-class travel, which critics claimed were unnecessary, as well as a sweetheart deal on a luxury condo rental from the wife of an energy lobbyist (Grunwald 2018). While this does not dilute the importance of concern or even alarm in some cases, it means that there is time for those who are concerned and alarmed about the rollbacks to plan and act before further environmental damage becomes permanent and irreversible. (As of this writing, Pruitt has resigned or been fired, but the policies of the EPA require ongoing vigilance from those concerned about the environment.)

CULTURE AND BASIC IDEAS ABOUT NATURE

Within rich democratic nations, where media shape public opinion that in turn influences official policy, public awareness is primarily focused on what happens within national borders. Disasters in less developed countries do not usually make news in the United States. For example, the American public is familiar with the damage from oil spills from the Exxon Valdez in 1989 and the British Petroleum oil spill of 2010. But receiving less attention than the 2010 Gulf of Mexico BP oil spill was an oil spill in China following a pipeline explosion in July 2010 that affected an offshore area of about four hundred square miles. Oil spills in the Niger Delta over a period of decades are estimated to have exceeded the 2010 US BP spill, with very little success resulting from legal action taken by the Nigerian government against Shell Oil Company (Amnesty International 2015). Avowedly probusiness U.S. administrations are unlikely to aid Nigeria. It is easier to see how economic interests in profits and jobs trump concerns about the environment in such faraway cases than it is to recognize political self-serving behind rhetoric about jobs and gross national product within our own borders.

However, even within the United States, observers and participants in environmental discourse, particularly those who scorn corporate greed and dismiss apparent public ignorance, may not fully understand the depth of disagreement. For those to whom the environment and its preservation are obvious values, with or without their relation to human well-being, the shortsightedness in how the U.S. government, business, and public have waivered in sustaining coherent policies of preservation may be difficult to understand. This is not merely a question of the time span over which benefits or utilities are considered, because not everyone is able or can afford to take a long view. And neither can aesthetics decide these issues for everyone because people who defend industrial pollution or deny climate change in favor of preserving their basic livelihoods may not have the leisure or inclination to appreciate natural beauty. Of course, this says something about them ethically, in terms of their individual and collective virtues, but many would now consider it unfairly elitist to criticize degraded aesthetic choices by people whose daily existential pressures do not allow them to develop aesthetic standards in regard to natural environments and nonhuman living things. Common sense about what appears to be necessary can easily coexist with ugliness and cruelty.

People's lives and traditions tend to be deeply imbued with their fundamental perspectives on the environment, not only in terms of their political actions but in differences in core beliefs. Andrew Hoffman in "Climate Science as Culture War" argues that contemporary denial of the reality of climate change is not purely a matter of cognition and cannot be shifted by piling on additional facts. These facts are perceived by the 71 percent of Americans who in 2009 were skeptical about the scientific consensus (that the earth's climate is changing) as an attack on capitalism and some of these people's core values that are shaped by their reference groups and prior ideologies. Hoffman relates how after the 1997 Kyoto Treaty threatened the most powerful companies in the fossil fuel industry, the subject of climate change became aligned with liberal or conservative positions on a slate of issues, such as abortion, gun control, health care, and evolution. Climate change is not about pollution by toxic chemicals but about the effects of CO_2, an otherwise benign substance that is extremely common throughout nature. Taking the problem seriously requires a paradigm shift in worldviews, such as belief in the goodness of a caretaking God or confidence in the friendliness of nature (Hoffman 2012). Hoffman expands his use of research by social psychologists in *How Culture Shapes the Climate Debate* to explain that when people's values and identities are activated, they react to threatening information emotionally, with responses that not only bypass intellectual deliberation but occur much faster than cognitive processing of ideas (Hoffman 2015, 15–33).

JOHN LOCKE ON THE NATURAL ENVIRONMENT

One contrast in basic beliefs about the relation of humankind to nature that is relevant to the contemporary culture wars over climate change becomes evident in comparing John Locke's early modern view with that of contemporary indigenous people. Let's now take them in turn. Locke was sufficiently aware of the physical environment to retreat from London to Essex in his later years because of what we would now consider its pollution. And he seems to have enjoyed rides through the countryside during his retirement at Oates, the home of Lady Masham and her husband, Sir Francis (Cranston 1957, 215–33, 449–83; Scharfstein 1980, 99–100, 346). But nowhere throughout his writings does Locke say anything indicating that he viewed nature aesthetically or thought that undeveloped land, animals, or vegetation had any value in themselves.

In the *Second Treatise of Government*, which in many ways became the framework for development and expansion after the thirteen colonies became the United States of America, Locke set himself the task of justifying the existence of individually owned private property, in the state of nature, after God had given mankind the earth and all of its fruits in common. He wrote:

God, as King David says (Psalms cxv.16), has given the earth to the children of men—given it to mankind in common. This is clear, whether we consider natural reason, which tells us that men, once they are born, have a right to survive and thus a right to food and drink and such other things as nature provides for their subsistence, or revelation, which gives us an account of the grants that God made of the world to Adam and to Noah and his sons. Some people think that this creates a great difficulty about how anyone should ever come to own anything. I might answer that difficulty with another difficulty, saying that if the supposition that God gave the world to Adam and his posterity in common makes it hard to see how there can be any individual ownership, the supposition that God gave the world to Adam and his successive heirs, excluding all the rest of his posterity makes it hard to see how anything can be owned except by one universal monarch. But I shan't rest content with that, and will try to show in a positive way how men could come to own various particular parts of something that God gave to mankind in common, and how this could come about without any explicit agreement among men in general. (Locke [1689] 2017, chap. 5, sec. 25)

Thus, according to Locke, God gave all of the earth to all of mankind, and this gift and possession is more than a question of Adam and Noah having received it and passed it on to their descendants. The question is how individuals can own anything out of this gift without getting the consent of everyone else.

Though men as a whole own the earth and all inferior creatures, every individual man has a property in his own person [i.e., owns himself]; this is something that nobody else has any right to. The labour of his body and the work of his hands, we may say, are strictly his. So when he takes something from the state that nature has provided and left it in, he mixes his labour with it, thus joining to it something that is his own; and in that way he makes it his property. (Locke [1689] 2017, chap. 5, sec. 27).

Overall, it is work that creates ownership and this extends to land: a man owns whatever land he tills, plants, improves, cultivates, and can use the products of (Locke [1689] 2017, chap. 5, sec. 31). That is, private property is the result of mixing things with the labor of individuals, who already own themselves and their own labor. Locke's focus here is on how there come to be owners, not on what can be owned. This is important for subsequent history because it connects labor with ownership, without restriction on *what* can be owned. The overriding importance of value added through labor is thereby enshrined.

Locke continues his justification of private property with claims that if things, including land, have not been worked on, they have no value. Thus:

It is labour, then, that puts the greatest part of value upon land, without which it would scarcely be worth anything. (Locke [1689] 2017, chap. 5, sec. 43)

> This appropriation of a plot of land by improving it wasn't done at the expense
> of any other man, because there was still enough (and as good) left for oth-
> ers—more than enough for the use of the people who weren't yet provided for.
> In effect, the man who by his labour "fenced off" some land didn't reduce the
> amount of land that was left for everyone else: someone who leaves as much
> as anyone else can make use of does as good as take nothing at all. Nobody
> could think he had been harmed by someone else's taking a long drink of
> water, if there was the whole river of the same water left for him to quench his
> thirst; and the ownership issues concerning land and water, where there is
> enough of both, are exactly the same. (Locke [1689] 2017, chap. 5, sec. 31)

Thus, work creates ownership, provided that there is "enough and as good"
left over for others. Locke could not conceive of a condition of human
existence in which there would not be "enough and as good" left over.
Scarcity of natural resources as a limitation to acquisition was not a factor in
his economic analysis—in his seventeenth century, the world was there for
the taking. Although waste was not permitted, the use of precious objects as
money could legitimately provide a store of value just in case an owner had
acquired more than he could use. Locke begins his derivation of money with
a humble agricultural example. but in the next section he has introduced full-
blown money into the state of nature:

> If he traded his store of nuts for a piece of metal that had a pleasing colour, or
> exchanged his sheep for shells, or his wool for a sparkling pebble or a di-
> amond, and kept those—the metal, shells, pebbles, diamonds—in his posses-
> sion all his life, this wasn't encroaching on anyone else's rights. . . . What
> would take him beyond the bounds of his rightful property was not having a
> great deal but letting something spoil instead of being used. That is how
> money came into use—as a durable thing that men could keep without its
> spoiling, and that by mutual consent men would take in exchange for the truly
> useful but perishable supports of life. (Locke [1689] 2017, chap. 5, secs. 46
> and 47)

Putting all this together, work creates ownership of land (other objects
also, but the subject of environmentalism has a focus on land) that is otherwise of little value and an individual can own as much as he can work on and
use. But he can defer his use indefinitely if he sells some of the products of
his work for money. And there is an apparently unlimited amount of land.
Given the history of U.S. expansion and dispossession of Native Americans,
the Lockean creed amounted to a freedom to acquire and work on land that
was not limited by the presence or claims of prior inhabitants. Rather, the
only limitation was the amount of work or development that could be ex-
pended. Also, although Locke uses examples of individuals who labor, it
should be understood that the core idea that is relevant for subsequent history
includes entrepreneurs who employ workers. Ownership directly secured by

workers through their labor was and still is automatically transferred to their employers. Locke understood the rhetorical force of simple examples involving common workers, and he made good use of them as examples in his political philosophy. In real life, he was reasonably affluent, owning property that he rented; he never labored on anything himself.

Locke had European property ownership and acquisition in mind. When it came to "the Indians in America," he did not recognize their legitimate ownership of land because they had not worked it as Europeans might/soon would. "It is important to keep America in mind, because America even now is similar to how Asia and Europe were in the early years when there was more land than the people could use, and the lack of people and of money left men with no temptation to enlarge their possessions of land" (Locke [1689] 2017, chap. 8, sec. 108).

THE STANDING ROCK VIEW OF WORKING THE ENVIRONMENT

The Standing Rock Sioux Tribe and their allies lost a protracted protest against the Dakota Access Pipeline (DAPL) in February 2017, when President Trump signed an executive order putting an end to an environmental impact assessment that President Obama had ordered for the purpose of finding alternate routes for an easement for the pipeline. (Trump earlier sold stock in companies involved in the construction of DAPL, although one of their CEOs had contributed one hundred thousand dollars to his campaign.) Construction of DAPL would cost $3.8 billion to carry about 470,000 barrels of oil over 1,172 miles from North Dakota wells, through South Dakota and Iowa, to a shipping port in Illinois. This route runs under Lake Oahe on the Standing Rock Sioux Indian reservation. Protesters claimed that DAPL would put the reservation's only supply of drinking water at risk of oil spills and contamination, increase carbon emissions, and harm sacred sites. DAPL was estimated to create about eight thousand (temporary) jobs, generate state tax revenues, and lower energy costs (Sampathkumar 2017). By June 2017, DAPL Facts announced the following:

> How much of the Dakota Access Pipeline is complete?
> Construction is complete. Dakota Access Pipeline began commercial service June 1, 2017, transporting crude oil from the Bakken/Three Forks production areas in North Dakota to a storage and terminalling hub outside Pakota, Illinois. (Dakota Access Pipeline Facts 2016–2017)

But one year after President Trump's February 2017 executive order, the *Guardian* published the following announcement by Chief Arvol Looking

Horse, nineteenth keeper of the sacred bundle and spiritual leader of the
Lakota, Dakota, and Nakota people:

> Standing Rock is everywhere. Our collective water has been assaulted for
> many generations to the possible point of no return. Our Elders foretold of a
> Black Snake and how the Water of Life—"Mni Woc'oni," which is our first
> medicine—would be affected if we did not stop this oncoming disaster. Mni
> Woc'oni is part of our creation story, and the same story that exists in many
> creation stories around Mother Earth.
>
> When we say "Mni Woc'oni"—Water of Life—people all over the world
> are now beginning to understand that it is a living spirit: it can heal when you
> pray with it and die if you do not respect it. We wanted the world to know
> there have been warnings in our prophecies and, as we see it, those warnings
> are now taking place. It was said water would be like gold. It was said that our
> spirit of water would begin to leave us.
>
> We are at the crossroads. (Looking Horse 2018)

Regarding his general EPA policy, Scott Pruitt is a devout follower of a
Southern Baptist conservative Christian church in Broken Arrow, Oklahoma.
His senior pastor, Nick Garland, said in clarification of Christian Evangelical
support of Pruitt's nomination in 2016, "The Lord God took the man and put
him in the Garden of Eden to work it and take care of it." Pruitt has said, "It's
like having a beautiful apple orchard that could feed the world, but the
environmentalists put up a fence around the apple orchard and say, 'Do not
touch the apple orchard because it may spoil the apple orchard'" (Leber
2018). It is astounding that the conflict between the perspective of indigenous people who do not commodify the natural environment and those who
seek to profit from it has not changed since Locke presented what was to
become the prevailing view, in 1689! Other Christians, including Pope Francis, have endorsed humankind's stewardship regarding the environment
(Burton 2014). But with development and construction as proxies for what
Locke called "labor," what indegenous people have not themselves developed remains available for the taking by those who have no interest in, or
respect for, their reasons for not developing it—it seems not even to occur to
them to consider the intrinsic value of the environment.

THE SOCIAL COMPACT AGAIN AND HOLISTIC
WEATHER AND CLIMATE

Contemporary environmental issues are now so vast as to affect every area of
human and nonhuman life, including food, soil, air and water purity, aesthetics, consumer product manufacture, recycling, and waste disposal, just to
name a few. Storms, oil spills, and basic ideas that minimize the importance
of the natural environment have been the main subjects of this chapter.

Underlying themes have been the attenuation of government regulation and human causes of climate change that range over the entire planet. Continuing with the suggestion in chapter 6 that natural disasters in society and unnatural disasters in nature have the same causes, it may be useful to conclude with a focus on weather here. But first, another look at the role of government is in order.

If the federal government abdicates environmental preservation by delegating the issue to state and local government, then, to the degree possible, environmental preservation becomes a social contract issue between people and government on those levels. However, as noted, the environment is not divided into state or city/town boundaries, and there is no assurance that local government will be more preservationist than federal government. Also, where government represents the public at the cost of business, business is likely to prevail, regardless of the level of representation. So perhaps the abdication of government from environmental protection and preservation is simply a historical development that has resulted from tensions between business and democratic representation, which cannot be resolved. The EPA was arguably strongest right after Nixon set it up. He set it up because millions of Americans expressed concern about their environment. But, perhaps eclipsed by protests against the Vietnam War, that expression was not sustained. The success of the EPA could not be sustained for more than a few years given consumer demand and the eagerness of fossil fuel providers to fulfill it and exert influence over government.

When all forms of government abdicate performance in a vital area, the realm of the social compact can reassert itself. Intentional resistance against government passivity regarding destruction of the environment would need to issue from the realm of the social compact. There are many nongovernmental institutions that could form coalitions and negotiate with business entities to curtail pollution or correct their activities. Decentralization from strong federal authority may need to be reiterated in processes of decentralization from local authorities, not to result in anarchy, but in other connections between organizations that already have strong support among citizens. The present breakdown in the EPA's mission and authority as a spokes-organ for the environment may reflect a change in the structure of the social order that no longer positions governmental authority on one pole and the people as a mass on the other. The people are not a mass but already organized as workers, students, consumers, and citizens, including indigenous citizens, who are concerned for the public good. In other words, maybe the United States does not need the EPA in order to preserve and protect its environment, and if there are sufficient collective wills to accomplish that, it can be done without central or even local government regulation and enforcement. This is a suggestion, not a blueprint.

And now about the weather and climate. Although details are not yet filled in and the best models for prediction and timing have not yet been fully worked out, there is a scientific consensus that climate change is likely to affect hurricane frequency and intensity, as well as coastal storm surges (Sneed 2017; Union of Concerned Scientists 2018). The current scientific consensus is that climate change is partly or mainly human made, by the greenhouse gasses of carbon dioxide (from fossil fuels) and methane (from livestock) (Environmental Protection Agency 2018; Union of Concerned Scientists 2018). This entails that both disasters in society and what humans view as disasters in the natural environment have human causes. A holistic understanding of weather and climate is therefore indicated.

It has been traditional for the concept of weather to be limited to immediate surroundings or places of immediate interest. Weather is local. Climate encompasses both immediate and global contexts and everything in between, over longer periods of time. This means that weather can also be viewed as global in ways that vastly overflow national, local, and neighborhood boundaries, because weather is part of climate. In that sense, the entire human collectivity or commonwealth is the cause of planetary weather that has different national and local and neighborhood expressions at the same time. Over time, global climate encompasses both global weather and local weather. There is no effective government organization capable of uniting nations for global policies concerning global climate. Government treaties and their signatories come and go, and there has never been an international weather treaty with clear penalties for violation (Georgetown Law 2018). This is a planetary commonwealth issue, an imagined global social compact. Private and nonprofit organizations should continue to strive for their governments' participation in international treaties seeking to mitigate the effects of climate change, and it is laudatory for them to do that. However, future strategies might require direct protest against the largest corporate polluters, such as litigation, demonstration, and varied forms of persuasion, including consumer boycotts, talking heads, talking voices, academic theorists, and education.

We have seen that fossil fuel emissions contribute to global climate. Global climate is experienced as local weather at any given time, which includes intense storms. Fossil fuel development also results in accidents that directly degrade the environment, as well as damage to the environment in the process of development, such as the effect of the DAPL on Sioux land and water. Global climate, local climate, local weather, and fossil fuel development and consumption are therefore part of the same system. Contrary to the traditional western view of modernity, humankind is not apart from nature as an unlimited resource, but part of nature as a condition for its own well-being and survival. This is the holistic picture that more people need to understand.

REFERENCES

Albeck-Ripka, Livia, and Kendra Pierre-Louis. 2018. "America before Earth Day: Smog and Disasters Spurred the Laws Trump Wants to Undo." *New York Times*, April 21. https://www.nytimes.com/2018/04/21/climate/environmental-disasters-earth-day.html.

Allen, Erika. 2014. "April 22, 1970: The First Earth Day Draws Millions." *New York Times*, April 22. https://www.nytimes.com/times-insider/2014/04/22/april-22-1970-the-first-earth-day-draws-millions/.

Amnesty International. 2015. "Niger Delta: Shell's Manifestly False Claims about Oil Pollution Exposed." November 13. https://www.amnesty.org/en/latest/news/2015/11/shell-false-claims-about-oil-pollution-exposed/.

Archambault, Dave, II. 2016. "Standing Rock Sioux Chairman: Dakota Access Pipeline 'Is Threatening the Lives of My Tribe.'" *Democracy Now*, August 23. https://www.democracynow.org/2016/8/23/standing_rock_sioux_chairman_dakota_access.

Baker, Peter. 2017. "Does Donald Trump Still Think Climate Change Is a Hoax? No One Can Say." *New York Times*, June 2. https://www.nytimes.com/2017/06/02/us/politics/climate-change-trump-hoax-scott-pruitt.html.

Burton, Tara Isabella. 2014. "Pope Francis's Radical Environmentalism: Exploiting the Earth "Is Our Sin," the Pontiff Says." *Atlantic*, July 11. https://www.theatlantic.com/international/archive/2014/07/pope-franciss-radical-rethinking-of-environmentalism/374300/.

Cranston, Maurice. 1957. *John Locke: A Biography*. London: Longmans Green.

Dakota Access Pipeline Facts. 2016–2017. "How Much of the Dakota Access Pipeline Is Complete?" https://daplpipelinefacts.com/dt_articles/how-much-of-the-dakota-access-pipeline-is-complete/.

Diaz, Andrea. 2018. "A Sperm Whale That Washed Up on a Beach in Spain Had 64 Pounds of Plastic and Waste in Its Stomach." CNN, April 11. https://www.cnn.com/2018/04/11/health/sperm-whale-plastic-waste-trnd/index.html.

Ebinger, Charles K. 2016. "6 Years from the BP Deepwater Horizon Oil Spill: What We've Learned, and What We Shouldn't Misunderstand." Brookings, April 20. https://www.brookings.edu/blog/planetpolicy/2016/04/20/6-years-from-the-bp-deepwater-horizon-oil-spill-what-weve-learned-and-what-we-shouldnt-misunderstand/.

Environmental Protection Agency. 2018. "Greenhouse Gas Emissions." https://www.epa.gov/ghgemissions/global-greenhouse-gas-emissions-data.

Flechas, Joey. 2017. "How Hurricane Irma Blew Away the Beach in Miami Beach." *Miami Herald*, September 19. http://www.miamiherald.com/news/weather/hurricane/article174225591.html#storylink=cpyIn.

Georgetown Law. 2018. "International Environmental Law Research Guide." January 4. http://guides.ll.georgetown.edu/c.php?g=273374&p=1824812.

Glusac, Elaine. 2007. "How Travelers Can Help Hurricane-Damaged Islands." *New York Times*, April 3. https://www.nytimes.com/2018/04/03/travel/volunteer-vacations-caribbean.html.

———. 2018. "How Travelers Can Help Hurricane-Damaged Islands." *New York Times*, April 4. https://www.nytimes.com/2018/04/03/travel/volunteer-vacations-caribbean.html.

Grunwald, Michael. 2018. "The Myth of Scott Pruitt's EPA Rollback: His Ethics Woes Are Overshadowing the Central Fact of His Tenure: He Hasn't Done Much." *Politico*, April 7. https://www.politico.com/magazine/story/2018/04/07/scott-pruitt-epa-accomplishments-rollback-217834.

Hoffman, Andrew John. 2012. "Climate Science as Culture War." *Stanford Social Innovation Review* 10 (4): 30–37. http://dx.doi.org/10.2139/ssrn.2944200.

———. 2015. *How Culture Shapes the Climate Debate*. Stanford, CA: Stanford University Press.

Kotch, Alex. 2017. "Surprise! The Four GOP Representatives behind Bill to Abolish EPA Are Backed by Fossil Fuel Industry." *DeSmogBlog*, February 16. https://www.desmogblog.com/2017/02/16/gaetz-four-gop-representatives-bill-abolish-epa-backed-fossil-fuel-industry.

Leber, Rebecca. 2018. "Scott Pruitt Is Gutting the EPA Because He Thinks It's God's Plan: Is True Environmentalism 'Do Not Touch'?" *Mother Jones*, February 26. https://www.

motherjones.com/environment/2018/02/scott-pruitt-is-gutting-the-epa-because-he-thinks-its-gods-plan/.

Locke, John. [1689] 2017. *Second Treatise of Government*. Ed. Jonathan Bennett. Early Modern Texts. http://www.earlymoderntexts.com/assets/pdfs/locke1689a.pdf.

Looking Horse, Chief Arvol. 2018. "Standing Rock Is Everywhere." *Guardian*, February 22. https://www.theguardian.com/environment/climate-consensus-97-per-cent/2018/feb/22/standing-rock-is-everywhere-one-year-later.

Perkins, Devin N., Marie-Noel Brune Drisse, Tapiwa Nxele, and Peter D. Sly. 2014. "E-Waste: A Global Hazard." *Annals of Global Health* 80 (4): 286–95. https://doi.org/10.1016/j.aogh.2014.10.001.

Pope, John. 2017. "Remembering the BP Oil Spill, a Disaster of Historic Proportions." *Times-Picayune*, December 5. http://www.nola.com/300/2017/12/the_bp_oil_spill.html.

Popovich, Nadja, Livia Albeck-Ripka, and Kendra Pierre-Louis. 2017. "67 Environmental Rules on the Way Out under Trump." *New York Times*, October 5. https://www.nytimes.com/interactive/2017/10/05/climate/trump-environment-rules-reversed.html.

Rothman, Lily. 2017. "Here's Why the Environmental Protection Agency Was Created." *Time*, March 22. http://time.com/4696104/environmental-protection-agency-1970-history/.

Sampathkumar, Mythili. 2017. "Dakota Access Pipeline Explained: What Is It, Why Are People Protesting It and What Happens Next?" *Independent*, January 24. https://www.independent.co.uk/news/world/americas/dakota-access-pipeline-facts-explained-pros-cons-protests-what-next-a7544451.html.

Scharfstein, Ben-Ami. 1980. *The Philosophers: Their Lives and the Nature of Their Thought*. Oxford: Basil Blackwell.

Sneed, Annie. 2017. "Was the Extreme 2017 Hurricane Season Driven by Climate Change? Global Warming Already Appears to Be Making Hurricanes More Intense." *Scientific American*, October 26. https://www.scientificamerican.com/article/was-the-extreme-2017-hurricane-season-driven-by-climate-change/.

Talbot, Margaret. 2018. "Scott Pruitt's Dirty Politics: How the Environmental Protection Agency Became the Fossil-Fuel Industry's Best Friend." *New Yorker*, April 2. https://www.newyorker.com/magazine/2018/04/02/scott-pruitts-dirty-politics.

Union of Concerned Scientists. 2018. "Scientists Agree: Global Warming Is Happening and Humans Are the Primary Cause." January 9. https://www.ucsusa.org/global-warming/science-and-impacts/science/scientists-agree-global-warming-happening-humans-primary-cause#.WuDIcZep7cs.

White House. 2018. "Presidential Message on Earth Day." April 22. https://www.whitehouse.gov/briefings-statements/presidential-message-earth-day-2018/.

Williams, Dennis C. 1993. "The Guardian: EPA's Formative Years, 1970–1973." EPA Web Archive. https://archive.epa.gov/epa/aboutepa/guardian-epas-formative-years-1970-1973.html.

World Vision. 2017. "Hurricane Irma: Facts, FAQs, and How to Help." February 14. https://www.worldvision.org/disaster-relief-news-stories/hurricane-irma-facts#strength.

Chapter Eight

Homelessness and Monetization

Stories about underground dwellers were already flourishing when the first New York City subway line opened in 1904. The expansion of extensive sewers and steam pipes systems had brought a newfound fascination with what laid below the streets. From Jules Verne's 1864 novel "Journey to the Center of the Earth" to George Gissing's 1889 book "The Nether World," literature was brimming with tales of people living in isolation or trapped under the surface, peaking in 1895 with "The Time Machine," in which H. G. Wells described a fictional subterranean species called the "Morlocks." (Taille 2015)

An epicure dining at Crewe
Found quite a large mouse in his stew.
Said the waiter, "Don't shout,
And wave it about
Or the rest will be wanting one too!" (Anonymous)

The problem of homelessness strains a purely material property–based interpretation of the social contract. We need Locke's expanded version of property that is "life, liberty, and estate," as discussed in chapter 5, to provide a theoretical foundation for addressing the needs of homeless people. This chapter begins with the scope and nature of the problem of homelessness, followed by its history, the role of the public–private distinction in aversion to homeless people, a distinction between needs-based and symbolic materialism, and discussion of solutions that are consistent with a social contract capitalistic system.

THE SCOPE AND NATURE OF HOMELESSNESS

Few doubt that homelessness is a practical problem in the early twenty-first-century United States. But nobody knows for sure how many people in the United States are homeless. According to the 2015 report of the National Alliance to End Homelessness, there were about half a million homeless people in the United States, with a national rate of about eighteen per ten thousand (National Alliance to End Homelessness 2015). By 2017, the official count had increased for the first time since 2010, to 534,000 (Stanford 2018). Such counts are compiled based on the total number of people seeking social services or shelter on one given night. Left out are those who do not seek services or live in shelters, which includes people living on the streets, in their vehicles, sleeping on relatives' and friends' couches, or camping in parks and rural areas. Taking these situations into account, in 2009 the National Coalition for the Homeless placed the yearly homeless figure at approximately 3.5 million people, of which 1.35 million were children (National Coalition for the Homeless 2009).

Anecdotal experience is both relative and important in considering homelessness as a problem, because reports of an overwhelming presence of homeless people may accurately reflect life in some communities but exaggerate the problems of others. For instance, the National Alliance to End Homelessness estimated 120 homeless people per ten thousand in Washington, DC, and seven per ten thousand in Mississippi (National Alliance to End Homelessness 2015). Exact and uniform measures aside, it seems accurate to consider homelessness in the U.S. context as a serious societal problem for a large number of people. Most observers and analysts suggest that although varied conditions are unpredictable in different ways, the problem has not been solved and there is little reason to believe that it will be solved in the foreseeable future.

The exposure resulting from being without shelter from the elements and lacking privacy from other people in public is a form of suffering. Suffering is bad, and the suffering of children is very bad. People ought to respond with aid when others, children especially, suffer. The conditions in which the suffering occurs or its causes are a practical problem, if they can be corrected by certain kinds of response.

Many academics in the United States have some direct experience with homelessness near their campuses and where they reside. But homelessness is hardly a "cutting edge" or "hot" topic. For instance, in academic philosophy, besides a scattering of articles, there has been only one book-length treatment since 1999 (Abbarno 1999). The question is, why have radical philosophers, teachers against oppression, philosophers of class and economics, and even social and political philosophers ignored homelessness? Part of the answer may be that many scholars in the humanities, including philosophers, believe that homelessness is mainly a practical problem that belongs to public policy administrators, government officials, charities, and volunteers, who already have social technologies, funds, and sufficient motivation to solve it. These scholars are well informed that there are different homeless populations such as substance abusers, the mentally ill, the hard-core unemployed, and female heads of households and that these populations have different needs that are variably addressed by different kinds of social aid programs. They are aware of recent successes: Housing First programs (U.S. Interagency Institute on Homelessness 2018; National Alliance to End Homelessness 2015); increased housing opportunities for homeless veterans (U.S. Department of Veteran Affairs 2018; U.S. Interagency Institute on Homelessness 2016); alternative forms of housing such as tents and Conestoga wagons in some Western states (Mukerjee 2018). They understand that recessions, great recessions, and depressions that are unavoidable parts of the business cycle affect the number of homeless people when jobs are lost and housing payments cannot be met, against a background of scarcity in affordable or very cheap housing. They note that interests of local government contractors, and property owners may unfairly and unethically obstruct solutions to practical problems of homelessness (New York Times Editorial Board 2015). And the special vulnerabilities of homeless people to cruel, violent attacks, sometimes even by students, have led some states to classify them as hate crimes (Goldberg 2014). Less disturbing, but still distressing, a certain number of students on our campuses are rumored to be sheltered only through couch surfing or sleeping in their cars, or else out in the open (Ehrmann 2017).

Failure to be alarmed by homelessness suggests moral complacency among the esteemed, comfortable, healthy, abled, and residentially flourishing part of the population. Members of the great majority that has housing do not think that they are responsible for the problem of homelessness or that it is an urgent problem. They may conclude that all of the complexities and causal factors associated with homelessness result in deprivations and conflicts that can be addressed with practical, humane measures by knowledgeable experts—even though that has not yet occurred. Those subject to almost constant eviction may be more anxious about homelessness because it could happen to them (Desmond 2016). There is also an aesthetic and affective element. The problem of homelessness is unattractive because homeless people often exhibit behavior that is offensive or rude and their appearance fails to conform to broad norms of grooming and dress. In sum, most of the housed probably would prefer to avoid thinking about the problem of homelessness.

HISTORICAL ASPECTS OF HOMELESSNESS IN
THE UNITED STATES

Since the 1980s, homeless people in the United States have been stereotyped
as drug addicted, alcoholic, mentally ill, criminal, or too lazy to work. Contemporary application of this general pathologization usually posits the
homeless as passive objects who *in their mere existence* fail to meet, or
violate, the life norms of law-abiding citizens who have homes, families, and
jobs (DePastino 2003). Americans are good at what Ian Hacking has called
"making people up," and the identification of someone as a "homeless person" puts a stereotype to work, although identification is not the same as
identity. Positive identities are rarely on display among today's homeless, but
to the extent that they are, they constitute resistance against the negative
stereotyped identification. It has not always been thus.

In the late nineteenth and early twentieth centuries, the homeless were
vocally opposed to middle-class values and modern progress; in defending
and valorizing their itinerant lifestyles, they actively contributed to their
social outcast status. Overall, American homeless people have always lived
in distinct subcultures, made up of interactions among themselves, survival
in public spaces in society, and interactions with social service and law
enforcement personnel. In emphasizing the natural sociality of human beings, it is often assumed that the homeless are something like "strays." But
the well-documented historical and contemporary existence of subcultures
among the homeless attests to the fact that, despite their lack of stable or
permanent dwelling places, homeless people are not without the sociality
connoted by ideas of "home" (Hopper 2003; Wasserman and Claire 2010).

The conflict between housed normativity and homelessness was not a
subject in public awareness until after the Civil War. The Civil War produced
a large number of veterans who could not secure steady employment in one
place. They took to the roads and railroads as "tramps." The freedom of these
tramps from wage labor became part of an ideology for single men without
families. They actively and vocally resisted what some saw as a national
social movement toward domestic organization around a male breadwinner.
A family man was seen as "feminized" by his role and thereby deprived of
property in the labor of his wife and children, which belonged to him under
an older system of patriarchy (DePastino 2003, 115–16). The idea was widely circulated that "the reckless, free life of the army" had given these tramps
"a taste for wandering and a distaste for every species of labor" (DePastino
2003, 18–19). And there was something enviable about their freedom.

So as not to romanticize the independent, rebellious lifestyles of such
tramps and hoboes, it should be remembered that between the Civil War and
the 1930s, the concept of unemployment as an effect of downturns in the
business cycle was not fully developed. For that concept to take root, em-

ployment had to be viewed as a healthy and positive social norm and supported as a public value. The public consensus that most people ought to have paid work, with government safety nets to take up gaps in the business cycle, did not develop until the Depression of the 1930s. During the Great Depression, fifteen million or one-third of the nonfarm workforce was unemployed. Only one-quarter of unemployed families—whites only—received relief, and hundreds of thousands or perhaps millions were homeless. Communities of shacks, known as "Hoovervilles," sprung up throughout the United States; the largest, covering eight or nine acres with a population of 1,200, endured in Seattle from 1931 to 1941 (Gregory 2009).

After World War II, federal housing programs and the G.I. Bill supported education for productive employment and individual home ownership in suburbia—again, for whites only. Such programs were in part motivated by uneasiness about the social instability that could result if the thirteen million returning troops were left to fend for themselves as tramps or hoboes (DePastino 2003, 226–30). But many of the single men who were excluded from this boom continued to occupy single rooms (SROs) in cheap hotels in large cities. In the early 1980s, the Reagan administration introduced austerity measures to cut funding for social services and subsidized housing. In the name of "urban renewal," most forms of SRO housing were demolished or converted into condominiums. Consequently, not enough housing was available for the urban poor and more began living on the streets (a population that notoriously included former mental institution residents) as a permanent fixture of American urban life (Rossi 1989, 27–44).

There was a dramatic shift in the demographics of the homeless from the late nineteenth to the late twentieth century. Before the Great Depression, the voice of hoboes and "forgotten men" was precisely an assertion of their own identity as not being women, black, Asian, Italian, Polish, and so forth. During the Great Depression of the 1930s and after dislocation caused by the demolition of cheap housing, homeless women and children received new attention, as did homeless families, who remain ongoing contemporary casualties of housing scarcity—along with military veterans, nonwhites, and the elderly. The large numbers of children and teenage runaways among the contemporary homeless increases the overall vulnerability of this entire population (Barak 1991, 66–71; Anderberg 2011). However, although each disadvantaged component of the homeless population has advocates and scholars who study their counterparts among the housed, the distinct needs of homeless categories become invisible under the homeless label.

HOMELESSNESS AND THE PUBLIC–PRIVATE DISTINCTION

In the twenty-first century, it is no longer expected that everyone has to have or belong to a home containing a heterosexual nuclear family with a sole male breadwinner. A diversity of lifestyles is broadly accepted without controversy and people move freely, especially renters. But people possess places. Those who do not possess places continue to be relentlessly stereotyped by the pathologies of drug and alcohol addiction, mental illness, criminality, and laziness. Because these pathologies are not limited to those who are homeless, it makes sense to focus on the fact that the homeless today are primarily, as some advocates call them, *the unhoused*, or those without dwellings under their control. But this is not to imply that being unhoused is a simple condition.

Being unhoused, despite broad mobility and diversity, violates a societal distinction between public and private. Sleeping, eating one's self-prepared food, washing, excreting, engaging in sexual acts, and taking care of one's personal possessions are daily biological and physical functions and activities that are part of what is private. Exceptions are made for picnics, camping, tailgate parties, scripted displays of nudity, and high art installations, but all of those activities are recreational or optional and not part of humdrum, daily, serious, socially responsible life in society.

It is expected that people will perform their daily biological and physical functions within walls, shielded from public view. There are two parts to this expectation: the majority of the public, who perform those functions in their dwellings, do not wish to view others performing them in public; the functions are expected to be shielded from public view as a primary requirement not only for respectability in terms of social status, but for respect to one's person, as deserving privacy. Thus, the homeless are forced by their circumstances to perform a radical unconventionality that is deemed by the majority not only to fall beneath respectability but to be unworthy of individual respect. The majority is not so much concerned about the literal lack of the shielding walls experienced by the unhoused—they don't care that the privacy of the unhoused is constantly violated—but is offended by what they can see in the absence of these walls. And because of this direct contradiction of one of its most broad assumptions about civilized life, the public assumes that the homeless are criminal, not only in the bare fact of their unhoused status, but with a disposition to commit crimes against housed persons. What the public overlooks is that the walls it takes for granted as respectably dividing what is biologically and physically private from what is public cost money. The public does not focus on the fact that the homeless or permanently unhoused cannot afford housing, which results in a kind of "let them eat cake" attitude toward the homeless.

Having a home ensures a private space that is necessary not only for filling biological needs—what Marxists call the reproduction of labor—but for social and political activities outside of the private space. When writers emphasize the importance of a private space for autonomy and distinctively human flourishing (Schrader 1999), the home or private dwelling is viewed as an instrumentality for what is done outside the home (Betz 1999). For instance, there is a long Euro-American history of the requirement of property ownership to vote. Homeless people are now permitted to vote by listing nominal addresses, such as a park or street corner, although Nonprofit Vote recommends that a shelter address be used (Nonprofit Vote 2018). But despite enough numbers to constitute a political interest, few homeless people do in fact vote or think about their situation as an issue to be addressed through political voice.

While many marginally employed Americans are in reality unhoused (Ehrenreich 2001), about 25 percent of the homeless are employed (National Coalition for the Homeless 2013; Gowan 2010). However, the social services now available to the unhoused often require long hours of travel by public transport and long hours waiting in line. Single women with young children who are homeless usually cannot arrange for the child care that would enable them to work. While in principle the homeless could both work and participate politically, their unhoused condition results in inconveniences merging into hardships that are practical barriers to such activities taken for granted among the housed (Nunez 2010). Even a cursory understanding of the condition of being unhoused in contemporary society reveals its tedious and wasteful complexity (Orwell [1933] 2001).

Aversion to those who perform their biological functions in public is an immediate surface reaction. The biological functions at issue, especially excretion and sleep, occur on the basis of need, which human beings are helpless in being driven to fulfill. Both the homed and homeless have the same needs. It is important to emphasize that these needs must be fulfilled and that homeless people have no choice but to fulfill them in public (Waldron 1991–1992). But those whose needs cannot be fulfilled in ways that disguise their necessity are a source of contempt from others, perhaps because they remind them of their own needs that they fulfill in private. When needs are fulfilled in private, they can be put out of mind in public, but their public visibility disrupts that order. That is, we can all pretend together that we are naturally clean and groomed and do not excrete disgusting substances, but even mere sliding glances at those who are in plain view dirty, ungroomed, publicly excreting, and sleeping embarrass those who look. Human helplessness about universal needs becomes an obvious means for manipulation and coercion of the extreme poor in general. And if the homeless have special needs, such as addictions, their vulnerability is exacerbated. Through interactions shielded from wider public view, the needs of the extreme poor are visible to others who have the will and ability to manipulate their satisfaction in exchange for whatever they want from them—usually some form of day work or sex work (Vanderstaay 1992, 51–54).

BASIC-NEED MATERIALISM AND SYMBOLIC-VALUE MATERIALISM

In contemporary western culture, some kinds of physical things that cost money are required to satisfy universal basic human material needs, for example, adequate food and shelter for privacy, security, and protection from weather. In contrast to this basic-need materialism is a *symbolic-value materialism* concerning physical objects that are desired more for their nonmaterial properties than for their need-satisfying material ones. The material-need-satisfying properties may not even be noticed by average consumers of, for example, exotic bottled waters, designer jeans, or luxury houses and hotel rooms. Jean Baudrillard describes such consumers negatively:

> They have turned consumption into a dimension of status and prestige, of useless keeping up with the Joneses or simulation, of potlatch which surpassed use value in every way. A desperate attempt has been made from all sides (official propaganda, consumer societies, ecologues and sociologues) to instill in them sensible spending and functional calculation in matters of consumption, but it is hopeless. (Baudrillard 1983, 45)

At the same time that the relatively affluent satisfy their basic needs by practicing their symbolic-value materialism, they share a tendency to remain unaware of the reality of basic-need materialism or to deny it. For example, while eating a gourmet meal in a high-end restaurant, the service and ambiance, how the food is presented, how it tastes, and seeing and being seen by other patrons may be more important than nutrition and hunger. Those who can afford more expensive versions may have a slight contempt for tap water, simple food, and plain lodging, contempt that ignores the basic material-need-satisfying properties of the humble versions of such objects. And that contempt and oversight subtly imply that those who consume the more expensive versions do not have the same basic needs as those who make do with the humble versions. If one dismisses and contemns cheap food and lodging, it is a small extension of the attitude toward those things to look down on those who either have to make do with them or cannot even get them. The contempt and oversight of universal basic material needs is a form of denial of those needs, to the extent that the needs are material. Everyone needs the materials of water, food, and shelter, but the focus on the nonmaterial values of objects providing them (for the sake of status and prestige) can contribute to a delusion that one's basic needs are psychological and social only, and not at all physical. Symbolic-value materialism may also be minimalist in "less is more" styles of consumption, such as tiny houses and tree houses that cost hundreds of thousands of dollars and tiny portion sizes in expensive restaurants. As minimalist lifestyle statements, such items are extremes in symbolic-value consumption, which are hardly comparable to the "less is less" dwellings of those who live in the small spaces of their vans, cars, shacks, or older mobile homes. The difference is the element of choice in the fashionable cases and economic constraint in poorer ones—owners choose the posh tiny houses and tree houses, but the other dwellings are usually occupied as last and only resorts.

Having a home goes beyond both basic- and symbolic-value materialism into universal psychological and social needs. All human beings share a need for a life with others, for relationships with relatives, friends, animals, and neighbors, which usually occur in the same physical locations. In a nonnomadic society such as ours—even those who move frequently make a permanency of their temporary locations—these psychological and social connections are importantly connected to the idea of home as materially located in a constant place. The strong normativity of having a *relation-place*—"Thou shalt have a home"—is a kind of absolute. Those who struggle along with cheap food and substandard housing may suffer within the range of harshness, exploitation, and cruelty that afflicts the poor, but they are still accorded minimal respect, as in the expression "working poor." To be a member of the "working poor" may entail many disadvantages, but it is also likely to garner charitable praise as "deserving."

The analysis thus far explains the reaction of the majority to the homeless, but it does not address the apparent intractability of the present problem of homelessness. To understand the apparent inability to solve this problem, we might further examine basic-need materialism among the "homed." There is something peculiar about basic-need materialism at this time because symbolic-value materialism has made it very difficult for *anyone* in a full-blown capitalistic consumer society to satisfy their basic needs and only that. The affluent may preciously get back to basics in consuming versions of Third World foodstuffs and living among and wearing handmade artifacts, as well as decluttering and downsizing. But the lower middle class and poor spend a great deal of time and energy attending to their own basic material needs via symbolic-value materialist products. Despite the nearly ubiquitous distribution of standardized types of things, everyone has to figure out the quickest, most gratifying, and cheapest ways to get what they "need." Multiplying labor-saving devices and ever-new electronic marvels increasingly result in less leisure time—and that means there is less time to sleep and fulfill other basic needs. So basic needs may not be met even by those who are able to practice symbolic-value materialism.

There are few high-quality, simple forms of food and housing, and consumers make their choices according to competing pulls of advertising, marketing, peer pressure, and how much money they have. The huge number of choices for even insignificant objects is less a matter of freedom than a bewildering fog that each person has to cut her way through before uniting with the right thing for her. All consumer products are the result of multiple prior transactions between capital and labor. Housing is not only shelter but an investment that can turn out badly, and the cheapest food is often the most highly processed and least nutritious. This system may not guarantee or even offer basic-need fulfillment to anyone. A trivial trope for this is faculty parking at a state university. For several hundred dollars a year, one may purchase a faculty parking permit. But the permit does not come with a designated space, so it is merely permission to park any place within a number of lots—if one has the time to search for a spot and the luck to find one. If bodies are like cars, a homeless person is like someone with a car who cannot afford the permit, and is thereby banned from the scramble to park and get on with her life.

The elimination of contemporary homelessness would likely require the construction of basic, cheap housing and the mass production of unprocessed nutritious food for a population of several million people. This could be done for a modest profit if government and charities were the purchasers on behalf of the homeless. However, there is no tradition or financial infrastructure for producing such objects. Instead, the present system supports high prices for substandard welfare slum housing, dormitory-style emergency shelters, food pantries, and food stamps that are begrudged by those who don't need them. For both housing and food, the extreme poor are given limited access to some of the products of symbolic-value materialism. But after being filtered through profit-seeking contractors, the housing available to the homeless may not only lack the unnecessary frills of shelter but also lack necessities of structural safety, security, and hygiene (Nunez 2010; New York Times Editorial Board 2015). Food stamps give the homeless no less and no more than the same access to the wall of potato chips that the rest of us enjoy.

In our society, no effort is made and little financial incentive exists to efficiently satisfy basic material needs and do only that. Any success in such projects would be politically opposed by those who profit from the production of products catering to symbolic-value materialism—hence the limerick epigraph to this chapter. Part of the motivation for tearing down SROs and giving developers free reign to create expensive housing where they stood was the belief that maintaining, improving, or increasing housing stock for the "disaffiliated" single male poor would be met by an increase in demand, to the detriment of the general work ethic and the American family (DePastino 2003, 240–43). We have already seen how the basic-need frustration of the homeless is to some extent shared by the homed, but privately, within their homes. In reality, now as then, the numbers of their consumers would swell if more basic need objects were available—to the detriment of those who profit from symbolic-value materialism.

HOW HOMELESSNESS COULD BE MONETIZED

As discussed earlier, the social contract is property based, having been composed at a time when conceivable citizens were male heads of households who owned property. Homeless people usually do not own property, and their condition of homelessness entails that they do not have control over or possession of dwellings for themselves. As a result, in a narrow sense of property as material possession, instead of a broad sense to include life and freedom as well as material possession, homeless people fall out of the social contract because they have no recognized property meriting official protection. Indeed, it is customary for police officers to discard their possessions when they apprehend the homeless, even though federal court rulings have upheld their property rights (Holland 2016).

The problem of homelessness is almost by definition a problem of a lack of housing. It may not be coincidental that recent rises in the official count of homeless people, as mentioned at the beginning of this chapter, are the effect of recent decreases in the availability of affordable housing—a 60 percent decrease in inexpensive housing stock is said to have occurred from 2010 to 2016 (Jan 2017). But housing varies in what counts as a house in different locales, and for this and other reasons, homelessness might not be caused by a shortage of housing, just as famine may not be caused by a shortage of food. The solution to homelessness has the same form as the solution to famine: provide housing/provide food. But many contemporary Americans are intolerant of making gifts to select groups of people. There may be strong humanitarian as well as individual-rights reasons for the broad Lockean interpretation of the social contract to include government protection of individual ownership of life and liberty (see chapter 5). The provision of housing to the homeless may not be justifiable in a private-property society on the grounds that because they need housing and are suffering without it, the government should provide them with housing. But it can be justified on the grounds that their lack of housing obstructs their freedom and endangers their lives. It is on these grounds that housing subsidies could be made available or more available and accessible for people who are currently homeless. The problem with this solution to homelessness is that it would likely increase the numbers of homeless people, as many on the verge of homelessness learned that reaching a condition of homelessness would entitle them to government housing subsidies. A more creative solution might therefore be worth considering.

GUARANTEED HOUSING INCOME

There were, in 2016, over two hundred million Americans who were qualified to vote. Each of those qualified voters, including even several million homeless people, could receive a guaranteed housing income (GHI) to be spent only on housing. Payments from the GHI program could vary depending on housing costs in different localities. It would likely be a substantial part of the U.S. federal budget, which was about 4.5 trillion for 2018 (Balance 2018).

The justification for a U.S. GHI for all qualified voters is that it would allow everyone to increase their housing costs beyond that, if they wanted to, and not incur the usual resentment and resistance to entitlement programs. The majority who are already able to afford housing would receive extra income, to spend, save, or invest as they saw fit. Any U.S. GHI would need to be tailored to the broad values within the United States, in contrast to proposals and programs in countries that already have more robust social nets, such as recent trials of basic income in Finland (Peter 2018). Because only those qualified to vote would benefit, conservatives fearful of undocumented immigrants taking advantage of such a system would be reassured. Since all qualified voters would receive a GHI, and most, except for the one percent, would welcome the increase to their yearly income, those same conservatives would benefit. Some of the distributed GHI would be recaptured in income tax payments from those in middle and upper brackets. Most important in our capitalistic system, the spending on new housing would be a substantial stimulus to the economy because the homeless and very poor would likely spend all of their GHI funds; those who worked for the construction companies would spend their salaries, and their employers would buy land and building materials and invest profits.

The economic benefit of GHI in a capitalistic system is that it would provide stable incentives for developers and builders to construct low-cost housing, and with that stability would come sufficient political muscle to push back against real estate interests opposed to cheap housing. It's possible that the segment of the population now on the verge of homelessness would not try as hard to generate income on their own, but that is unlikely given symbolic-value materialism. The same reasons that those who can afford to buy food or eat in restaurants do not exploit the opportunities to get free meals from soup kitchens and food pantries would deter unnecessary recourse to new cheap housing. Those barely hanging on, pre-GHI, would be more financially secure. The former homeless would still be poor, but now housed. The corruption and decrepitude of the current shelter system in cities such as New York would become redundant if "shelter housing" were no longer a publicly financed option (Tempey 2016). Overall, a GHI would monetize the condition of homelessness.

Without such monetization of homelessness that created new incentives for the construction of cheap housing, we are left with ameliorative and charitable solutions to homelessness that are ad hoc and community based. In any given community, housed residents have to decide whether the unhoused are part of their community or not. Shared-species humanity and presence would dictate that the unhoused are part of the same community as the housed. Given general community values, this means that for some it becomes a moral obligation to help those unhoused and ameliorate their suffering. When that is not done and opportunities to help have not been taken, over time the condition of the unhoused becomes unjust. The result is that the housed members of the community become collectively unjust. So moral imperatives to house the homeless remain, although they are probably not as strong as new financial incentives would be. A GHI financed and regulated by the federal government would be a solution to homelessness in the realm of the social contract. Voluntary and charitable efforts to assist homeless people are social compact projects, if they are not patronizing or condescending; they require recognition of the unhoused as members of the same community or commonwealth as the housed. This commonwealth would be the entire community of housed and unhoused, which is viewed as a valuable entity to which each member should contribute and which benefits each member (see chapter 5).

Either homelessness is viewed as a community problem that needs to be solved with immediate additional housing, or homelessness is accepted in its present state of there being unhoused people. So what should be done if homelessness is accepted? Jeremy Waldron and others have considered whether the occupation of public spaces by homeless people constitutes harm to the community. If the homeless are part of the community, then they should have a say in what is acceptable use of public space, and their mere occupation of it, while annoying and offensive to some, would not be considered a harm. Waldron writes:

> So long as people live among us in a condition of homelessness, our normative definitions of community must be responsive to their predicament; and it must be responsive, not only in articulating some vague sense of social obligation to "do something" about the problem, but in accepting that the very definition of community must accommodate the stake that the homeless have—as community members—in the regulation of public place. (Waldron 2000, 111)

REFERENCES

Abbarno, G. John M., ed. 1999. *The Ethics of Homelessness: Philosophical Perspectives.* Atlanta: Rodopi.
Anderberg, Kirsten. 2011. *21st Century Essays on Homelessness.* Ventura, CA: Seaward Press.

Balance. 2018. "US Federal Budget Breakdown." April. https://www.thebalance.com/u-s-federal-budget-breakdown-3305789.

Barak, Gregg. 1991. *Gimme Shelter: A Social History of Homelessness in Contemporary America.* New York: Praeger.

Baudrillard, Jean. 1983. *In the Shadow of the Silent Majorities, Or, The End of the Social and Other Essays.* Trans. Paul Foss, John Johnston, and Paul Patton. New York: Semiotext(e).

Betz, Joseph. 1999. "The Homeless Hannah Arendt." In Abbarno (1999), 217–32.

DePastino, Todd. 2003. *Citizen Hobo: How a Century of Homelessness Shaped America.* Chicago: University of Chicago Press.

Desmond, Matthew. 2016. "Letter from Milwaukee, Forced Out: For Some Americans Eviction Never Ends." *New Yorker*, February 8.

Ehrenreich, Barbara. 2001. *Nickel and Dimed: On (Not) Getting By in America.* New York: Henry Holt.

Ehrmann, Chris. 2017. "Homeless College Students a Growing Concern on Campuses." *US News*, June 25. https://www.usnews.com/news/best-states/michigan/articles/2017-06-25/homeless-college-students-a-growing-concern-on-campuses.

Goldberg, Eleanor. 2014. "States Classify Attacks Against Homeless ss 'Hate Crimes' to Curb Rising Violence." *Huffington Post*, Aug 29. https://www.huffingtonpost.com/2014/08/29/homeless-hate-crimes_n_5732660.html

Goldmacher, Shane. 2016. "America Hits New Landmark: 200 million Registered Voters." *Politico*, October 19. https://www.politico.com/story/2016/10/how-many-registered-voters-are-in-america-2016-229993.

Gowan, Teresa. 2010. *Hobos, Hustlers, and Backsliders: Homeless in San Francisco*, Minneapolis: University of Minnesota Press.

Gregory, James. 2009. "The Great Depression in Washington State: Hooverville and Homelessness." Pacific Northwest Labor Civil Rights Project, University of Washington. https://depts.washington.edu/depress/hooverville.shtml.

Holland, Gale. 2016. "Seize a Homeless Person's Property? Not So Fast, a Federal Judge Tells L.A." *Los Angeles Times*, April 13. http://www.latimes.com/local/lanow/la-me-ln-homeless-injunction-20160413-story.html.

Hopper, Kim. 2003. *Reckoning with Homelessness.* Ithaca, NY: Cornell University Press.

Jan, Tracy. 2017. "America's Affordable-Housing Stock Dropped by 60 Percent from 2010 to 2016." *Washington Post Wonkblog*, October 23. https://www.washingtonpost.com/news/wonk/wp/2017/10/23/americas-affordable-housing-stock-dropped-by-60-percent-from-2010-to-2016/?utm_term=.be05b0e92d88.

Mukerjee, Subir. 2018. "Conestoga Huts Offer More Options for Housing the Homeless." MRSC, Local Government Success, April 23. http://mrsc.org/Home/Stay-Informed/MRSC-Insight/April-2018/Conestoga-Huts-for-Housing-the-Homeless.aspx.

National Alliance to End Homelessness. 2015. "The State of Homelessness in America." April 1. http://www.endhomelessness.org/library/entry/the-state-of-homelessness-in-america-2015.

National Coalition for the Homeless. 2009. "How Many People Experience Homelessness?" July. http://www.nationalhomeless.org/factsheets/How_Many.html.

———. 2013. "Homeless Employment Report: Findings and Recommendations." http://www.nationalhomeless.org/publications/index.html.

New York Times Editorial Board. 2015. "Homeless in New York City, an Unending Crisis." *New York Times*, May 7. http://www.nytimes.com/2015/05/07/opinion/homeless-in-new-york-city-an-unending-crisis.html?_r=0.

Nonprofit Vote. 2018. "Voting and Homelessness." https://www.nonprofitvote.org/voting-in-your-state/special-circumstances/voting-and-homelessness/.

Nunez, Ralph da Costa. 2010. *A Shelter Is Not a Home . . . or Is It? Family Homelessness in New York City.* New York: White Tiger Press.

Orwell, George. [1933] 2001. *Down and Out in Paris and London.* London: Penguin Classics.

Peter, Laurence. 2018. "Finland's Basic Income Trial Falls Flat." BBC News, April 23. http://www.bbc.com/news/world-europe-43866700.

Rossi, Peter H. 1989. *Down and Out in America.* Chicago: University of Chicago Press.

Schrader, David E. 1999. "Home Is Where the Heart Is: Homelessness and the Denial of Moral Personality." In Abbarno (1999), 49–64.

Stanford, Daphne. 2018. "Homelessness in America: What Will It Take for the Crisis to Abate?" *International Policy Digest*, January 1. https://intpolicydigest.org/2018/01/01/homelessness-america-will-take-crisis-abate/.

Superson, Anita M. 1999. "The Homeless and the Right to Public Dwelling." In Abbarno (1999), 147–48.

Taille, Anthony. 2015. "The Truth about New York's Lendendary Mole People." *Naratively*, October 29. http://narrative.ly/the-truth-about-new-yorks-legendary-mole-people/.

Tempey, Nathan. 2016. "Nearly 9 out of 10 Family Homeless Shelters in NYC Have an 'Immediately Hazardous' Problem." *Gothamist*, January 6. http://gothamist.com/2016/01/06/homeless_shelters_still_decrepit.php.

U.S. Department of Veteran Affairs. 2018. "Homeless Veterans." April. https://www.va.gov/homeless/.

U.S. Interagency Institute on Homelessness. 2018. "Housing First Checklist: A Practical Tool for Assessing Housing First in Practice." April. https://www.usich.gov/tools-for-action/housing-first-checklist.

Vanderstaay, Steven. 1992. *Street Lives: An Oral History of Homeless Americans*. Philadelphia: New Society.

Waldron, Jeremy. 1991–1992. "Homelessness and the Issue of Freedom." *UCLA Law Review* 39:295–324.

———. 2000. "Homelessness and Community." *University of Toronto Law Journal* 50 (4): 371–406. https://www.jstor.org/stable/825960.

Wasserman, Jason Adam, and Jeffrey Michael Clair. 2010. *At Home on the Street: People, Poverty and a Hidden Culture of Homelessness*. Boulder, CO: Lynne Rienner.

Chapter Nine

Immigration and Expulsion

Empires were not democratic, but were built to be inclusive of all those who came under their rule. It is not the same with nations, which are founded on the fundamental distinction between who is in and who is out—and therefore harbour a tendency toward ethnic purification. This makes them much more unstable than empires, for that tendency can always be stoked by nativist demagogues. (Dasgupta 2018)

Of those men who have overturned the liberties of republics, the greatest number have begun their career by paying an obsequious court to the people; commencing demagogues, and ending tyrants. (Hamilton [1787] 2008)

As a nation, we began by declaring that "all men are created equal." We now practically read it, "all men are created equal, except negroes." When the Know-Nothings get control, it will read, "all men are created equal, except negroes, and foreigners, and Catholics." When it comes to this I should prefer emigrating to some country where they make no pretense of loving liberty—to Russia, for instance, where despotism can be taken pure, and without the base alloy of hypocrisy. (Lincoln 1855)

Rana Dasgupta may be correct in diagnosing the end of the nation-state, which unlike empires has never been inclusive but bases its identity on borders both figurative and literal. Dasgupta believes that the nation-state is doomed because money travels globally and governments can no longer control the most powerful economic interests that are never completely within the borders of any one nation (Dasgupta 2018). However, if the world is moving toward global government, it won't happen overnight, and in the meantime generations will need to cope with changes in the remnants of rich western nation-states, immigration being an urgent concern for U.S. citizens, residents, and immigrants.

There are push-and-pull theories of immigration that in a general sense make it difficult to understand why immigrants would be eager to come to the United States at this time. Those who are fleeing poverty or political oppression (push) are not likely to encounter unwavering hospitality if they are poor or people of color. Those who are attracted for economic reasons and greater freedom (pull) and arrive with relative privilege would seem to face moral dilemmas about their position in opposing political battles about inclusion and exclusion. Those in between might not be so badly off in their countries of origin or find more stable destinations. However, although some categories of immigration to the United States have declined recently, with fewer Muslims and Mexicans arriving, immigration is likely to remain robust. The pull for immigrants who can improve their lives in the United States at this time is very specific for those pursuing predesignated education and job opportunities and goals, as well as refugees and others urgently seeking protection (Cilluffo and Cohn 2018).

There have been many twists and turns in U.S. immigration policy and the treatment of immigrants. The reality is that even in the periods when immigrants were officially welcomed, through inclusive immigration laws and Statue of Liberty rhetoric, except for some Anglo-Saxons, immigrants belonging to identifiable national, ethnic, or racial groups have never been treated well upon arrival. Their success over generations has always followed hard work and struggles against prejudice, discrimination, and obstacles to education, employment, and civic status. This chapter will begin with that history, followed by consideration of contemporary attitudes of expulsion and policies of deportation, including the position of DACAs (Deferred Action Childhood Arrivals) and the history of Mexican immigrants. It will conclude with a discussion of the civic virtue of hospitality.

THE HARSH HISTORY OF U.S. IMMIGRATION

Benjamin Franklin was not welcoming toward German arrivals to Pennsylvania. He wrote, "Why should Pennsylvania, founded by the English, become a Colony of Aliens, who will shortly be so numerous as to Germanize us instead of our Anglifying them, and will never adopt our Language or Customs, any more than they can acquire our Complexion" (Franklin 1751). Notice what we would today call Franklin's racism, a signal and mechanism for unfair treatment. In that tradition, we should not be surprised that President Trump is said to have asked why the United States can't have more immigrants from Norway, instead of "shithole countries" such as Haiti, El Salvador, and countries in Africa (Dawsey 2018). Trump might not have known that in the late nineteenth century, most Scandinavians were regarded with suspicion, and because only the most dangerous jobs were available to them, they could not buy life insurance. James J. Hill, a railroad tycoon, said, "Give me snuff, whiskey and Swedes and I can damn well build a railroad down to hell" (Wenzel 2018).

PROJECTIONS OF RACE AND ETHNICITY ONTO U.S. IMMIGRANTS

In discussing the discrimination against non-Anglo-Saxon U.S. immigrants who are now privileged as racial whites, the point is not to suggest that their oppression was comparable to that of African Americans, Native Americans, or Asian Americans, but to show how U.S. nativist attitudes toward immigrants have generally been quite negative. From the beginning, U.S. immigrant groups were *othered* as ethnic and racial groups fundamentally different from those already in residence. We can take it as a premise that race in the biological sense is constructed, with a long history of racist interjections into scientific theories, until the biological sciences themselves finally recognized that the concept of race had no independent scientific foundation (Zack 2018, 47–73). But ethnicity continues to be accepted as an empirical way to divide human groups. However, in terms of immigration, ethnic groups are also to a degree invented, and labels are imposed on new arrivals in ways that would have been irrelevant in their places of origin.

The U.S. Census invented the Hispanic/Latino category, which includes a diversity of groups from Central and South America, but not Spaniards from Spain, although Spain is the national origin of the language spoken throughout most groups in this ethnic category. The Hispanic/Latino census category includes U.S. residents from Puerto Rico, Mexico, Cuba, Argentina, and Brazil and all other countries in South America. While many U.S. residents from Cuba and Argentina identify as racially white, many of those with different Hispanic/Latino backgrounds are not perceived as white, and they often view themselves as people of color. So not only does this census category arbitrarily combine distinct groups, but it is not a purely ethnic category, in contrast to a racial one, as census forms stipulate (Alcoff 2000, 2018). Census researchers themselves have considered revisions of how to count the Hispanic/Latino group more accurately, thereby recognizing that the addition of the category in 1970 was an invention (Haub 2012).

A second example of the imposition of racial-ethnic identities is how Middle Eastern and North African (MENA) immigrants have been categorized by the U.S. government in the post-9/11 United States (Sheth 2017). The new and intense focus on members of these groups as threats to national security has been accompanied by beliefs that they can be identified by physical appearance, a form of racialization or treating them as a race. That racist hate crimes have been triggered by articles of clothing, which are expressions of ethnicity, shows how racism and ethnicism may be extended to group members who are already citizens (Muslim Advocates 2017).

In U.S. immigration history, the strongest factor in the invention of non-white ethnicity and race for non-Anglo-Saxon immigrants has been real or politicized worries about job loss for established residents, dressed up as patriotism with dog whistles for white purity. These factors have been formalized in immigration policies and laws. The great waves of European immigration to the United States in the nineteenth and twentieth centuries were met by expectations that new immigrant groups would conform to dominant culture, which they largely did in buying into the American Dream. That is, assimilation was presented as a value to immigrants, and most accepted it.

IMMIGRATION AND LAW AND POLICY

The history of U.S. immigration and immigration law tells its own story about the invention of American ethnic groups. From the colonial period to the early nineteenth century (1620–1820), most arrivals were from Great Britain (England, Ireland, Scotland, and Wales), France, the Netherlands, and the Palatinate region of southwest Germany. From 1820 to 1880, about fifteen million of those who came to be called "old immigrants" arrived from Sweden, Norway, Denmark, what is now the Czech Republic, and Northern Ireland. They settled in families in the rural Northeast and Midwest. Chinese men arrived to the West Coast, usually to hostile reception by whites; after about three hundred thousand had arrived, Congress passed the Chinese Exclusion Act in 1882 and further Chinese immigration was banned. From 1880 to 1920, about twenty-five million people, the largest wave yet, arrived from eastern and southern Europe on great steamships from Italy, Russia, Greece, Hungary, and Poland. Most in this wave were single adults who became the labor pool for factories in urban America through World War II.

U.S. continental expansion, agricultural development and production, and industrialization required workers for new mines, farms, and ranches, as well as factories, but this period of growth eventually petered out. The Immigration Act of 1924 imposed quotas of 2 percent of the same group already residing in the United States for each immigrant group. New arrivals were screened for skills in manual labor and the professions or family relations to U.S. citizens. The civil rights movement of the 1960s resulted in the 1965 Hart-Celler Immigration and Nationality Act. Quotas were rescinded, but there was a cap of 170,000 visas a year. Occupational and familial preferences from the 1924 act were retained, but restrictions due to "race, sex, place of birth or place of residence" were outlawed. New immigrants from Korea, China, India, Pakistan, the Philippines, South and Central America, and Africa began to arrive, and those from Europe decreased (Cornell University Legal Information Institute 2017). Enter the beginning of the non-white U.S. racial majority, the so-called browning of America.

ACCEPTANCE AND DISCRIMINATION FOR U.S. IMMIGRANTS

White Anglo-Saxon Protestants have received the best immigrant reception throughout U.S. history, except for Scots and Irish. The attitudes toward southern and eastern Europeans and Jews were comparatively harsh, as was the treatment of Chinese men; black immigrants from Africa and the Caribbean encountered racism already in place against African Americans; Asians have not been fully assimilated, despite or because of the "model minority" status accorded to some. Space does not permit a comprehensive history here, but worth noting are certain highlights and low points of the historical narrative that privileges Anglo-Saxons, followed by other northern Europeans, followed by southern and eastern Europeans. Of course, Asians, Middle Easterners, Africans, and Latin/Hispanic American immigrants experienced more severe prejudice and discrimination. But a focus on the European groups makes the case for a fundamental inhospitality to immigrants, apart from the persistent nonwhite racism that is ever ready in the wings to ratchet up ill will and exclusion.

After English Puritans arrived at Plymouth Rock on the *Mayflower* in 1620, eighty thousand English settled in Virginia, Maryland, Massachusetts, Connecticut, and Rhode Island by 1742 (Klein 2008b). They displaced Dutch, Native American, and Spanish occupants who were there first. (There were also twenty indentured servants on the *Mayflower*, and in 1619 the governor of Jamestown had imported twenty African slaves who had been pirated from a slave-trading Portuguese ship [Hashaw 2007, xv–xvi].)

Over the next 150 years, specifically English customs, speech, dress, and folk culture set the norms for U.S. society in New England, the South, Mid-Atlantic states, and the Southwest. Restraint in public display and recreation and the nuclear family structure became associated with civic respectability (Fischer 1989). During the colonial period, Americans bought about one-fourth of British exports of finished goods, many of which were luxuries purchased on credit, such as fabrics, tea, fancy clothes, and fine furniture (Breen 2004, 185). English law and representative government were evident in the U.S. Constitution and Bill of Rights (Haft 1995, 472–78).

The Revolutionary War and the War of 1812 with England interrupted commerce. But soon after, English foreign investment developed U.S. land, industry, railroads, mining, and cattle ranching. Eight of the first ten American presidents were English, and English Americans became a plurality (greater in number than any other group) in the executive, legislative, and judicial branches of government (Haft 1995, 475–76). From 1997 to 2006, about thirteen thousand British persons immigrated to the United States each year, of which over eight thousand became citizens (Klein 2008b). Assimilation was never a problem for individual English immigrants. The U.S. and UK governments were allies during World Wars I and II, the cold war, and the First Gulf War, as well as in post-9/11 military actions in Afghanistan and Iraq (Haft 1995, 476).

Additional Anglo-Saxon groups had varied success compared to the English. The Scots-Irish, or Ulster Irish, descended from two hundred thousand Scottish lowland Presbyterians whom the English government settled in Northern Ireland during the 1600s. Upon their first arrival in New England in 1717, they were considered "illiterate, slovenly, and filthy" and themselves "nurtured a profound hatred for the English." But they were fully assimilated by the late 1700s (McLemore and Romo 2005, 63–64). Distinct from this group were the Scots, many of whom were prisoners taken during the English Civil War or criminals sent to work on tobacco plantations in South Carolina, where they were a third of the state population by the 1790 census (Dobson 1994, 4–5). Scots continued to arrive throughout the nineteenth century, often in clans who settled in West Virginia, Kentucky, and Tennessee, with many to live in rural poverty (Hess 1995). Since colonial times, Welsh immigrants were welcomed because they were skilled workers (Welsh Americans 2008). Similarly, Manx from the Isle of Man, Australians, New Zealanders, and Canadian immigrants have assimilated easily (Isle of Man Government Treasury 2011; Parkin 1980, 163; Klein 2008b; Fednukiw 1995, 244).

The present population of thirty-nine million Irish Americans are believed to be mainly descended from the 3.2 million Roman Catholic "potato famine Irish" who arrived in the United States from 1841 to 1890 to settle on the East Coast (U.S. Census Bureau 2010). Many were peasants, escaping starvation and English economic and political oppression. About 40 percent of those who traveled below deck, in *steerage*, died on the way. There were large numbers of young single women who worked in domestic service, and others became schoolteachers throughout the country (Ireland Story 1998; Schaefer 2011).

Nineteenth-century Irish Catholic immigrants were not accepted as white but viewed as an inferior racial group. Samuel F. B. Morse, inventor of the telegraph, in 1834 published *A Foreign Conspiracy Against the Liberties of the United States*, vilifying the Irish as illiterate and claiming that the pope was planning to move the Vatican to the Mississippi River Valley. By the Civil War, Irish gangs or "fire companies" were attacking African Americans as their competitors for jobs; they also resisted their draft to the Union side, particularly during the Draft Riots of 1863. (Members of some fire companies later participated in the Fenian movement for Irish independence [Kenny 2000, 124–27].)

Following Ireland's independence from Britain in 1921, Irish Americans asserted themselves as superior to Italian, Polish, and Slovak Roman Catholic immigrants, as well as blacks (Ignatiev 1995; Schaefer 2011). Through the patronage system, Irish Americans became well represented in police and fire departments in New York City, Boston, Chicago, and other cities. The Irish came to be regarded as racially white and became more inclusive themselves. (Saint Patrick's Day is now celebrated throughout the United States, without much regard for the real "Irishness" of participants [Blessing 1980, 529–39, 545].)

Americans with German ancestry number over forty million, the most numerous U.S. ethnic group, who by the twenty-first century were mostly third generation or later (U.S. Census Bureau 2010). Until the twentieth century, German Americans were not fully assimilated, but retained their distinct social institutions, including newspapers (almost one thousand by 1900), political groups, and singing societies (thirty in San Francisco in 1890) (Bergquist 2005). But international politics intervened. Germany was a U.S. enemy during World War I, and the political fallout included anti-German propaganda in the United States, which accelerated German American assimilation. The German-American National Alliance, representing German interests in the United States, dissolved under congressional pressure, and the number of German organizations, including newspapers, quickly shrank. During the 1930s, before World War II, and then during the war, eleven thousand German Americans were interned or removed from the West and East Coasts and relocated to over fifty closed "camps" throughout the United States and Hawaii. Still, the patriotism of German Americans was generally unquestioned, and many fought in the U.S. military. Two twentieth-century U.S. presidents had German ancestry: Herbert Hoover, who served after World War I, and Dwight D. Eisenhower, who served after World War II (Carlson 2003; Kazal 2004; Schaefer 2011, 165–66). After World War II, English-speaking German immigrants have been able to assimilate immediately, including over one hundred thousand who arrived to the United States from 1990 to 2010 (Homeland Security 2010; Harzig 2008).

About sixteen million Americans claim Italian descent. Italians had explored the New World before Italy became a united country in 1861: in the fifteenth and sixteenth centuries, Cristoforo Colombo, Giovanni Caboto, Amerigo Vespucci (from whose first name *America* was derived), and Giovanni de Verranzzano all explored and charted parts of what would be the United States; Father Marcos da Niza explored Arizona. There were Italian glass bead makers in Jamestown, silk producers in Georgia, and landowners in Maryland. Filippo Mazzei, a Tuscan physician, shared his interest in agricultural science with his neighbor, Thomas Jefferson. More than one thousand Italians fought in the Revolutionary War. The fourteen thousand Italians in the United States before the Civil War were artisans, artists, teachers, musicians, and political refugees. Constantino Brumidi painted frescoes in the Capitol rotunda from 1852 to 1877, and Antonio Meucci from Florence invented a version of the telephone twenty-six years ahead of Alexander Graham Bell; the first Italian church in the United States was founded in 1866 in New York City. Despite such cultural contributions, skin-color discrimination against Italians was virulent in the South throughout the nineteenth century, including segregation, attempts to substitute Italian laborers for slaves, and lynchings (Parrillo 2008; Candeloro 1992, 173–74).

About five million Italians arrived between 1880 and 1920, from Sicily and parts of the impoverished *Mezzogiorno*, east and south of Rome. They came for *pane e lavoro*, and many were single males who returned to Italy. After the Depression of the 1930s and the reign of Benito Mussolini in Italy, Italian immigration to the United States slowed, but it picked up again after World War II. Italian immigrants often settled near neighbors from Italy, in Philadelphia, New Orleans, New York, and Boston. Culture was based on *famiglia* and the church, including many festivals throughout the year. Early generations worked at unskilled jobs and in family-owned and -run restaurants, shoe repair shops, barbershops, and dry and green groceries. Job security came with success in union organizing (Parrillo 2008; Klein 2008a; Candeloro 1992).

Italian immigrants were not themselves initially optimistic that they would assimilate. This partly accounts for the Italian American presence in organized crime. The ongoing sensationalization of those activities in the media and popular entertainment has depended on their identity as a distinctive group. But long before *The Sopranos*, stereotypes of Italian Americans as criminals were common. In New Orleans on March 14, 1891, eleven Italians were hung or shot by a mob after the death of a policeman. The *New York Times* wrote in an editorial,

> These sneaking and cowardly Sicilians, the descendants of bandits and assassins, who have transported to this country the lawless passions, the cut-throat practices, and the oath-bound societies of their native country, are to us a pest without mitigation. Our own rattlesnakes are as good citizens as they. . . . Lynch law was the only course open to the people of New Orleans to stay the issue of a new license to the Mafia to continue its bloody practices. (*New York Times*, March 16, 1891; quoted in Woolf 2015)

Fifty Italians were lynched in the United States between 1890 and 1920. Italians were also subject to deportation. After the Wall Street Bombing of 1920, in which thirty-eight died, thousands of Italians were arrested and hundreds deported (Woolf 2015).

Researchers now agree that criminal stereotyping and suspicion of Italian Americans was unjustified and impeded their progress in politics as well as business. Third- and fourth-generation Italian Americans are now well represented in the professions, and by 2000 their median family income was higher than the national median. As assimilated generations moved to the suburbs and generally assumed a white racial identity, "Little Italy" disappeared from many American cities (Guglielmo and Salerno 2003; U.S. Census Bureau 2010; Klein 2008a; Candeloro 1992).

Forty percent of Jews in the world live in the United States. (Israel has only 20 percent, making up 80 percent of its population.) Jewish Americans are now a small, religiously identified ethnic minority who have been successful in American secular society, politics, the arts, academia, law, medicine, and the media. Until the end of World War II, Jews were considered a racial group, although there are no uniform physical traits shared by all Jews. Most Jews in the United States have northern and eastern European ancestry, but there are also Jews from the Mediterranean region and North Africa. One-third of all Jewish Americans have no religious affiliation and do not observe Jewish religious practices. (The term *Judaization* refers to shared culture and history as a basis of Jewish identity [Porter 2008; Shapiro 1992].) After World War II and the Nazi attempt to exterminate all Jews as a race, suggestions that Jews are racially nonwhite have been viewed as anti-Semitic. Almost all American Jews now identify as white Americans (Brodkin 1998).

In the early twentieth century, some mainstream Americans reacted to Jewish financial success and political radicalism with virulent anti-Semitism that did not distinguish between eastern European Jews and the already established German Jews. All Jews were accused of being clannish, vulgar, greedy, physically inferior, and so forth. American Jews supported the Jews remaining in eastern Europe during World War I, who were subject to famine, expulsion, and pogroms. After World War II, Jewish Americans continued to prosper and by the 1970s were no longer subject to explicit, organized anti-Semitism (Goran 1980, 586–97).

Scholars differ about whether the new immigrant/ethnic groups who have arrived since the late twentieth century will go through the same processes of assimilation as Scots, Irish, Germans, Italians, and Jews. Sociologists Richard Alba and Victor Nee (2005) have been optimistic that past patterns will in time repeat, with a net result of assimilation. However, new MENA immigrants face problems of post-9/11 suspicion and fears of terrorism that were not as widespread and intense earlier. And undocumented immigrants from Latin America, especially Mexico, have been targeted by changes in immigration enforcement policy and political promises of "building a wall" under President Donald Trump's administration. In addition, Muslim religious affiliation and practice among MENA immigrants and a general racialization of Hispanic/Latino immigrants have come up against new expressions of American white Christian nationalism during and after the 2016 political campaign (Gidda 2016).

The other side of mainstream establishment barriers to assimilation of immigrants after 1990 is that electronic communications and air travel make it easier for them to maintain ties with relations in places of origin. Many members of these groups send money and consumer items back to their countries of origin, and ongoing contact supports retention of their original cultural identities (Rebala 2015). Thus, the incentive for non-Anglo-Saxon and nonwhite immigrants to assimilate may be further weakened by the strength of their national identities of origin, along with hate crimes and suspicion by government and the public. However, assimilation is largely an issue of culture and identity. In a pluralistic democratic society, cultural assimilation need not be required by the majority of those who have been here longer, or by dominant groups.

EXPULSION/DEPORTATION

The terms *expulsion* and *deportation* are used interchangeably to mean removal from a nation by the state (Henckaerts 1995, 5). After 9/11, discourse about immigrant issues seems to have sharply pivoted from considerations of assimilation and identity to expulsion/deportation. Two million were deported under the Bush administration following 9/11 (Marshall 2016). During the first seven years of the Obama administration, government data record 2.5 million official deportations, a historical record that does not include voluntary "self-deportations" or those not admitted. Over the first year of the Trump administration, deportations at the border decreased, but internal deportations (from within the United States) increased. The net effect as of March 2018 was a 6 percent drop in deportations from 2016 to 2017, which many attribute to Trump's anti-immigrant rhetoric (Huth 2018). Consider these campaign remarks:

> When Mexico sends its people, they're not sending their best. . . . They're sending people that have lots of problems, and they're bringing those problems [to] us. They're bringing drugs. They're bringing crime. They're rapists. And some, I assume, are good people. (Announcement of candidacy for Republican nomination for president at Trump Tower Atrium, New York, June 16, 2015)

> Donald J. Trump is calling for a total and complete shutdown of Muslims entering the United States until our country's representatives can figure out what is going on. According to Pew Research, among others, there is great hatred towards Americans by large segments of the Muslim population. (Written statement on December 7, 2015, before a rally aboard the aircraft carrier USS *Yorktown* in Mount Pleasant, South Carolina)

I saw him. He was, you know, very emotional. And probably looked like—a nice guy to me. His wife, if you look at his wife, she was standing there. She had nothing to say. She probably—maybe she wasn't allowed to have anything to say. (Comment to ABC News about Khizr Khan and his wife, Ghazala, on July 29, 2016, after Khan challenged candidate Trump, implying that their Muslim faith required Ghazala's silence. Ghazala Khan said that she had been too distraught to speak while standing in front of a huge photo of their son, Humayun Khan, a Muslim U.S. Army captain who had been killed in Iraq in 2004.)

Appreciate the congrats for being right on radical Islamic terrorism, I don't want congrats, I want toughness & vigilance. We must be smart! (Tweet after news broke about the mass shooting at the Pulse nightclub in Orlando on June 12, 2016.) (all quotes from Newsday.com 2016)

This rhetoric has alarmed many insofar as it seems to run counter to even hypocritical references to the United States as "a nation of immigrants."

Trump continued with anti-immigrant ideology in his 2018 State of the Union address when he said, "In recent weeks, two terrorist attacks in New York were made possible by . . . chain migration." Couched as "protection for the nuclear family," he advocated curtailment of family reunification through immigration as one of four pillars of the Trump administration's immigration policy. The three other pillars were a path to citizenship for 1.8 million "Dreamers" and those undocumented immigrants who would otherwise qualify for the Obama-era DACA program, twenty-five billion dollars for a wall along the Mexican border, and ending the visa lottery in favor of a merit-based immigration system (Plott 2018). Trump may not have understood the visa lottery insofar as its pool consists of applicants who are already prescreened for eligibility for admission. He said in a speech to graduates of the FBI Academy on December 15, 2017, "They give us their worst people, put them in a bin . . . they're picking the worst of the worst, congratulations you're going to the US" (CBS News 2017).

Expulsion is thus more than the act of physical removal, because it involves attitudes and policies toward selected immigrant groups. The discourse and practice of expulsion raises existential questions: Who will be let in, and once in allowed to remain? Of those already in the United States, who can be deported? These are not questions about national security, which is often used to frame them in favor of expulsion and deportation, but issues of human security: can non-European immigrants and their descendants experience their lives in the United States on the basis of a permanent right to stay here?

Under the Trump administration, discussion of deportation has focused on the expulsion of undocumented Mexican immigrants and on different versions of a travel ban against Muslim countries, portrayed as sources of

"Radical Islamic Terrorism" in campaign rhetoric. A ruling by the U.S. Supreme Court on the third version of Trump's travel ban is pending as of this writing, and observers predict that the court will not interpret the ban in terms of what Trump said during his campaign, implying that Trump's ban will hold (Liptak and Shear 2018).

HISTORICAL ASPECTS OF MEXICAN AMERICAN EXPULSION

There is a history of arbitrary Mexican American deportation, accompanied by racist rhetoric and justification in terms of job scarcity. Between 1929 and 1936, in response to unemployment pressures of the Depression, President Herbert Hoover's administration cut immigration by 90 percent and deported almost 1.8 million Mexican Americans, including many who were already US citizens (Balderrama and Rodríguez 2006). People were rounded up through unconstitutional raids. In the words of California State Senator Joseph Dunn, who began an investigation in 2004, "The Republicans decided the way they were going to create jobs was by getting rid of anyone with a Mexican-sounding name" (Wagner 2017). During President Dwight D. Eisenhower's administration in 1955, as many as 1.3 million Mexican Americans were deported as undocumented in "Operation Wetback" (Blakemore 2018). However, Mexico has traditionally been the biggest source of U.S. immigration. Through the Bracero program from 1942 to 1964, 4.3 million Mexicans legally immigrated to the United States, followed by 430,000 immigrants arriving in the 1960s, 780,000 in the 1970s, and 3 million in the 1980s (Durand, Massey, and Zenteno 2001).

With or without documentation, Mexican Americans are an integral part of the U.S. population. At 56.6 million, Hispanic Americans are 17.6 percent of the U.S. population, and 63.4 percent of them are of Mexican origin (U.S. Census Bureau 2016). That is not surprising. The United States and Mexico share the largest border for both countries. The Mexican-American War (1846–1848) was prosecuted by the administration of President James K. Polk through the doctrine of "manifest destiny" so that the United States could occupy the entire continent. Mexico lost the war and with that one-third of its national territory, including large parts of California, Utah, Nevada, Arizona, and New Mexico. Texas had already become independent from Mexico in 1836 and was not yet a part of the United States, but Mexico recognized its American annexation at the Treaty of Guadalupe Hidalgo (History.com 2018; Guardino 2017).

DACAs

Beginning in August 2012, DACA applicants were accepted on a rolling basis, subject to these requirements: arrival in the United States before age sixteen; continuous residence in the United States without legal status since June 15, 2007; at least fifteen but not older than thirty-one at application; enrollment in school, high school graduation, or GED or honorable discharge military status; no convictions for felonies or multiple or serious misdemeanors; no threat to national security or public safety. Estimates of the number of those eligible for DACA were 1.7 million in 2012, and the figure estimated in 2018 is 1.8 million. Without DACA, undocumented young people who were brought to the United States as children would be subject to automatic deportation. If deportation is deferred, successful DACA applications can include permission to work or attend school, with renewal every two years. The Pew Hispanic Center estimates that there are 11.2 million unauthorized immigrants in the United States, including 4 million under age thirty, not all of whom are eligible to apply for DACA. The demographics of DACA recipients do not resemble Trump's portraits of terrorists and criminals, and he has indicated as much: 97 percent are working or in school; their average age of arrival was six years old; eight hundred thousand had been accepted in the program by 2018, with nine hundred serving in the military; less than 0.2 percent had been convicted of crimes (Passel and Lopez 2012).

However, President Trump canceled the DACA program in 2017, and Congress failed to present a new plan because an agreement could not be reached about immigration reform more generally, which included the construction of a wall between the United States and Mexico. The immigration status of DACAs remains in judicial limbo. The U.S. Supreme Court has declined opportunities to rule on Trump's rollback, and lower federal courts have granted extensions for the administration to show why its rollback is not arbitrary (Jordan 2018). Until then, new DACA applications must be accepted.

The DACA situation is not unique to the United States. Recently in the UK, attention has been focused on commonwealth citizens from Jamaica and Barbados who arrived as children but never applied for UK naturalization paperwork or UK passports. Now in their sixties, after spending their adult lives living and working in the UK, because these individuals are not "on the system," they are ineligible for full social services and subject to deportation (Gentleman 2018). More broadly, expulsion or threats thereof create uncertainty and conflict throughout society (Anderson, Gibney, and Paoletti 2011).

THE SOCIAL COMPACT AND HOSPITALITY

The foregoing account of U.S. immigration policies establishes Anglo dominance among residents. Those European groups who have been able to assimilate to Anglo norms have achieved secure citizenship. But others—and here it is difficult not to see influences of how the public perceives race and ethnicity—are subject to the politics of the moment. It may be that immigration policy related to deportation has always been subject to turbocharged politics, where concern about employment can be manipulated by racism and ethnicism for votes. Nevertheless, it is odd that a "nation of immigrants" now in its fourth century has not yet constructed a fair, benevolent, and stable immigration policy. For instance, it is not self-evident that native-born workers have more rights to jobs than immigrant residents, if only because employment is not a constitutional right.

The American idea of a nation of immigrants has never encompassed real cosmopolitanism or the kind of pluralism that allows cultural differences to coexist without penalty to those who have not assimilated their lives to dominant cultural patterns. It is unlikely that as the representative democracy it continues to be the United States will be able to construct stable immigration reform. So this places in the realm of the social compact questions about how to regard and behave toward those who reside here but were born abroad. We have seen that even legal immigrants may be regarded with suspicion and prejudice. We need to recognize such immigrants as full citizens or prospective citizens and extend them the same respect and inclusion that those born in the United States are presumed to merit. This should not be difficult to do in a culture that values the self-made individual, without regard to lineage or unearned privilege. But it remains an ideal that foreign-born citizens and prospective citizens not be treated as foreigners.

The question remains of how citizens and residents should think about those among them who do not have documentation that entitles them to live, work, and learn in the United States. At my university, the following posting was approved by the administration:

> Deferred Action for Childhood Arrivals (DACA) students
>
> We have heard from numerous students, faculty and staff members that they are concerned about potential changes to immigration laws, especially as it relates to undocumented students and those covered under the Deferred Action for Childhood Arrivals policy. We want to be very clear that we support all UO students, regardless of their immigration status. While it is too soon to speculate on what may happen in the future, the University of Oregon remains committed to the DACA policy and providing an inclusive campus that values global citizenship and engagement. International students, scholars, and faculty members as well as undocumented and DACA students continue

to be protected by the same privacy laws and university policies as US citizens. (International Student and Scholars Services 2018)

This statement does not resist the federal government but instead positively asserts a welcoming and protective attitude. Whether my colleagues and our administrators would agree with my interpretation, this statement fills a gap for justice in the social contract. It is in the realm of the social compact and shows an intention to practice the collective and individual virtue of *hospitality*. Of course, we cannot know the outcome of a situation in legal limbo, but some form of hospitality to DACAs has the support of many in higher education at this time (Rock 2017; Quilantan 2018; Redden 2018).

Hospitality is a biblical virtue with clear connections to immigration. Elizabeth McCormick and Patrick McCormick (2006) suggest that in a Christian country, biblical references to the duty of hospitality to strangers could be framed to shift immigration debates from issues of national security to moral issues. While not all strangers can be admitted, those whose presence is irregular but law abiding should not be subject to punishment for their mere presence or denied social services. Hospitality in this religious sense is analogous to Christian ideas of land stewardship in relation to politics.

Religious Americans do not always have a way to translate their beliefs into government programs in a two-party system where politics requires nets that will reliably take up as many voters as possible, according to existing common denominators. But some progressive religious concerns are shared throughout a wider secular public. Unless the voting public can be inoculated against catchphrases such as "Radical Islamic Terrorism" and dehypnotized from the fantasy that hordes of *Mexican* drug-dealing, murdering rapists are out to get them, even Christian moral virtues will not be practiced. However, in shared religious and secular modes of resistance to the electoral results of cheap catchphrases, there is time for moral reflection and argument, and that is where the value of hospitality could be regained. Indeed, it may be part of the dynamic of politics as contest that the best ideas are formed by the opposition after a loss.

Hospitality in terms of present undocumented immigrants generally, and DACAs specifically, is not an issue of open borders—how far open national borders ought to be is another subject—but an issue of how to treat people who are already within our borders and not known to be criminals. Within the nation, trespass is not a crime, unless it is in violation of an injunction to desist or has been committed with intent to commit a crime. Unlawful presence is not itself a crime unless it can be proved beyond a reasonable doubt that the manner of entry was unlawful (Snider 2014). Hospitality toward the undocumented would require commensurable due process on a national level. However, under the Trump administration, internal deportations of undocumented immigrants have not been reassuring in this regard (Shear and Nixon 2017). Ongoing ICE (Immigration and Customs Enforcement) raids and fear of deportations in Mexican immigrant communities create constant stress, despite considerable support for DACAs. DACAs for the most part do not look like white Europeans, so the rollback and support have overtones of racial/ethnic injustice and projects of social justice.

Seyla Benhabib (2004) in *The Rights of Others* discusses hospitality as a cosmopolitan right derived from Immanuel Kant's 1795 essay "Perpetual Peace: A Philosophical Sketch." Unlike individual rights within nations and rights between sovereign nations, cosmopolitan right pertains to rights between individuals and nations not their own. Hospitality as a cosmopolitan right is a claim individuals have, rather than an obligation of others toward them. Kant's idea of cosmopolitan right is based on shared occupancy of the ultimately finite space of the world. However, according to Kant, this right is a claim to a temporary sojourn, only, and not a right to permanent residence.

Might it be possible to apply cosmopolitan right to DACAs after they were originally granted permission to remain for two years? And might not an argument be made that given all things equal, including law-abidingness and adequate resources, those granted temporary sojourns in two-year increments would be able after a certain number of such periods to apply for permanent occupancy, that is, for citizenship? If the answer is some form of absolute refusal, it may be possible to soften it with appeals to a more general form of hospitality, as a virtue for those who are already citizens. If hospitality cannot be effectively applied to immigrants already present, then depending on their legal status, these immigrants would have social contract claims. But there is a fragile structure in this situation, because after deportation there is no legal status for such claimants. This suggests that hospitality as an obligation of citizens may motivate litigation by lawyers, employers, and relatives. Advocates generally would be acting in the social compact realm as good citizens, an ideal that will be taken up in the conclusion of this book. Such action would be a crossover from social compact to social contract.

REFERENCES

Alba, Richard, and Victor Nee. 2005. *Remaking the American Mainstream: Assimilation and Contemporary Immigration*. Cambridge, MA: Harvard University Press.

Alcoff, Linda Martín. 2000. "Is Latina/o Identity a Racial Identity?" In *Hispanics/Latinos in the United States: Ethnicity, Race, and Rights*, ed. Jorge J. E. Gracia and Pablo De Greiff, 23–44. New York: Routledge, 2000.

———. 2018. "Latinos Beyond the Binary." http://www.alcoff.com/content/beyondbinary.html.

Anderson, Bridget, Matthew J. Gibney, and Emanuela Paoletti. 2011. "Citizenship, Deportation and the Boundaries of Belonging." *Citizenship Studies* 15 (5): 547–63. DOI:10.1080/13621025.2011.583787.

Balderrama, Francisco, and E. Raymond Rodríguez. 2006. *Decade of Betrayal: Mexican Repatriation in the 1930s*. Albuquerque: University of New Mexico Press.

Benhabib, Seyla. 2004. *The Rights of Others: Aliens, Residents and Citizens.* Cambridge: Cambridge University Press.

Bergquist, James M. 2005. "German-Americans." In *Multiculturalism in the United States: A Comparative Guide to Acculturation and Ethnicity*, ed. John D. Buenker and Lorman A. Ratner, 53–76. Westport, CT: Greenwood.

Blakemore, Erin. 2018. "The Largest Mass Deportation in American History." *History Stories*, March 23. https://www.history.com/news/operation-wetback-eisenhower-1954-deportation.

Blessing, Patrick J. 1980. "Irish." In *Harvard Encyclopedia of American Ethnic Groups*, ed. Stephan Thernstrom, 524–45, 695–97. Cambridge, MA: Harvard University Press.

Breen, T. H. 2004. *The Market Place of Revolution: How Consumer Politics Shaped American Independence.* New York: Oxford University Press.

Brodkin, Karen. 1998. *How Jews Became White Folks: And What That Says about Race in America.* New York: Routledege.

Candeloro, Dominic. 1992. "Italian-Americans." In *Multiculturalism in the United States: A Comparative Guide to Acculturation and Ethnicity*, ed. John D. Buenker and Lorman A. Ratner, 173–92. Westport, CT: Greenwood.

Carlson, Allan C. 2003. "The Peculiar Legacy of German-Americans." *Society*, January/February, 77–99.

CBS News. 2017. "President Trump Slams Visa Lottery Program at FBI National Academy Graduation Ceremony." YouTube.com, December 16. https://www.youtube.com/watch?v=FSmiNaCDX-U.

Cilluffo, Anthony, and D'Vera Cohn. 2018. "7 Demographic Trends Shaping the U.S. and the World in 2018." Pew Research Center, April 25. http://www.pewresearch.org/fact-tank/2018/04/25/7-demographic-trends-shaping-the-u-s-and-the-world-in-2018/.

Cornell University Legal Information Institute. 2018. "Immigration." https://www.law.cornell.edu/wex/immigration.

Dasgupta, Rana. 2018. "The Demise of the Nation State." *Guardian*, April 5. https://www.theguardian.com/news/2018/apr/05/demise-of-the-nation-state-rana-dasgupta.

Dawsey, Josh. 2018. "Trump Derides Protections for Immigrants from 'Shithole' Countries." *Washington Post*, January 12. https://www.washingtonpost.com/politics/trump-attacks-protections-for-immigrants-from-shithole-countries-in-oval-office-meeting/2018/01/11/bfc0725c-f711-11e7-91af-31ac729add94_story.html?utm_term=.e798f9cb5a95.

Dobson, David. 1994. *Scottish Emigration to Colonial America, 1607–1785.* Athens: University of Georgia Press.

Durand, Jorge, Douglas S. Massey, and Rene M. Zenteno. 2001. "Mexican Immigration to the United States: Continuities and Changes." *Latin American Research Review* 36 (1): 107–27. https://www.jstor.org/stable/2692076.

Fednukiw, Marianne. 1995. "Canadian Americans." In *Gale Encyclopedia of Multicultural America*, ed. Judy Galens, Anna Sheets, and Robyn V. Young, 238–51. Detroit: Gale Research.

FindLaw.com. 2018. "Trespass to Land." https://injury.findlaw.com/torts-and-personal-injuries/trespass-to-land.html.

Fischer, David Hackett. 1989. *Albion's Seed: Four British Folkways in America.* Oxford: Oxford University Press.

Franklin, Benjamin. 1751. "Observations Concerning the Increase of Mankind, Peopling of Countries, etc." http://www.columbia.edu/~lmg21/ash3002y/earlyac99/documents/observations.html.

Gentleman, Amelia. 2018. "'I've Been Here for 50 Years': The Scandal of the Former Commonwealth Citizens Threatened with Deportation." *Guardian*, February 21. https://www.theguardian.com/uk-news/2018/feb/21/ive-been-here-for-50-years-the-scandal-of-the-former-commonwealth-citizens-threatened-with-deportation.

Gidda, Mirren. 2016. "How Donald Trump's Nationalism Won Over White Americans." *Newsweek*, November 15. http://www.newsweek.com/donald-trump-nationalism-racism-make-america-great-again-521083.

Goran, Arthur A. 1980. "Jews" In *Harvard Encyclopedia of American Ethnic Groups*, ed. Stephan Thernstrom, 571–88. Cambridge, MA: Harvard University Press.

Guardino, Peter. 2017. *The Dead March: A History of the Mexican-American War.* Cambridge, MA: Harvard University Press.

Guglielmo, Jennifer, and Salvatore Salerno, eds. 2003. *Are Italians White? How Race Is Made in America.* New York: Routledge.

Haft, Sheldon. 1995. "English Americans." In *Gale Encyclopedia of Multicultural America*, ed. Judy Galens, Anna Sheets, and Robyn V. Young, 471–85. Detroit: Gale Research.

Hamilton, Alexander. [1787] 2008. "To the People of New York State." Federalist Paper 1. http://avalon.law.yale.edu/18th_century/fed01.asp.

Harzig, Christiane. 2008. "German Americans." In *Encyclopedia of Race, Ethnicity and Society*, ed. Richard T. Schaefer, 1:540–44. Thousand Oaks, CA: Sage.

Hashaw, Tim. 2007. *The Birth of Black America: The First African Americans and the Pursuit of Freedom at Jamestown.* New York.: Caroll and Graf/Avalon.

Haub, Carl. 2012. "Changing the Way U.S. Hispanics Are Counted." Population Reference Bureau. http://www.prb.org/Publications/Articles/2012/us-census-and-hispanics.aspx.

Henckaerts, Jean-Marie. 1995. *Mass Expulsion in Modern International Law and Practice.* The Hague: Martinus Nijhoff.

Hess, Mary A. 1995. "Scottish and Scotch-Irish Americans." In *Gale Encyclopedia of Multicultural America*, ed. Judy Galens, Anna Sheets, and Robyn V. Young, 1198–1210. Detroit: Gale Research.

History.com. 2018. "Mexican-American War." https://www.history.com/topics/mexican-american-war.

Homeland Security. 2010. "Yearbook of Immigration Statistics." http://www.dhs.gov/files/statistics/publications/LPR10.shtm.

Huth, Lindsay. 2018. "Immigration Under Trump: By the Numbers Immigrants Appear to Be Responding to the President's Hard-Line Rhetoric." USNews.com, March 13. https://www.usnews.com/news/data-mine/articles/2018-03-13/fewer-crossing-border-fewer-deported-immigration-under-trump.

Ignatiev, Noel. 1995. *How the Irish Became White.* New York: Routledge.

International Student and Scholar Services. 2018. "Deferred Action for Childhood Arrivals (DACA) Students." University of Oregon. https://isss.uoregon.edu/immigration/faqs-daca.

Ireland Story. 1998. http://www.wesleyjohnston.com/users/ireland/.

Isle of Man Government Treasury, Economic Affairs Division. 2011. "Isle of Man Census Report."https://www.gov.im/media/207882/census2011reportfinalresized_1_.pdf.

Jordan, Miriam. 2018. "U.S. Must Keep DACA and Accept New Applications, Federal Judge Rules." *New York Times*, April 23. https://www.nytimes.com/2018/04/24/us/daca-dreamers-trump.html.

Kazal, Russell A. 2004. "The Interwar Origins of the White Ethnic: Race, Residence, and German Philadelphia, 1917–1939." *Journal of American Ethnic History* 23 (4): 78–131.

Kenny, Kevin. 2000. *The American Irish: A History.* Harlow, UK: Pearson.

Klein, Jennifer M. 2008a. "Sicilian Americans." In *Encyclopedia of Race, Ethnicity and Society*, ed. Richard T. Schaefer. Thousand Oaks, CA: Sage. http://dx.doi.org/10.4135/9781412963879.n511.

———. 2008b. "United Kingdom, Immigrants and Their Descendants in the United States." In *Encyclopedia of Race, Ethnicity and Society*, ed. Richard T. Schaefer. Thousand Oaks, CA: Sage. http://dx.doi.org/10.4135/9781412963879.n565.

Lincoln, Abraham. 1855. "Letter to Joshua Speed." Abraham Lincoln Online. http://www.abrahamlincolnonline.org/lincoln/speeches/speed.htm.

Liptak, Adam, and Michael D. Shear. 2018. "Key Justices Seem Skeptical of Challenges to Trump's Travel Ban." *New York Times*, April 25. https://www.nytimes.com/2018/04/25/us/politics/trump-travel-ban-supreme-court.html.

Marshall, Serena. 2016. "Obama Has Deported More People Than Any Other President." ABC News, August 9. http://abcnews.go.com/Politics/obamas-deportation-policy-numbers/story?id=41715661.

McCormick, Elizabeth, and Patrick McCormick. 2006. "Hospitality: How a Biblical Virtue Could Transform United States Immigration Policy." *University of Detroit Mercy Law Review* 83 (5): 857–900.

McLemore, S. Dale, and Harriet D. Romo. 2005. *Racial and Ethnic Relations in America.* Boston: Pearson Education.

Muslim Advocates. 2017. "Map: Recent Incidents of Anti-Muslim Hate Crimes." June 18. https://www.muslimadvocates.org/map-anti-muslim-hate-crimes/.

Newsday.com. 2016. "Donald Trump Speech, Debates and Campaign Quotes." November 9. https://www.newsday.com/news/nation/donald-trump-speech-debates-and-campaign-quotes-1.11206532.

Parkin, Andrew. 1980. "Australians and New Zealanders." In *Harvard Encyclopedia of American Ethnic Groups*, ed. Stephan Thernstrom, 163–64. Cambridge, MA: Harvard University Press.

Parrillo, Vincent N. 2008. "Italian-Americans." In *Encyclopedia of Race, Ethnicity and Society*, ed. Richard T. Schaefer. Thousand Oaks, CA: Sage. http://dx.doi.org/10.4135/9781412963879.n307.

Passel, Jeffrey S., and Mark Hugo Lopez. 2012. "Up to 1.7 Million Unauthorized Immigrant Youth May Benefit from New Deportation Rules." Pew Hispanic Center. https://consulmex.sre.gob.mx/boise/images/stories/2012/medios12/phunauthorized-immigrant-deportation.pdf.

Plott, Elaina. 2018. "Trump's Immigration Plan Receives a Chilly Reception." *Atlantic*, January 31. https://www.theatlantic.com/politics/archive/2018/01/trump-bets-on-immigration-in-the-state-of-the-union/551936/.

Porter, Jack Nusan. 2008. "Jewish Americans." In *Encyclopedia of Race, Ethnicity and Society*, ed. Richard T. Schaefer. Thousand Oaks, CA: Sage. http://dx.doi.org/10.4135/9781412963879.n314.

Quilantan, Bianca. 2018. "Colleges Can't Completely Shield Undocumented Students If DACA Lapses: Here's What They Can Do." Chronicle of Higher Education, February 26. https://www.chronicle.com/article/Colleges-Can-t-Completely/242643.

Rebala, Pratheek. 2015. "This Map Shows Where Immigrants Send the Most Money Home." Time Labs, September 9. http://labs.time.com/story/where-immigrants-send-the-most-money-home/.

Redden, Elizabeth. 2018. "DACA Lives, but for How Long?" *Inside Higher Ed*, March 5. https://www.insidehighered.com/news/2018/03/05/daca-continues-now-colleges-and-students-face-uncertainties.

Rock, Amy. 2017. "Colleges Pledge to Protect DACA Students after Program Repealed." *Campus Safety Magazine*, September 6. https://www.campussafetymagazine.com/university/colleges-protect-daca-students/.

Schaefer, Richard T. 2011. *Race and Ethnicity in the United States*. Upper Saddle River, NJ: Prentice Hall.

Shapiro, Edward. 1992. "Jewish-Americans." In *Multiculturalism in the United States: A Comparative Guide to Acculturation and Ethnicity*, ed. John D. Buenker and Lorman A. Ratner, 149–72. Westport, CT: Greenwood.

Shear, Michael D., and Ron Nixon. 2017. "New Trump Deportation Rules Allow Far More Expulsions." New York Times, February 21. https://nyti.ms/2lrcgKg.

Sheth, Falguni. 2017. "The Racialization of Muslims in the Post-9/11 United States." In The Oxford Handbook of Philosophy and Race, ed. Naomi Zack, 342–51. New York: Oxford University Press.

Snider, Brett. 2014. "Is Illegal Immigration a Crime? Improper Entry v. Unlawful Presence." FindLaw.com, July 9. https://blogs.findlaw.com/blotter/2014/07/is-illegal-immigration-a-crime-improper-entry-v-unlawful-presence.html.

U.S. Census Bureau. 2010. "Quick Facts."https://www.census.gov/quickfacts/fact/table/US/PST045217.

———. 2016. "Facts for Features: Hispanic Heritage Month 2016." October 12. https://www.census.gov/newsroom/facts-for-features/2016/cb16-ff16.html.

Wagner, Alex. 2017. "America's Forgotten History of Illegal Deportations." *Atlantic*, March 6. https://www.theatlantic.com/politics/archive/2017/03/americas-brutal-forgotten-history-of-illegal-deportations/517971/.

Welsh Americans. 2008. http://www.facebook.com/pages/Welsh-American/1429853057 15399.

Wenzel, Robert. 2018. "On Immigrants from 'Shithole' Countries." *Target Liberty*, January 11. http://www.targetliberty.com/2018/01/on-immigrants-from-shithole-countries.html.

Woolf, Christopher. 2015. "A Brief History of America's Hostility to a Previous Generation of Mediterranean Migrants—Italians." *PRI's The World*, November 26. https://www.pri.org/stories/2015-11-26/brief-history-america-s-hostility-previous-generation-mediterranean-migrants.

Zack, Naomi. 2018. *Philosophy of Race: An Introduction*. Cham, Switzerland: Palgrave-Macmillan.

Conclusion

The Uncertainty and Duty of Inclusive Citizenship

Today's ceremony, however, has very special meaning. Because today we are not merely transferring power from one Administration to another, or from one party to another—but we are transferring power from Washington, D.C. and giving it back to you, the American People. (Trump 2017)

On 29 March 2017, *New York* magazine published a story by investigative reporter Yashar Ali that cited three people who independently said they overheard former President George W. Bush walk away from 45th President Donald Trump's 20 January 2017 inauguration ceremony, saying, "That was some weird shit." According to reports, three unnamed witnesses heard Bush refer to the 45th president's inauguration using the phrase. (Palma 2017)

It is not your responsibility to finish the work of perfecting the world, but you are not free to desist from it either. (*Pirkei Avot* [Fundamental Principles/ Ethics of the Fathers], 2:21; see Chabad.org 2018)

This book has been working toward inclusive citizenship through its public aspects, which include implied political and social agreements, the social contract between the people and government, and the social compact among the people. The social contract works well when government functions and is responsive to requests for change and greater inclusion from the people. When government breaks the social contract because it fails to function or fulfill its obligations to citizens and others, there is an indecisive period of time that can be a form of revolution or a regrouping among citizens to influence government change. In an electoral democracy with a two-party system, voting can create regime change. Voting one party in and the other out is tantamount to a revolution. To conclude this book, ironies, media, and uncertainties in recent political changes will be considered first, and we will end with the *duty* of citizenship.

POLITICAL IRONIES, MEDIA, AND UNCERTAINTIES

The first two epigraphs show how real life has ironic twists and turns that would be unbelievable in fiction. President Trump said he was giving power back to the American people in his inaugural address, and the strength of the resistance against his administration within the social compact realm may prove him prescient (if not sincere). The public popularity of former President George W. Bush's remark that he found the entirety of Trump's inaugural address weird shows how the extreme relativity of our political judgments turns yesterday's conservatives into today's liberals. When Steve Bannon said he was on a mission to destroy the Republican Party and that Trump was an imperfect vessel for his grand schemes, it was assumed that he assumed reactionary white conservative nationalists would take over, not Democrats (Phelan 2017). Either political leaders are a lot smarter and more devious than most observers imagine or history ends up outsmarting us all, as yesterday's devils become teddy bears today.

Hegelian scholars have been reminding us for a while that the consequences of human actions often do not coincide with their intentions (Pippin 2010). The net effect of such uncertainty and instability is that cultural and political criticism about present events, as in the foregoing chapters, may not be a reliable process. An analysis that is coherent today may become comically irrelevant by the events of tomorrow. There is no solution to this problem because it is built into social reality as we experience it over time. But there may be more enduring truths to be gleaned from analyses of present social structures and forms, rather than their contents.

I have noticed since the 1991 Senate confirmation hearings for Clarence Thomas as a U.S. Supreme Court justice that there is a new phenomenon in mass media news, namely, the jumbo news story (JNS). The Thomas hearings captured everyone's attention for a period of time extending beyond the normal news cycle of a day or two. Not only were television audience numbers high, but the hearings became the main topic of conversation away from the tube. This JNS was followed by the Oklahoma City bombing, the scandal involving President Clinton and Monica Lewinsky, the O. J. Simpson murder trial, the death of Princess Diana, 9/11, the War on Terror, Hurricane Katrina, the Great Recession, Edward Snowden, and the Haitian earthquake. The normal news cycle endures during a JNS, but items dart in and out of a collective attention that remains permanently distracted by the JNS. Nevertheless, as riveting as these JNS events were, every one eventually lost steam and people went on with their lives apart from them. The bad news in that was how easily the public forgets, but that was also the good news because people do have lives with their own major events and dramas requiring their attention.

However, at a certain time during the presidential election campaign of 2016, the current JNS did not end but instead merged into the subsequent JNS about the Trump administration. The resulting super JNS (SJNS) is what many of us are obsessively riveted by and living with today (May 2018). This experience is partly expressed when it is said that political reality has become a reality television show. Not only is the reality for politicians viewed by the audience as constant news, but the reality of life for the audience is shaped by the show. What we hear and read and view from media is what we experience over increasing parts of our lives, including our conversations, work, emotional reactions, and dreams. There are also new or heightened forms of activity, such as registering to vote, participating in demonstrations, reading more op-ed pieces and other analyses, and making academic work and teaching more relevant to the issues of the day. Some of this for some people, such as immigrants facing deportation, has drastic consequences for their lives, but those kinds of problems are different from the issue of constant attention. Injustice has a longer history than reality television.

The good news from the advent of SJNSs is that many who were indifferent before now care about political events. The bad news is that as people and activities have become politicized, politics, which is a contest, has expanded to take over much of life that was previously not political. The news awaiting assessment is that, as politics has expanded, so has our relationship with news media, which in many instances is part and parcel of entertainment media, or vice versa. The worse news here is that serious events are not separated out from frivolous ones, and the spectatorship and influence in real life of SJNSs may not leave room for sober contemplation and assessment. The forms of news media, such as public radio and television and legitimate news sources, present plenty of analysis, but they also face the challenge of getting caught up in partisanship. (For example, as of this writing, it is difficult to assess President Trump's foreign policy with Syria and North Korea, because his supporters are inclined to think of a Nobel Peace Prize, while his critics are inclined to view his actions abroad as reactions to the SJNS of investigations and litigation concerning his campaign's involvement with Russia.)

There is also a structural difference between shared mass media and more individualized social media that allow for opinion and resolve to be formed very privately, without the checks of institutional news services or conversation within a larger audience. Online, everyone can be in contact with anyone at any time and everyone can experience anything at any time. However, this has not meant that people randomly seek out information or contacts. In *The Square and the Tower*, Niall Ferguson (2018) traces the history of human networks from ancient times to the present, showing how informal lines of communication may bypass and even overpower official hierarchical structures. The internet enables or facilitates this kind of networking, and sometimes it is used to invent new content, as well as new wants or demands, but it does not wholly create or determine all interests and motivations. People who go to the square or log onto the internet already know what or whom they are looking for.

In December 2016, a North Carolina man drove six hours to a Washington, DC, pizzeria, where he fired an assault-type weapon, scaring employees and patrons. His aim was to investigate widespread online conspiracy reports, known as "Pizzagate," that claimed Hillary Clinton was running a child sex-slave business in the basement of that restaurant. The restaurant had no basement, and the shooter, who was later sentenced to four years in prison, conceded at the scene that "the intel on this wasn't 100 percent" (Haag and Salam 2017). More seriously, in April 2018, a mostly white federal jury convicted three Kansas men calling themselves "The Crusaders" for conspiring before the 2016 election to use a weapon of mass destruction to bomb an apartment complex and mosque inhabited by Somali refugees. They had been infiltrated by a paid FBI informant who taped their conversations, but the jury did not find entrapment. Evidence included online searches for news about Trump during the campaign and a focus on his criticism of the FBI and "Radical Islamic Terrorist" Muslims, whom the Crusaders constantly called "cockroaches" (Smith 2018). The expansion of inflammatory politics into what is accepted as news online is overall a great threat to U.S. public safety.

The Republican focus on "Radical Islamic Terrorism" to the neglect of radical white male American terrorism is both political and racist—racism is activated to turbocharge politics. Recent statistics support an assessment that more deaths from terrorist acts within the United States are caused by white males than Muslims. In 2015, *Time* reported a study by the New America Foundation that since 9/11 white extremists had killed twice as many Americans as Jihadists (Plucinska 2015). Such terrorists tend to be lone males who self-activate based on what they read online. The combination of politics, racism, the internet, and isolation, as well as a lack of effective screening for gun purchases, is a very great threat to public safety. These perfect storms of structural factors that can be benign or containable taken singly do not yet appear to have the full attention of the public, although aspects of them do appear to be on the FBI's radar. U.S. Attorney General Jeff Sessions issued the following statement after the Kansas conspiracy verdict: "The defendants in this case acted with clear premeditation in an attempt to kill people on the basis of their religion and national origin. That's not just illegal—it's immoral and unacceptable, and we're not going to stand for it" (Smith 2018).

The problem with the expansion of politics as engagement in party contests is that there is insufficient time and attention paid to what would be the best course of action for groups and individuals in the nation. This competitive nature of politics did not begin in 2016. In *How Democracies Die*, Steven Levitsky and Daniel Ziblatt recount how a month after U.S. Supreme Court Justice Antonin Scalia died on February 13, 2016, President Obama nominated Appellate Judge Merrick Garland to fill Scalia's position. Since 1866, whenever a president had nominated a Supreme Court justice, the Senate had allowed it to proceed. But this time Senate Republicans refused to follow that custom and insisted that the president to be elected in November 2016 fill that seat. That did happen when President Trump's nominee was rapidly approved a year later (Levitsky and Ziblatt 2018, 146). Levitsky and Ziblatt interpret this episode as an example of norm breaking and a lack of political forbearance that threatens democracy. However, if we also consider how such partisan defiance of norms reflects the expansion of politics as contest, more than democracy is threatened. What is at stake in the long term is the functioning and stability of government, which politics can now disrupt regardless of which party is in power.

The title of this book and its general sense that author and readers can reach a consensus about democratic values in the realm of the social compact is not without its own dangers. All revolutions are conducted from within that social compact realm. As we know, literal revolutions can be bloody. In terms of its political principles, the South in the Civil War was launching a revolution based on states' rights, and had they won, within the South it would have taken its place in history as the second U.S. revolution. Within the resulting United States, it would probably have been called the "War of Independence," only slightly modifying for internal use what the British still call what we call the "Revolutionary War," that is, the "American War of Independence." Because the South lost and the United States more or less reunited, we call it the "Civil War." But during and soon after the Civil War, it was called "War of the Rebellion" or the "Great Rebellion" (Foote 1866; Greeley 1864.) Livitsky and Ziblatt (2018) suggest that the North–South reconciliation following Reconstruction was based on white supremacy and the willingness of northern Republicans to overlook the virulent antiblack racism of southern Democrats. That complicity persisted until the civil rights movements.

After the initial success of civil rights legislation of the mid-1960s, there has been a return to the hearts-and-minds conflict in race relations, with alarming outbursts of violence, as in relentlessly episodic and largely unpunished police killings of unarmed young black men. An intensified criminalization of black men, both in reality and in stereotyping, began with what Vesla Weaver (2007) has called "frontlash" in 1980s conservative reactions to nonwhite formal equality. Weaver argues that when exaggerated portrayals of black crime became a political issue, harsher sentencing laws for nonviolent drug crimes followed, which increased the black population in the expanding U.S. prison system (Zack 2015). Insofar as the Civil War was a battle over slavery defined by race, it has never really ended.

On the social compact level of demonstrations and discourse, all now remains nonviolent, and a political victory will and should keep violence at bay. But the truth of the matter is that no participants really know what they are in for until their project is complete, and projects of liberation are very difficult to complete. The philosophical view is that we may to the best of our ability create an informed view of current events, but we do not have either control of those events or of how future events will lead to reassessment. However, the historical progression of events doesn't end with this philosophical uncertainty and lack of knowledge. Within this historical process, we have duties to reciprocate the millions of ways we benefit from living in our parts of society that are part of larger parts to which so many people contribute administratively, materially, and culturally. We are, as Aristotle said, political animals. And even though our excellence may not lie in our political activity, we are obligated to participate in political activity. We are obligated to fulfill the duties of citizens to the best of our abilities. We have a duty to be good citizens.

GOOD CITIZENS

There are two sides to citizenship: how the government recognizes and treats citizens and what citizens themselves do. There are also two kinds of citizens: those who are recognized as citizens by the government and other citizens, those who ought to be recognized as citizens but are not yet or who make claims and contributions that are the activities of citizens. For examples, black slaves were citizens because they helped build the United States, and DACAs are citizens because they have grown up possessing the rights and expectations of future citizens (see chapter 9); women were citizens before they got the right to vote; African Americans were citizens before the civil rights movements, even as they were called "second-class citizens." Felons who are not permitted to vote after release from prison are citizens. Active terrorists and criminals are also citizens, but bad ones.

This broad view of citizenship that includes those not recognized as citizens by the government is necessary for the social compact. At different times, there are situations in which people are not yet recognized but should be recognized as citizens on existing legal or moral grounds (slaves, women before the 1920s, African Americans before civil rights legislation, DACAs today). Overall, the criteria are residence and contributions. It is not necessary to be able to vote in order to be a citizen, although the ability to vote is the main official honor accorded to citizens.

The formal criteria for good versus bad citizens are not self-evident, and much of that assessment depends on concrete circumstances. The importance of good citizens derives from their power to improve society. If someone is able to vote, then voting is a necessary condition for being a good citizen. But as Judith Shklar (1991) has persuasively argued, voting is not sufficient for being a good citizen. Shklar explicates citizenship as standing or status, nationality, good citizenship, and ideal republican citizenship that has historically involved participation in ruling. Standing includes the abilities to vote and earn, and Shklar claims that standing has been the most important aspect of citizenship, which has dominated citizenship aspirations:

> The significance of the two great emblems of public standing, the vote and the opportunity to earn, seems clearest to these excluded men and women. They have regarding voting and earning not just as the ability to promote their interests and to make money but as the attributes of an American citizen. And people who are not granted these marks of civic dignity feel dishonored, not just powerless and poor. They are also scorned by their fellow-citizens. The struggle for citizenship in America has, therefore, been overwhelmingly a demand for inclusion in the polity, an effort to break down excluding barriers to recognition, rather than an aspiration to civic participation as a deeply involving activity. (1991, 3)

Missing from Shklar's emphasis on standing is the urgency of the content of what creates standing. Voting can change government in ways that directly affect the individual citizen, and earning is often a matter of the ability to survive. Thus, standing or status is more than honorific or ceremonial.

Shklar describes the good citizen as someone who actively participates in politics on national and local levels, speaks out against unjust or imprudent public policies, and listens to opposing arguments and tries to assess their merits; the good citizen is a patriot, but also a whistle-blower as need be (1991, 4–8). Here, we get close to the core importance of citizenship and what makes good citizenship. Listening is particularly important within the divisions of an agonistic turbocharged two-party system. No one would be expected to listen to political counterparts who spew unreflective hatred. But insofar as listening is a form of respect, there are a large number of contemporary white Republicans who continue to support Trump because they feel disrespected by elites (Hohmann 2018). This means that those perceived to be elite have an obligation to respectfully listen to them and try to understand what makes them feel disrespected, instead of dismissing them on the grounds of their political conclusions. Compared to the issues at stake in national and global politics, feeling disrespected may seem like a relatively trivial matter, especially insofar as women and people of color among perceived elites have gotten used to it. But, for a number of reasons, not the least of which is a systemic ongoing loss of social and majority status associated with being white and nonelite, feeling disrespected may have overriding psychic importance. This importance may be exaggerated or even irrational, but for many nonelite white Americans, their only defense against their experience of the dishonor of disrespect may be to vote defiantly. It's an empirical question whether listening more to these complainants will change their voting patterns, but they are nonetheless entitled to respectful hearings by good citizens who disagree with them politically.

The good citizen is of course free to be a partisan in a party system, especially during an age of extreme politics. But in addition to hearing and evaluating opposing positions, she has a duty, as a citizen, to make her citizenship decisions on the basis of what there is good reason to believe is good for the whole nation or commonwealth to which she belongs. She contributes her work to this end without allowing a desire to win to trump the rules of the contest. The good citizen works on both a social contract and a social compact level. At times, it may not be possible to distinguish between these two levels. For example, the National Popular Vote Interstate Compact (NPVIC) is a current movement among state governments to transfer their electoral votes in a general election to the candidate with the highest popular votes (NPVIC 2018). The relation between states and the federal government occurs within the social contract. But that the initiative is called a compact among the states brings our attention to the independence of states from the central government in key issues, such as the structure of national elections. Citizens actively supporting the NPVIC are themselves working within their social contract with the state, but again they are supporting their state's social compact standing among other states.

The good citizen is involved in perfecting the nation or commonwealth as an intrinsically valuable process in itself. Caring about what others experience, good citizens are concerned to welcome new members into the whole, a concern that translates into responsible hospitality to immigrants (as we saw in chapter 9).

The main problem with turbocharged politics and any exaggerated political contest is that it can leave out the reason for the contest and the work that winners should be committed to doing. Too many of our elected and appointed political officials do not seem to have thought about what policies would be best for the nation, state, or locality they are pledged to represent, lead, or adjudicate over. They do not evaluate policies involving race, immigration, environmentalism, health care, gun control, or reproductive and LBGTQ rights on the basis of how they preserve individual rights and benefit the whole. Their major concerns are politically partisan issues—get reelected, support their patrons, support other party members, further an ideology. Such officials are not ideal republican citizens or even good citizens in the ordinary sense, and good citizens are likely to vote them out of public service.

Good citizenship requires a moral dimension, as well as knowledge and action. A good citizen is capable of constructing moral criticism against government officials and policies that may be legal but nonetheless harm innocent people or inflict cruel punishment or use torture as an interrogation technique (Chappell 2018). Nevertheless, if politics continues to be as oppositional as present disagreements between Republicans and Democrats are, regime change through voting can go either way every few years. This means that politics will continually be a source of unpredictability and instability for many important institutions in society. Leaders in business and education, to name but two areas, usually find it necessary to plan long term, as do individuals. Citizens will need to design projects and plan their lives with some insulation from the unpredictability of binary political victories and defeats. This will either be political neutrality or new kinds of action in the realm of the social compact.

Political contest leading to regime change has moral dangers and temptations that even liberatory leaders may not avoid. For instance, the loss of innocence resulting from knowledge of how Cambridge Analytica furnished material for the manipulation of votes cannot be repaired, and Democrats may be tempted to use such techniques in future elections (see chapter 3). It is the task of good citizens to apply a broad moral consensus that manipulation of political views is a type of fraud that should be avoided, no matter how good the end results may be. Civic morality is not a political weapon but a source of values that can inform political life if enough good citizens make themselves heard. Civic morality can also inform aspects of life that in normal times are external to politics.

REFERENCES

Chabad.org. 2018. "Pirkei Avot: Ethics of the Fathers." https://www.chabad.org/library/article_cdo/aid/680274/jewish/Pirkei-Avot-Ethics-of-the-Fathers.htm.

Chappell, Bill. 2018. "'I Don't Believe That Torture Works,' CIA Nominee Gina Haspel Tells Senators." *NPR Two-Way*, May 9. https://www.npr.org/sections/thetwo-way/2018/05/09/609681289/gina-haspel-confirmation-hearing-cia-nominee-faces-senators-questions.

Ferguson, Niall. 2018. *The Square and the Tower: Networks and Power from the Freemasons to Facebook.* New York: Penguin.

Foote, Henry S. 1866. *War of the Rebellion; Or, Scylla and Charybdis.* New York: Harper & Bros.

Greeley, Horace. 1864. *The American Conflict: A History of the Great Rebellion in the United States of America, 1860–64.* 2 vols. Hartford, CT: O.D. Case & Co.

Haag, Matthew, and Maya Salam. 2017. "Gunman in 'Pizzagate' Shooting Is Sentenced to 4 Years in Prison." *New York Times*, June 22. https://www.nytimes.com/2017/06/22/us/pizzagate-attack-sentence.html.

Hohmann, James. 2018. "Trump Voters Stay Loyal Because They Feel Disrespected." *Washington Post*, May 14. https://www.washingtonpost.com/news/powerpost/paloma/daily-202/

176 *Conclusion*

2018/05/14/daily-202-trump-voters-stay-loyal-because-they-feel-disrespected/5af8aac530fb0425887994cc/?utm_term=.354f9a944ab7.

Levitsky, Steven, and Daniel Ziblatt. 2018. *How Democracies Die.* New York: Crown.

NPVIC (National Popular Vote Interstate Compact). 2018. "Agreement Among the States to Elect the President by National Popular Vote." May. https://www.nationalpopularvote.com/written-explanation.

Palma, Bethania. 2017. "Did George W. Bush Describe President Trump's Inauguration as 'Some Weird Sh*t'?" *Snopes,* 31 March. https://www.snopes.com/news/2017/03/31/bush-trumps-inauguration-weird-sht/.

Phelan, Matthew. 2017. "Inside Trump's Breitbart Brain." *New Republic*, March 15. https://newrepublic.com/article/140956/inside-trumps-breitbart-brain.

Pippin, Robert. 2010. "Hegel's Social Theory of Agency: The 'Inner-Outer' Problem." In *Hegel on Action*, ed. Arto Laitinen and Constantine Sandis, 3–50. London: Palgrave-Macmillan.

Plucinska, Johanna. 2015. "Since 9/11, White Right-Wing Terrorists Have Killed Almost Twice as Many Americans in Homegrown Attacks Than Radical Islamists Have, according to Research by the New America Foundation." Time.com, June 25. http://time.com/3934980/right-wing-extremists-white-terrorism-islamist-jihadi-dangerous/.

Shklar, Judith N. 1991. *American Citizenship: The Quest for Inclusion.* Cambridge, MA: Harvard University Press.

Smith, Mitch. 2018. "Kansas Trio Convicted in Plot to Bomb Somali Immigrants." *New York Times,* April 18. https://www.nytimes.com/2018/04/18/us/kansas-militia-somali-trial-verdict.html.

Trump, Donald J. 2017. "The Inaugural Address." WhiteHouse.gov, January 20. https://www.whitehouse.gov/briefings-statements/the-inaugural-address/.

Weaver, Vesla. 2007. "Frontlash: Race and the Development of Punitive Crime Policy." *Studies in American Political Development* 21 (2): 230–65. DOI:10.1017/S0898588X07000211.

Zack, Naomi. 2015. *White Privilege and Black Rights: The Injustice of U.S. Police Racial Profiling and Homicide.* Lanham, MD: Rowman & Littlefield.

Index

black life: expectancy, rise from
1900–2015, 39; poverty rate, decrease
from 1960–2011, 39; as precarious, 36,
38
Black Lives Matter, 34–35, 36. *See also*
police
black-white dating, decline in racism
about, 39
black women: as intersection, 28; as
protected class, 28–29; voted for
Hillary Clinton, 73
Blue Lives Matter, 35. *See also* police
bots, anti-Clinton, 48
boundaries, governmental and natural,
116–117, 127
BP. *See* British Petroleum oil spill
Bread and Roses Strike, 1912, 60
Breitbart News Network, 47–48
British Petroleum oil spill, 2010, 117–118,
121
Brown, Michael, 34
Burke, Edmund, 88
Burke, Kenneth, 20; on Hitler's rhetoric,
52–53
Burke, Tarana, 73
Bush, George W.: on elites, 45;
"ownership society," U.S., 92; on
Trump's inaugural address, 167, 168.
See also 9/11, Bush memorial service
Bush administration, deportations during,
156

Cambridge Analytica, as scraping data, 48,
55, 175
capitalism, problems with supplanting, 37,
50
Caputi, Mary, 71
Chadwick, Andrew, 21
changes, big-picture, 36
Chile, 2010 earthquake, 103–104. *See also*
Chile and Haiti, earthquake comparison
Chile and Haiti, earthquake comparison,
104–105, 109
Chinese Exclusion Act, 1882, 150
Chomksy, Noam, on Occupy Wall Street,
56
citizen or citizens. *See* good citizens
citizenship. *See* inclusive citizenship

Citizens United v. FEC, 13, 55. *See also*
political campaigns
civic morality, as source of value, 175
civil rights: activists, 2; movements,
achievements of, 27–28
Civil War, names for, 171
class: components, 44, 45; culture wars
(*see* culture, wars and class); ethnicity
and race substituted for, 50, 53;
ignorance of, 43, 52; politicization of
cultural aspects of, 49, 50–51;
privileged, assets of, 51; reality of, 44;
resistance and struggle, Marxist idea of,
52; self-knowledge of, compared to
race, 43–44; turbocharged politics, and,
45–46, 73. *See also* class differences;
political class; race and class;
turbocharged politics
class differences: discomfort with, in U.S.,
44; organically developed and
turbocharged, difference between, 55.
See also class
Clean Air Act, 1970, 119
clean air policies, complications of, 119
Clean Water Act, 1972, 119
climate, as global and long-term, 128. *See
also* social compact
climate change: as cause of natural
disasters, 98, 128; as "Chinese hoax,"
117; empiricism in science of, 97; as
politicized, 97, 117, 118; preparation
and economic interests, 122. *See also*
environmental preservation;
Environmental Protection Agency;
weather
Clinton, Bill: fiscal conservatism of, 46;
health care, 12; Monica Lewisky
scandal, and, 168; on social contract, 85
Clinton, Hillary, 13, 61, 73; "Pizzagate,"
170. *See also* 2016 election
Coates, Ta-Nehisi, 37–38
colleges and universities, contribution to
U.S. society, 43, 50–51
colonialism. *See* settler colonialism
Comey, James, 87
commonwealths, 91; structure of, 93;
within nations, 92, 94. *See also* social
contract
communities, as real and imaginary, 20

www.ingramcontent.com/pod-product-compliance
Lightning Source LLC
Chambersburg PA
CBHW030650270326
41929CB00007B/292